Wittgenstein Reads Weininger

Otto Weininger was one of the most controversial and widely read authors of fin-de-siècle Vienna. He was both condemned for his misogyny, self-hatred, anti-Semitism and homophobia and praised for his uncompromising and outspoken approach to gender and morality. For Wittgenstein, Weininger was a "remarkable genius." He repeatedly recommended Weininger's *Sex and Character* to friends and students and included the author on a short list of figures who had influenced him.

Hitherto the nature of Weininger's philosophical influence on Wittgenstein has remained a matter of speculation. The purpose of this new collection of essays is to explore the various ways in which Wittgenstein absorbed and responded to Weininger's ideas. Written by an international team of experts on Wittgenstein and Weininger, the volume is especially timely in the light of recent translations of Weininger's work and will appeal to anyone interested in the history of twentieth-century philosophy, and the literary and cultural history of fin-de-siècle Vienna.

David G. Stern is Associate Professor in the Department of Philosophy at the University of Iowa.

Béla Szabados is Professor in the Department of Philosophy and Classics at the University of Regina.

"the immunity of the strxr allows for the predj. of the content."

* 147 dualism

mystical withdraw fr social

Schulte 132 c̄ s/time view of W

136 dualism

137 LW / mysticis

Steiner 140 LW's essential li

ō uniform sense / m

[* tragedy 141-2 145ff biog

fatalism / trag. courage

need 4 it 157

Wittgenstein Reads Weininger

Edited by

DAVID G. STERN

University of Iowa

BÉLA SZABADOS

University of Regina

CAMBRIDGE
UNIVERSITY PRESS

PUBLISHED BY THE PRESS SYNDICATE OF THE UNIVERSITY OF CAMBRIDGE
The Pitt Building, Trumpington Street, Cambridge, United Kingdom

CAMBRIDGE UNIVERSITY PRESS
The Edinburgh Building, Cambridge CB2 2RU, UK
40 West 20th Street, New York, NY 10011-4211, USA
477 Williamstown Road, Port Melbourne, VIC 3207, Australia
Ruiz de Alarcón 13, 28014 Madrid, Spain
Dock House, The Waterfront, Cape Town 8001, South Africa

http://www.cambridge.org

First published 2004

Printed in the United States of America

Typeface ITC New Baskerville 10/13.5 pt. *System* LaTeX 2ε [TB]

A catalog record for this book is available from the British Library.

Library of Congress Cataloging in Publication Data

Wittgenstein reads Weininger / edited by David G. Stern, Béla Szabados.
p. cm.
Includes bibliographical references.
ISBN 0-521-82553-9 (hard) – ISBN 0-521-53260-4 (pbk.)
1. Weininger, Otto, 1880–1903 – Influence. 2. Wittgenstein, Ludwig, 1889–1951.
I. Stern, David G. II. Szabados, Bela, 1942–
B3363.W54W58 2004
193–dc22 2003065391

ISBN 0 521 82553 9 hardback
ISBN 0 521 53260 4 paperback

Contents

Contributors

Steven Burns Philosophy, Dalhousie University, Canada

Allan Janik The Brenner Archives Research Institute, University of Innsbruck

Joachim Schulte Philosophy, University of Bielefeld, Germany

David G. Stern Philosophy, University of Iowa, USA

Daniel Steuer Senior Lecturer in German, School of Humanities, University of Sussex, England

Béla Szabados Philosophy, University of Regina, Canada

Reading Wittgenstein (on) Reading

An Introduction

David G. Stern and Béla Szabados

Wittgenstein's Influences

In 1931, Ludwig Wittgenstein included Otto Weininger on a list he made of ten writers who had influenced him. He wrote:

> I think there is some truth in my idea that I am really only reproductive in my thinking. I think I have never *invented* a line of thinking but that it was always provided for me by someone else & I have done no more than passionately take it up for my work of clarification. That is how Boltzmann Hertz Schopenhauer Frege, Russell, Kraus, Loos Weininger Spengler, Sraffa have influenced me.[1]

The list appears to be arranged according to the chronological order in which they influenced Wittgenstein. One sign of this is the odd punctuation of the list, which is due to the fact that Wittgenstein first wrote just four names – "Frege, Russell, Spengler, Sraffa" – and added the other names, carefully arranged in order, above the line. The first three names are authors Wittgenstein read as a teenager; Frege and Russell first had an impact on him when he was in his early twenties. While Wittgenstein would certainly have known of Kraus and Weininger long before 1914, for both were famous and controversial in fin-de-siècle Vienna, their position on the list, and the fact that Kraus, Loos and Weininger all had an influence on the *Tractatus*, which was composed during the First World War, suggests that their influence should be dated to the war years, or immediately before. All three were important influences on Paul Engelmann and his friends in Olmütz with whom Wittgenstein stayed during an extended leave in the summer of 1916. Spengler's influence would have been after the publication of *The Decline of the West*, in 1918, while Wittgenstein first met Sraffa after returning to Cambridge in 1929. In most cases, while the precise nature of the influence is certainly debatable, the overall character is not.

In the case of Otto Weininger, however, we have very little firm evidence as to how he influenced Wittgenstein, or why. We do know that Wittgenstein read Weininger during the First World War, that he still thought highly of his writing late in life, and that, in the early 1930s, he repeatedly recommended reading Weininger to his friends and students. Desmond Lee, in a piece on Wittgenstein in 1929–31, writes that

> He had a great admiration for Weininger's *Sex and Character* and for the introduction to Hertz's *Mechanics.* Both of these he made me read, and I remember his annoyance at finding that the Weininger book was in a section of the University Library which required a special procedure for borrowing: he thought the implication was that it was in some way unfit for undergraduates and that that was nonsense.[2]

Around the same time, Wittgenstein recommended *Sex and Character* to G. E. Moore. In response to Moore's lack of sympathy for the book, Wittgenstein wrote:

> Thanks for your letter. I can quite imagine that you don't admire Weininger very much what with that beastly translation and the fact that W. must feel very foreign to you. It is true that he is fantastic but he is *great* and fantastic. It isn't necessary or rather not possible to agree with him but the greatness lies in that with which we disagree. It is his enormous mistake which is great. I.e. roughly speaking if you just add a "∼" to the whole book it says an important truth. However we better talk about it when I come back.[3]

However, Wittgenstein's letter does not further explain what he means by adding a negation sign to the whole book, or identify what he takes to be the "important truth" that emerges. Even if we include the passage quoted at the beginning, there are only a handful of additional references to Weininger in the Wittgenstein papers, and they do not, at first sight, cast much additional light on the nature of Weininger's significance for Wittgenstein.[4]

The first author to refer to the importance of Weininger for Wittgenstein was Georg Henrik von Wright,[5] who was also, as editor, responsible for the inclusion of our opening passage about Wittgenstein's influences in *Culture and Value*, first published in 1977. That book is, as he puts it, a selection from the numerous notes in Wittgenstein's manuscript material that "do not belong directly with his philosophical works although they are scattered amongst the philosophical texts. Some of these notes are autobiographical, some are about the nature of philosophical activity, and some concern subjects of a general sort, such as questions about art or about religion."[6] There are also repeated discussions of Wittgenstein's reading, and he refers to a much wider range of authors than he does in the *Philosophical Investigations* or *Tractatus*. For instance, the index of names includes Francis Bacon, Karl Barth, Ludwig Boltzmann, Josef Breuer, John Bunyan and Wilhelm Busch among the B's, Immanuel Kant, Gottfried Keller, Søren Kierkegaard, Heinrich von Kleist and Karl Kraus among the K's.

Von Wright's brief but helpful remarks on Wittgenstein's reading divide the writers he read into two groups. The first consists of philosophers in the narrow sense, the great figures in the history of philosophy. Here, Wittgenstein was not a "learned man":

> Wittgenstein had done no systematic reading in the classics of philosophy. He could read only what he could wholeheartedly assimilate. We have seen that as a young man he read Schopenhauer. From Spinoza, Hume, and Kant he said that he could get only glimpses of understanding. . . . it is significant that he did read, and enjoy, Plato. He must have recognized congenial features, both in Plato's literary and philosophical method and in the temperament behind the thoughts.[7]

This summary of Wittgenstein's views about the canonical philosophers finds some corroboration and qualification in Drury's records of conversations with Wittgenstein, which also allow us to add some names to this list: Kant and Berkeley are described as "deep," Leibniz as a "great man" well worth studying, and there are also references to Hegel and Marx.[8] Another canonical figure on Wittgenstein's reading list was William James. He thought very highly of William James's *The Varieties of Religious Experience*, and devoted so much time to the *Principles of Psychology* during the second half of the 1940s that he seriously considered using it as a text in one of his classes.[9]

On a number of occasions, Wittgenstein seems to have almost made a point of bragging about his lack of reading in the history of philosophy, or his lack of respect for the work of other philosophers. Thus we come across reports of comments to Drury and Leavis that seem to uneasily combine self-deprecation, humor and arrogance, and perhaps betray a certain anxiety. Consider the following recollections of discussions with Wittgenstein:

Drury: Did you ever read anything of Aristotle's?
Wittgenstein: Here I am, a one-time professor of philosophy who has never read a word of Aristotle![10]
[F. R. Leavis:] I was walking once with Wittgenstein when I was moved, by something he said, to remark, with a suggestion of innocent enquiry in my tone: "You don't think much of most other philosophers, Wittgenstein?" "No."[11]

The setting of these two exchanges might well have been partly responsible for the tone of Wittgenstein's responses. In the first, from Drury's notes on a conversation on an afternoon in Phoenix Park, Dublin, in the autumn of 1948, Drury had already quizzed him about the history of philosophy at some length, including Plato, Berkeley, Kant, Hegel, Kierkegaard, and Schopenhauer; in the second exchange, it is evident that there was considerable mutual mistrust between Wittgenstein and Leavis.[12]

On other occasions, Wittgenstein expressed a very different attitude:

Drury: "I sometimes regret the amount of time I spent in reading the great historical philosophers, at a time when I couldn't understand them."
Wittgenstein: "I don't regret that you did all that reading."[13]
Wittgenstein: "I have been wondering what title to give my book. I have thought of something like 'Philosophical Remarks.'"
Drury: "Why not just call it 'Philosophy'?"
Wittgenstein: (angrily) "Don't be such a complete ass – how could I use a word that has meant so much in the history of mankind. As if my work wasn't only a small fragment of philosophy."[14]

These remarks indicate, in a more congenial setting, a respectful attitude toward reading the great philosophers, and considerably more humility toward the philosophical tradition. At the same time, it is clear that Wittgenstein preferred to read relatively little but very closely, frequently returning to the books he knew best.

If philosophy were a cultural constant, then certain philosophical writings could be regarded as compulsory, regardless of the reader's time and place. But philosophy was not like that for Wittgenstein; as von Wright stresses, Wittgenstein was "much more 'history-conscious' than is commonly recognized and understood," and did not regard philosophy as a

> "historical constant", any more than science is, or art... His way of seeing philosophy was not an attempt to tell us what philosophy, once and for all, *is*, but expressed what for him, in the setting of his times, it had to be.[15]

Wittgenstein recommended books to his friends and students from which he thought they could benefit, taking into account their circumstances and problems:

> "It may be that you ought not to read Kierkegaard. I couldn't read him now. Kierkegaard is so long winded; he keeps on saying the same thing over and over again. I want to say, 'Oh, all right, all right – I agree, but please get on with it.'[16]

> "A book you should read is William James's *Varieties of Religious Experience*; that was a book that helped me a lot at one time."[17]

What emerges from these and other conversations, and from the wide range of literary references in his papers, is that Wittgenstein's interest in literature, *pace* Leavis, was far from "rudimentary," and that he had an unusual range and depth of understanding.[18] He read Dostoyevsky in Russian, Kierkegaard in Danish, Ibsen in Norwegian, and Augustine in Latin.[19] He could detect a bad translation of a passage of Augustine's *Confessions*, and supply a better one that made the point clear.[20]

Von Wright also tells us that Wittgenstein received "deeper impressions" from writers "in the borderlands between philosophy, religion, and poetry," and that these included:

> St. Augustine, Kierkegaard, Dostoyevsky, and Tolstoy. The philosophical sections of St. Augustine's *Confessions* show a striking resemblance to Wittgenstein's own way of doing philosophy. Between Wittgenstein and Pascal there is a trenchant parallelism which deserves closer study. It should also be mentioned that Wittgenstein held the writings of Otto Weininger in high regard.[21]

A crucial parallel between Pascal and Wittgenstein is the importance and priority of practice, of doing, rather than the traditional privileging of theory. There is a common emphasis in Pascal, Kierkegaard, and Tolstoy on the importance of trust and faith. Their personal and confessional style suggests a greater role for the personal in philosophy, an attitude that is in sharp contrast to the objective and scientistic posture of the dominant tradition. We might even say that in all these writers there is an attempt to struggle with pretension and self-deception as they struggle with philosophical problems. This is also true of Dostoyevsky; we get a very lively sense of this when we read Wittgenstein's insightful conversation with Bouwsma about "Notes from Underground," where the topic discussed is how, if at all, is it possible to write objectively about oneself.[22]

Despite these important and noteworthy affinities between Wittgenstein and the writers von Wright identifies that Wittgenstein did read intensively, only two of them, Schopenhauer and Weininger, appear on the list of influences with which we began. This strongly suggests that the list is highly selective, and that the writers who were included each had some particular significance for Wittgenstein. We know that Wittgenstein had once hoped to study with Boltzmann, and there are striking parallels between Boltzmann's and Wittgenstein's conceptions of philosophy.[23] The "picture theory" of the *Tractatus* is a development of Hertzian themes.[24] Wittgenstein knew the opening words of Hertz's *Principles of Mechanics*, which recommend the formulation of alternative notations as a way of dissolving philosophical problems, so well that he could recite them by heart, and at one time intended to quote from them for the motto to the *Philosophical Investigations*.[25] Schopenhauer's influence is evident in the *Tractatus*, especially in the treatment of the will. Similarly, Russell's and Frege's work informed Wittgenstein's Tractarian approach to logic, language and mathematics. Kraus's deep respect for language, his incessant battle against journalistic abuse of language, and his perspective on this abuse as an index of cultural malaise all left a deep mark on Wittgenstein's philosophy. Loos's influence can be traced on the style of both the *Tractatus* and the *Philosophical Investigations* inasmuch as Loos's practice of, and writings on, architecture and aesthetics are notable for the erasure of any sort of ornament and decorative elements as inappropriate for our era. Wittgenstein's attitude to his time was affected by Spengler's vision of the decline of the West, and his emphasis on seeing connections and the synoptic overview he aimed at have marked affinities with Spengler's methodology.[26] Sraffa's extended criticism of Wittgenstein is praised in the preface to the *Philosophical Investigations*; while the precise nature of their conversations must remain a matter for conjecture, we do know that he mocked the Tractarian idea that every proposition has a logical form,[27] and would have conceived of language as a practice, not a formal system.[28]

Why Weininger?

The issue of Weininger's connection with Wittgenstein is particularly charged because of Weininger's notoriety as the most widely read anti-Semite and antifeminist of fin-de-siècle Vienna. *Sex and Character*, published a few months before his suicide at the age of twenty-three, became a huge bestseller. The book includes an up-to-date synthesis of recent work on sexuality, a good deal of popular psychology, and an eccentric philosophical system. However, the equally important posthumous collection of essays, *Über die letzten Dinge*, was first translated into English in 2001,[29] and the first English translation of *Sex and Character* was not only poorly translated but also badly abridged. As a result, most Anglo-American philosophers have not been well placed to make sense of Weininger's significance for Wittgenstein, even though he enthusiastically recommended *Sex and Character* to G. E. Moore and other friends as a work of genius. With the publication of Steven Burns's translation of *On Last Things* and Ladislaus Löb's new translation of the full text of *Sex and Character*, the translation obstacles have been removed.[30] However, the pressing question remains: What did Wittgenstein and Weininger have in common philosophically that would illuminate the former's describing the latter as the source of "a line of thinking" that he "seized on with enthusiasm . . . for [his] work of clarification"?[31]

Weininger is an important figure for the study of literary modernism and the relationship between science and culture in the first half of the twentieth century. Both of his books were extremely widely read and went through many printings and translations. They were influential for a whole host of leading authors between the turn of the century and the Second World War, and remain a subject of continuing fascination. While there is little, in our judgment, that is genuinely original or admirable about his work, there is no doubt that it was a potent distillation of many of the most powerful prejudices of his time, presented not as opinion, but as a synthesis of scientific fact and philosophical insight. *Sex and Character* is a little like a highbrow version of *Men are from Mars, Women are from Venus* for turn of the century Vienna, with a good deal of racism, homophobia, and sexism thrown in. However, among Weininger's avid readers can be counted not only Wittgenstein, but also most of the leading literary figures of the years from 1903 to 1939, including such luminaries as Ford Maddox Ford, James Joyce, Franz Kafka, Karl Kraus, Charlotte Perkins-Gilman, Gertrude Stein, and August Strindberg. More recently, *Sex and Character* has also attracted renewed attention among historians of science as a Baedeker to views about science, sexuality, and gender at the time.[32] Weininger's psychoanalytic connections are another important aspect in the continuing interest in his work. Wittgenstein praised Weininger as a "remarkable genius," in part because Weininger was one of the first people outside Freud's inner circle to see "the future importance of the ideas which Freud was putting forward."[33] Quite apart from the old debate as to whether Fliess's ideas about universal bisexuality were stolen by Weininger via Freud, among the most interesting aspects of *Sex and Character* are its proto-psychoanalytic moments, such as the notion that the whore/madonna conception of Woman is the result of Man's projection: "Women have no existence and no essence; they are not, they are nothing. . . . Woman is nothing but man's expression and projection of his own sexuality."[34]

For obvious reasons, much of the Weininger literature is devoted to the debate between those who condemn Weininger out of hand for his prejudices and those who aim to rehabilitate his reputation. The following passages, the first from a website devoted to Weininger and the second from a Wittgenstein expert's homepage, provide good examples of these opposed positions:

> *Sex and Character* is one of the few masterpieces of modern times. In it, Weininger overflows with profound insight, deepest love, and awesome courage.[35]

> Otto Weininger, the misogynist nutcase by whom Wittgenstein was notoriously influenced.[36]

Our approach is rather different. In addition to casting light, not only on why Weininger mattered to Wittgenstein, but also on the problems surrounding talk of "influence" in philosophy, the essays in this book contribute to the project of understanding Weininger's reception, addressing both his cultural and intellectual significance and the fact that his work continues to provoke such extreme responses. Before turning to a review of the leading approaches to the relationship between Wittgenstein and Weininger, it will be helpful to first consider the parallels with Wittgenstein's relationship to another controversial citizen of fin-de-siècle Vienna: Sigmund Freud. Wittgenstein told Rush Rhees that he first read Freud shortly after 1919, and from that point on "Freud was one of the few authors he thought worth reading."[37] In the early 1940s Wittgenstein spoke of himself as a "disciple of Freud" and as "a follower" of Freud.[38] Nevertheless, he also thought of psychoanalysis as unscientific, and dangerous. Freud is full of pseudo-explanations, which are admittedly brilliant, clever, and charming – hence all the more dangerous.[39]

Freud wanted to replace the mythology in our "explanations" of human action. Similarly, Wittgenstein wanted to see through the mythology involved in philosophical attempts to understand language: do not be taken in by the surface grammar of language, but understand it through "use."[40] At the same time, Wittgenstein realized that Freud introduced a new mythology, which charmed and captivated, despite its unflattering nature. As McGuinness puts it, Wittgenstein "accepted and rejected Freud in equal measure, perhaps healthily."[41] His attitude to Weininger seems much the same: an attitude of ambivalence. He embraces and distances himself from Weininger in equal measure in the letter to Moore. Yet when it came to the list of influences, Wittgenstein included Weininger and left out Freud. What differences between Weininger and Freud account for this?

One response to this question starts from Freud's strategy of arguing that things that look different are really the same. For instance, he denies that there is any real difference between normal and abnormal behavior, in that both are to be explained in terms of deep unconscious forces. Wittgenstein's line of thinking is radically different. The following remark on Hegel is equally applicable to Freud:

> Hegel seems to me to be always wanting to say that things which look different are really the same. Whereas my interest is in showing that things which look

the same are really different. I was thinking of using as a motto for my book a quotation from *King Lear*: "I'll teach you differences."[42]

This indicates a deep difference between Weininger and Freud. While Freud thought of himself as a scientist and a reductionist, Weininger resisted both scientism and reductionism in his writings, where he insisted on differences of many kinds: between and among men and women, different temperaments, and cultures. Weininger, like Wittgenstein, was trained as a scientist, but became an antiscientistic thinker, opposed to those who extend scientific methods into areas where they are inappropriate. Hence Freud gives dangerous pseudo-explanations, while Weininger and Wittgenstein accent description, and depiction of facts and practices. Again, Freud is an essentialist, trying to bring all human behavior under one explanatory rubric, while Wittgenstein is an anti-essentialist. Weininger certainly looks like an essentialist, with his quasi-Platonic definitions of opposite Types, and his purported explanation of all character in terms of the Man-Woman dichotomy, but Wittgenstein may have found in Weininger's ever-inventive discovering of new distinctions an anti-essentialist movement of thought that he wished to clarify.

Wittgenstein may also have identified with the spirit in which Weininger wrote. Wittgenstein's struggle with hypocrisy, with self-deception in oneself and one's work, his emphasis on clarity and clarification as a value in itself, and his respect for the particular case are all relevant here. In the late 1940s, Wittgenstein contrasted Weininger with Kafka in the following terms: Kafka, he said, "gave himself a great deal of trouble *not* writing about his trouble," while Weininger, "whatever his faults, was a man who really did write about his."[43] Weininger wrote about problems in his own life, while Freud wrote about problems in other people's lives. Weininger worked on himself as he engaged in the activity of philosophizing and psychologizing, while Freud had the disengaged posture of the scientist. So Freud's scientism, essentialism, and his captivating new mythology are not only mistakes but also personal flaws:

The less somebody knows & understands himself the less great he is, however great may be his talent. For this reason our scientists are not great. For this reason Freud, Spengler, Kraus, Einstein are not great.[44]

Freud believed he had made a series of scientific discoveries, discoveries that provided for a scientific theory of the mind. Wittgenstein reads him as an inventor of an unscientific "way of thinking" that laid claim to the authority of a science; ultimately, psychoanalysis was not only a "powerful mythology"[45] but also a form of self-deception. Freud says: Think like this. Weininger and Wittgenstein say: Here is one way or line of thinking; now keep it in mind but think for yourself.

In sum, we have developed a parallel and a contrast between Wittgenstein's readings of Freud and of Weininger. Wittgenstein spoke of Freud's extraordinary scientific achievement and of himself as a disciple of Freud, terms of praise at least as strong as those he gave to Weininger. Yet he was an implacable critic of Freud's claims to have provided a scientific theory of the mind, or to have made scientific discoveries. This ambivalence is reminiscent of Wittgenstein's treatment of Weininger too, both in content and vocabulary. However, Weininger's writing helped Wittgenstein to resist the kind of essentialism and scientism that Freud, in his role as scientist of the mind, takes for granted.[46]

The Uses of Reading

Section 375 of the *Philosophical Investigations* consists of a series of Socratic questions about reading:

> How does one teach anyone to read to himself? How does one know if he can do so? How does he himself know that he is doing what is required of him?[47]

In answering them, Wittgenstein urges us to resist the inclination to turn inward, and the related attractions of a picture of reading as an inner process or activity, psychological or neurological. Sections 156 to 171 contain an extended examination of the concept of reading, a topic Wittgenstein repeatedly discussed. Here, he directs our attention to the skill of producing the right sounds as one looks at the words on the page; understanding what is read need not be part of this activity. In this sense of the word, it is possible to imagine a person who serves as a "reading machine," vocalizing correctly, but without any understanding of the text. One aim of this passage is to get the reader to distinguish between reading, in this reproductive sense, and reading with understanding; another is to combat the idea that "reading is just a special inner experience which you may or may not accompany by utterance out loud of the words you read."[48]

Perhaps these reflections on reading can shed light on Wittgenstein's ways of reading others' works as well as the difficulties he encountered in doing so. For once we distinguish reproductive reading from reading with understanding, and recognize that both of them are practical abilities, rather than a self-authenticating inner process, this leaves open the possibility that being well-read is no guarantee that one has understood what one has read. Reading and influence are complex notions. As we read Wittgenstein on reading we are reminded that "we also use the word 'to read' for a family of cases. And in different circumstances we apply different criteria for a person's reading."[49] To say of a person that we can read him or her like a book is to say that we understand that person very well – that he or she is transparent to us. But when the book is itself complicated and opaque, when it does not wear its meaning on its face, as it were, then we have a problem. Are we to understand "reading" in these circumstances as a process, or as an achievement, or both? As our various authors stress, there are many ways in which one can read and be influenced by an author.

The first assessments of Weininger's influence on Wittgenstein were relatively brief, rather general, and gave little attention to textual details and analysis. They also tended toward the purely biographical, without addressing the philosophical. Yet the relations between life and philosophy, influence and originality, are themselves themes that link Weininger and Wittgenstein.[50] Indeed, it is striking that the passage on Wittgenstein's influences, cited at the beginning of this introduction, is surrounded by remarks on influence and originality that have a strongly Weiningerian character.

Early Assessments

We now turn to a brief overview of the early literature on the relationship between Wittgenstein and Weininger. The principal authorities are Allan Janik, Rudolf Haller, Ray Monk, Brian McGuinness, and Jacques Le Rider. Haller and McGuinness primarily concern themselves with the *Tractatus*, while Janik, Le Rider and Monk also address the question of Weininger's subsequent significance for Wittgenstein.

In Allan Janik and Stephen Toulmin's *Wittgenstein's Vienna* (1973), one of the first discussions of the Wittgenstein-Weininger connection, Weininger makes only a brief appearance: they emphasize his negative view of femininity, and his influence on Karl Kraus.[51] However, by the end of the 1970s Janik had begun to argue that Weininger's significance for Wittgenstein was much more direct and far-reaching, for Janik reads Weininger as Wittgenstein's leading example of someone who tries to say what can only be shown:

> By looking at certain aspects of Weininger's work, one can discover an ethical position that asserts the sorts of things about "absolute value" that Wittgenstein admires but insists are unsayable.... Wittgenstein presupposes the validity of Weininger's ethical views in practice while he denies that these views can be put into words in the *Tractatus*.[52]

In a pioneering essay, Rudolf Haller further articulated this approach to the Wittgenstein-Weininger connection, arguing that Weininger influenced Wittgenstein philosophically in the *Tractatus*, exploring such philosophical common ground as their approaches to solipsism, the thesis that the soul of man is the microcosm, and the unity of logic and ethics. The latter is seen by Haller as the deepest affinity between the two thinkers in that "both believe that neither logical nor ethical rules can be established, but yet that both logical and ethical rules have an essential connection to the world and are thus one and the same."[53] Jacques Le Rider, in his *Le Cas Otto Weininger* (1982, 1985), on the other hand, construes Weininger's influence on Wittgenstein as purely personal. He denies there was any positive philosophical influence and argues that Wittgenstein's work amounts to a negation of Weininger's main theses.

Wittgenstein's biographers, Ray Monk and Brian McGuinness, also give their attention to this issue. McGuinness highlights the affinities between Weininger and the young Wittgenstein. Both were of Jewish descent and the theme of the influence of a person's Jewishness on his or her life recurs in their works; both were attracted to the idea that a man's character is something he cannot escape from.[54] McGuinness also suggests that the role of a theory of elements in the *Tractatus* is a Weiningerian echo. But what is of utmost importance, McGuinness maintains, for understanding why Weininger mattered to Wittgenstein, is the personal dimension. It was because "Weininger's thought about character, superficial and half-baked at times, came from a deep concern with ethical problems of his own life" that Wittgenstein later spoke of *Sex and Character* as an important book – for the questions it raised, not for its answers.[55] While McGuinness maintains in his biography, subtitled *Young Ludwig* (1988), that the influence was both existential and philosophical, he restricts the philosophical impact to the *Tractatus* and its source to Weininger's first book, *Sex and Character.*

The subtitle of Ray Monk's biography, *The Duty of Genius* (1990), refers to Monk's construal of the Wittgenstein-Weininger connection: he sees Weininger's ideas about the life of genius as shaping the kind of life that Wittgenstein led. Monk believes that of all the books Wittgenstein read in his adolescence, it was *Sex and Character* that "had the greatest and most lasting impact on his outlook."[56] *Sex and Character* rigorously separates love and sexual desire, insists that sexuality is incompatible with the honesty that genius demands, and takes an uncompromising view of everything except the products of genius. Weininger's peculiar twist on Kant's moral law not only imposes an inviolable duty to be honest but requires that everyone discover in themselves whatever genius they possess. Observing that Wittgenstein gave voice to these Weiningerian themes throughout his life, Monk maintains that Weininger's positive influence was primarily on Wittgenstein's convictions as to how he should lead his life.[57] However the connections Monk cites do not really answer the question about Weininger's impact on Wittgenstein's *philosophical* outlook. While Monk provides us with much evidence for ascribing a common outlook to Wittgenstein and Weininger, the question of precisely how Weininger influenced Wittgenstein's philosophy, and to what extent the influence goes beyond the particular ethical and cosmological themes that Wittgenstein took up in the *Tractatus* is not addressed.

Taken together, these early interpretations do give us a compelling picture of Weininger's impact on the young Wittgenstein and the *Tractatus.* They also provide a point of departure for a more detailed consideration of Weininger's influence in the *Tractatus*, and of the significance of the Weiningerian unity of logic and ethics. Weininger claims that

> Logic and ethics are fundamentally the same, they are no more than a duty to oneself. . . . All ethics are possible only by the laws of logic, and logic is no

more than the ethical side of the law. Not only virtue, but also insight, not only sanctity, but also wisdom, are the duties of mankind. Through the union of these alone comes perfection.[58]

The importance of this passage lies in its determination of what it is to be a moral agent: Only someone who can understand logic can be a moral agent.

A creature that cannot grasp the mutual exclusiveness of A and not A has no difficulty in lying; more than that, such a creature has not even the consciousness of lying, being without a standard of truth.[59]

Both Wittgenstein and Weininger paid close attention to the phenomena of hypocrisy and lying, and in strikingly similar ways: as occasions where we are confronted by problems of both logic and morality.[60] Wittgenstein touches on this Weiningerian theme in the *Tractatus*, where he characterizes logic, ethics and aesthetics as "transcendental":

Logic is not a body of doctrine, but a mirror-image of the world. Logic is transcendental.[61]

And further on:

Ethics is transcendental. (Ethics and aesthetics are one.)[62]

The standard reading of these gnomic identifications is that the use of the term "transcendental" provides the Kantian key to understanding them. Logic, ethics and aesthetics are all transcendental because they have to do with the conditions for the possibility of the world. Kant certainly gave pure reason a central place in his ethical system. But it is Weininger, not Kant, who draws the particular connections between logic and ethics that are of importance in the *Tractatus*. Taking seriously the deep connection between logic and ethics opens up an ethical perspective on Wittgenstein's struggles with logic and language. If confusion in our thinking is a kind of moral failure, then a struggle for clarity, transparency, and perspicuity is a moral struggle. For this reason, Wittgenstein writes that "clarity, transparency, is an end in itself,"[63] not only a means to other ends. Similarly, Weininger writes, "All error must be felt to be a crime. And so a man must not err. He *must* find the truth, and so he can find it."[64] Wittgenstein's works belong to the genre of *confessional* philosophical writing, the sort of writing that breaks down the distinction between the personal and the philosophical. Against this background, the strangest thing about the famous exchange between Wittgenstein and Russell – "What are you thinking about, logic or your sins?" "Both" – is that Russell was so puzzled by it that he made a joke of it.[65]

In this way, the Tractarian connection between logic and ethics is made clearer if we see the extent to which Wittgenstein's work on the *Tractatus* in 1916 is Weiningerian. However, the overall impression left by these initial assessments of Weininger's influence on Wittgenstein is that Weininger's personal impact had a deep and lasting influence on Wittgenstein as a man, but Weininger's philosophical impact was limited to sections 5.6 and 6.4 of the *Tractatus*.

Reassessments

Most early attempts to assess the precise nature of Weininger's influence on Wittgenstein looked for commonalities in content: views that could be attributed to Weininger, and identified as the source of Wittgenstein's own convictions. The results were relatively modest, and focused on a limited number of quite specific doctrines in the *Tractatus*. This collection of essays reassesses that influence, arguing that its nature, scope, and duration have been underestimated. In particular, and more positively, most authors aim to show not only how Weininger influenced Wittgenstein in 1916, or the early 1930s, but also how Wittgenstein's philosophy as a whole shows signs of that influence. One reason for this change in approach is that Weininger's extreme essentialism sits uneasily with his insistence on the enormous variation and particularity of individual cases, an aspect of his work that philosophers have not previously acknowledged.

Unable to see how Weininger's principal philosophical views might explain Wittgenstein's attribution of influence to Weininger, Monk's *Duty of Genius* and McGuinness's *Young Ludwig* emphasized biographical and existential concerns. While our contributors continue this discussion of the relationship between the doctrinal and the biographical, they also open up different ways of construing influence. Closer attention to Wittgenstein's reading of Weininger has led us to question common assumptions about the concept of influence, and its role in previous discussions of the Weininger-Wittgenstein connection. Each of the first three contributors to the volume, Szabados, Janik, and

Burns, identifies a number of shared lines of thinking, a cluster of common preoccupations, characterized by family resemblances. The second three contributors, Schulte, Steuer and Stern, are less sympathetic to the idea of replacing the search for a single shared line of thinking with a number of different and more open-ended connections. Schulte contends that the *Tractatus*' debt to Weininger may be quite specific and limited, while Weininger's broader influence may have been due to his style and methodology – the way he made use of the views of others – not his own views. Steuer and Stern both provide accounts of Weininger's influence on Wittgenstein in which Weininger's significance was not so much a matter of what Wittgenstein could assimilate in Weininger, but rather that Weininger provided the perfect statement of a position that enabled Wittgenstein to arrive at a position that was diametrically opposed. While this rough classification of our authors' methods is inevitably an oversimplification – for instance, Janik and Szabados also stress the idea that Weininger's importance for Wittgenstein was that he provided a strikingly stated alternative view, an "object of comparison"[66] – it may be helpful as an orientation to the range of approaches canvassed in this volume. Contributors also attend to striking similarities in the two authors' values, their conception of ethics, and the ways in which they wrote.

Taken together, our contributors offer a broader and deeper perspective on why Weininger mattered to Wittgenstein. Until now, most interpreters have begun from the premise that Weininger's importance to Wittgenstein was either as an example of egregious error – his extreme essentialism, his denigration of women – or as a positive influence in areas that one might consider nonphilosophical – his views about genius, his antimodernism. Each contributor, in one way or another, explores the much more interesting idea that Weininger was an important positive philosophical influence on Wittgenstein.

In "Eggshells or Nourishing Yolk? A Portrait of Wittgenstein as a Weiningerian," Béla Szabados draws our attention to the surprisingly large number of congenial "lines of thinking" that Wittgenstein found in Weininger. He concentrates on the textual evidence in Wittgenstein's writing, evidence that is not confined to the passages where Wittgenstein explicitly quotes or refers to Weininger. Drawing on parts of Weininger's writing that contain some of his best, but also least noticed, ideas Szabados sets out a wide variety of commonalities. This common ground includes their conception of clarification, their use of similes, their attention to particularity and individual difference, their anti-essentialism, their views about ideal types, and their diagnosis of philosophical error. He brings out these shared commitments by means of a close reading of passages from *Sex and Character* with passages from Wittgenstein's later works, especially the *Philosophical Investigations*, arguing that Wittgenstein's later philosophical procedures and ideas are interestingly and pointedly Weiningerian.

In "Weininger and the Two Wittgensteins," Allan Janik first provides a detailed account of Weininger's impact on Wittgenstein's thinking about the mystical and the problem of life in 1916, stressing the relationship between the two authors' ideas about the limits of language. Both Weininger and Wittgenstein take as a point of departure the idea that our most familiar ways of speaking and thinking tend to mislead us and tempt us to self-deception, both philosophical and personal. A central presupposition in Weininger's work is that we cannot trust conventional notions or values, an outlook that is worked out in particular detail in the case of gender and sexuality. Janik argues that the later Wittgenstein transforms Weininger's critique of conventional commitments about sex and character, and of our bewitchment by our preconceptions about race and gender, into a corresponding skepticism about conventional philosophical ideas about the nature of language. But while Weininger thinks we must overcome our animal nature, Wittgenstein's approach turns on acknowledging it. In particular, Wittgenstein draws our attention to the way primitive human knowledge turns on practical abilities, abilities that are prior to explicit rule-following. As a result, Wittgenstein aims to dissolve philosophical problems by directing our attention to practices, and so changing the way we look at things. Consequently, the notion that philosophizing is more a matter of the will than of the intellect, calling for a transition from a theoretical perspective to a practical point of view, is part of Wittgenstein's Weiningerian inheritance.

Steven Burns's "Sex and Solipsism: Weininger's *On Last Things*" begins with an overview of the principal themes of *On Last Things.* He gives particular attention to the Wittgensteinian aspects of Weininger's conception of the transcendental ego, his insistence on the subjectivity and absoluteness of the moral imperative, and his account of the primacy of culture over the techniques of modern science. Burns then turns to two interrelated themes in this material: Weininger's solipsistic view of love, and his assessment of solipsism. The first can be seen in Weininger's construal of Ibsen's use of the idea that the love of a woman can redeem a man, a leading theme for Ibsen, Goethe, and Wagner, among many others. Weininger, starting from a Kantian conception of autonomy, takes for granted the idea that nothing outside me can be of ultimate ethical value to me. So the redeeming value of Solveig's love for Peer at the end of Ibsen's *Peer Gynt* has nothing to do with the flesh and blood Solveig, or her love for him. Rather, Peer must be redeemed by "the Solveig within him." However, Weininger also argues that the existence of one's own ego can no more be disproved than it can be proved, and that while a refutation – or a proof – of solipsism is impossible, "to recoil from solipsism . . . is craven."[67] Burns argues that Wittgenstein's discussion of solipsism in the *Tractatus* can be better understood in the light of Weininger's simultaneous attraction to, and repulsion by solipsism: that, like Weininger, Wittgenstein does not attempt to prove, or refute, solipsism. Finally, Burns develops a Wittgensteinian reading of Weininger on self-love and self-hatred, arguing that Wittgenstein approached "Weininger's comparison of self-hatred and 'sonhood' in the way one might take a surprising but fruitful figure of speech." In this connection, he cites another striking Weiningerian comparison, a passage in which Weininger directly links the nature of morality to the fact that time only flows in one direction. "Thus the greatest of moral questions, whether to be honest or deceitful, whether to be honest with yourself or self-deceitful, whether to live by the truth or the lie, is closely related to the nature of time."

The question of the connections between Weininger's and Wittgenstein's approaches to time is also taken up by Joachim Schulte, in "Wittgenstein and Weininger: Time, Life, World." Unlike Burns, who treats their overlapping approaches to time and honesty as one of a family of resemblances between the two writers, Schulte proposes that Wittgenstein thought of Weininger as an influence because the *Tractatus* had taken a quite specific view from Weininger about the nature of time. Schulte proposes that if we are to identify a specific line of thinking in Weininger that Wittgenstein took over for his own purposes, it is Weininger's way of conceiving of the unidirectionality of time: Weininger connects the idea that one cannot return to the past with the capacity for ethical conduct. This, in turn, can be seen as the genesis of the Tractarian idea that "agreement with the world" is central to an ethical stance. However, the first three-quarters of Schulte's paper give a much more wide-ranging answer to the question of how Weininger influenced Wittgenstein. One reason for the difficulties we face in trying to understand what Wittgenstein got from Weininger, he suggests, is that there is no such thing as "Weiningerian thought." Of course, it is possible to identify any number of positions that are defended in his writing. But such summaries of what he wrote are misleading, since it is characteristic of Weininger that he took up other people's thoughts and made use of them for his own purposes:

> Weininger likes to tease his readers and to convey a concealed message by a subtle strategy of saying and apparently unsaying things at the same time. . . . it is not far-fetched to suppose that the author of such a deeply ironical and paradoxical work as the *Logische-philosophische Abhandlung* (another teasing title, if you are looking for more examples) might like the works of another writer reveling in (mostly unobvious) irony and paradox.

Janik, Burns, and Schulte emphasize the respect for limits in the two thinkers and tie this to their conception of the ethical. Daniel Steuer, on the other hand, suggests a seemingly opposed, but actually closely related, picture of the philosopher as the criminal, as a transgressor of limits, a traveler between different systems of thought. In "Uncanny Differences: Wittgenstein and Weininger as *Doppelgänger*," Steuer makes use of the notions of the "uncanny" and the "*Doppelgänger*" to shed light on the relationship between the two thinkers, drawing on Stanley Cavell's proposal that "a difference in which everything and nothing differs is uncanny." Examples of such a difference would be the difference between mechanical repetition and the repetition that is necessary to sustain life (the difference between the animate and the inanimate), or the difference between the feminine and the masculine, one of Weininger's main themes.

According to Freud the uncanny should be understood as the return of the familiar but repressed. The *Doppelgänger* is a special case of the uncanny: another person who represents a different version of oneself, one that includes possibilities that have been discarded – for good or bad reasons – in the course of one's own life. However, Weininger and Wittgenstein attach slightly different meanings to the *Doppelgänger* motif. Applying the notions of the uncanny and the *Doppelgänger* to the relation between Weininger and Wittgenstein leads Steuer to ask what Wittgenstein saw in Weininger that he had to give up, both philosophically and personally. Weininger's views on judgment, the quest for the self, and tragedy provide the basis for a detailed account of what Wittgenstein rejected by negating Weininger's form of thought. Concentrating on the chapters in *On Last Things* on "Science and Culture," and "Metaphysics," and on "Friedrich Schiller," as well as on Wittgenstein's recently published diaries from the 1930s, Steuer proposes that Wittgenstein took important ideas from Weininger, yet developed them into a diametrically opposed form and method. This results in what Steuer calls an aesthetic theory of judgment. In the course of this process Wittgenstein transforms Weininger's theory of double-life into a philosophical double perspective of general relativism on the one hand, and personal fundamentalism on the other.

David Stern's "Weininger and Wittgenstein on 'Animal Psychology'" takes up the question of the place of animals in Wittgenstein's later philosophy. Like Steuer, Stern highlights Weininger's significance for Wittgenstein as a point of departure for a view diametrically opposed to Weininger's, yet arising out of dialogue with Weininger. Weininger's essay on "Metaphysics" sets out to specify the ultimate symbolic significance of each type of thing in the world. Drawing on an "introspective-psychological" method, he aims to uncover what "the sea, what iron, what ants, what the Chinese mean, the *idea* which they represent."[68] The method turns on the idea of the human being as a microcosm: because everything is interpreted through our psychological categories, to say what everything in the world symbolizes is ultimately to talk about human characteristics. Weininger's most worked out example is the dog, which he maintains is the symbol of the criminal. Wittgenstein spoke highly of this essay in later life. Stern contrasts Weininger's conception of dogs as the image of the criminal with the questions about the differences between humans and animals, but especially dogs, in the opening paragraphs of Part II of the *Philosophical Investigations*, thus connecting the topic to central themes of Wittgenstein's philosophy, namely the differences between humans and animals, and the relationship between thought and language. Weininger's solipsistic conception of animals as reflecting his own fears and obsessions is contrasted with Wittgenstein's respect for the particularity of other kinds of living creatures. While Weininger lost sight of a world of differences in his projection of human concerns onto animals, Wittgenstein brings our attention to those very differences between the human animal and other animals.

Wittgenstein remarked that "People who are constantly asking 'why' are like tourists, who stand in front of a building, reading Baedeker, & through reading about the history of the building's construction etc etc are prevented from *seeing* it."[69] This could be negatively applied in a rather global way to discourage reading in the history of philosophy, or locally applied to our very reassessments in this book. But that would be unwarranted. For it is possible to study the history of a building and its construction with a view to seeing it better. Indeed, without a certain knowledge of its history, one may well be impoverished. That is to say, it is not only possible to do philosophy through doing history of philosophy, but that the price of doing one without the other is to weaken both of them. Reading Wittgenstein with an eye to his reading of Weininger illuminates not only a particular moment in the history of philosophy, but also helps us to see connections between philosophy and history that we might otherwise be prevented from seeing.

Notes

1. Wittgenstein, *Culture and Value*, 1980, 19; 1998, 16.
2. Flowers 1999, pp. 195–6.
3. Wittgenstein 1995, 250; letter dated 23 August 1931. See also Monk 1990, 312–13, Stern 2000, 387–98 or 2001, 254–62.
4. The Bergen edition of *Wittgenstein*'s *Nachlass* yields eight "hits" for a search for Weininger, but only four distinct references, as several of the entries are minor revisions of previous entries: (1) MS 111, 195; *Culture and Value*, 1980, 16; 1998, 23, 13 September 1931; see also MS 153a, 122r; (2) MS 115, 23; see also MS 146, 82; TS 228, 117; TS 230, 18; Wittgenstein 1969, 176, s.128; (3) MS 154, 16r, *Culture and Value*, 1980, 19; 1998, 16; (4) MS 173, 17r, *Culture and Value*, 1980, 84; 1998, 95, 30 March, 1950.
5. In "Ludwig Wittgenstein: A Biographical Sketch" (von Wright 1982, 33), first published in 1954.
6. *Culture and Value*, editorial preface, 1980, unpaginated; 1998, p. ix.
7. von Wright 1982, 33.

8. For Berkeley, Hegel, Marx, see Rhees 1981, 171, reprinted as Rhees 1984, 157–158. For Marx, see also Rhees 1981, 223, 226–31, reprinted as Rhees 1984, 202, 205–9.
9. On *Varieties of Religious Experience,* see Rhees 1981, 121, reprinted as Rhees 1984, 106. On the *Principles of Psychology,* see Monk 1990, 477–8. For further discussion of Wittgenstein and James, see Goodman 2002.
10. Rhees 1981, 172, reprinted as Rhees 1984, 158.
11. Rhees 1981, 63, reprinted as Rhees 1984, 50.
12. Leavis, in Rhees 1981, 72–3, 75–6, 79–80, reprinted as Rhees 1984, 59, 62, 65–7.
13. Rhees 1981, 171, reprinted as Rhees 1984, 157.
14. Rhees 1981, 173–4, reprinted as Rhees 1984, 160.
15. Von Wright 1982, 216.
16. Rhees 1981, 171, reprinted as Rhees 1984, 157–8.
17. Rhees 1981, 121, reprinted as Rhees 1984, 106.
18. Rhees 1981, 79, reprinted as Rhees 1984, 66. For a discussion of the literature with which Wittgenstein was familiar in his first eighteen years, see McGuinness 1988, 32–43; for a further indication of the range of Wittgenstein's reading, see Hallett 1977, 759–75.
19. For Dostoyevsky, see Pascal's memoir, in Rhees 1981, 34; Rhees 1984, 21; or Flowers 1999, 228. For Kierkegaard, see Lee's memoir, in Flowers 1999, 195. For Ibsen, see von Wright, quoted in Hallett 1977, 759.
20. Rhees 1981, 104, reprinted as Rhees 1984, 89–90.
21. Von Wright 1982, 33.
22. See Bouwsma 1986, 69–71; Szabados 1992, 7–11; Stern 2001, 246–8.
23. See McGuinness 2002, pp. 163–6.
24. See Stern 1995, s.2.1.
25. For further discussion of the relationship between Hertz and Wittgenstein, see Janik 2001, 147–69.
26. See Monk 1990, pp. 302–4.
27. See Malcolm 1984, 57–8.
28. For further discussion of the Sraffa connection, see Kitching and Pleasants 2002, pp. 7–9, 113–43, and 200–4.
29. While some Germanists maintain that *On Last Things* "had a greater impact on thought and letters" in German-speaking countries than *Sex and Character* (see Janik in Weininger 2001, x), the lack of an English translation has meant that most Anglophone commentators have either ignored it or seriously underestimated its significance; for instance, Sengoopta's book on Weininger, subtitled "Sex, Science and Self in Imperial Vienna" (2000; see 161, n. 1), makes no use of it. Except for the work of Allan Janik, it has been almost totally neglected in the Anglophone literature.
30. See Weininger 2001 and Weininger 2004. The new English translation of *Sex and Character* is the first translation of the full text of the book, including the very lengthy appendix in which Weininger cites, quotes, and discusses his sources.

31. Wittgenstein, *Culture and Value*, 1980, 19; 1998, 16.
32. See Sengoopta 1992, 2000.
33. Rhees 1981, 106, reprinted as Rhees 1984, 91.
34. Weininger 1906, 286, 300, based on Weininger 1980, 383, 402.
35. Kevin Solway, http://members.ozemail.com.au/~ksolway/ottow.html
36. T. P. Uschanov, http://www.helsinki.fi/~tuschano/lw/links/
37. Rhees, in Wittgenstein 1967, 41.
38. Ibid.
39. Wittgenstein, *Culture and Value*, 1980, 55; 1998, 62.
40. McGuinness proposes a reading along these lines at the end of his "Freud and Wittgenstein" (1982, 42–3.)
41. McGuinness 1982, 43.
42. Rhees 1981, 171, reprinted as Rhees 1984, 157.
43. Monk 1990, 498.
44. Wittgenstein, *Culture and Value*, 1998, 53 (not included in the 1980 edition).
45. Wittgenstein 1967, 50, 52.
46. For further discussion of the relationship between Freud and Wittgenstein along related lines, see Bouveresse 1995.
47. Wittgenstein 1953, s.375.
48. Anscombe 1991, 4.
49. Wittgenstein 1953, s.164.
50. For further discussion of the relationship between philosophy and biography, see Szabados 1992 and 1995 and the papers by Monk, Conant, Nordmann, and Stern in Klagge 2001.
51. Janik and Toulmin 1973, 70–4.
52. Janik 1985, 80, a reprint of Janik 1980.
53. Haller 1988, 97.
54. McGuinness 1988, 42.
55. McGuinness 1988, 40.
56. Monk 1990, 25.
57. Monk 1990, 23–5.
58. Weininger 1906, 159; Weininger 1980, 207.
59. Weininger 1906, 150; Weininger 1980, 193–4.
60. See Weininger 1906, 266, 268, 273–4, 342; Weininger1980, 358–9, 362, 368–70, 454; Weininger 1997, 142–50; 2001, 114–20; *Culture and Value*, 1980, 8, 24, 32, 33, 34, 35, 49; 1998, 11, 28, 37, 38, 39, 41, 56–7. See also Monk 1990, 3.
61. Wittgenstein 1922, 6.13.
62. Ibid., 6.421.
63. Wittgenstein, *Culture and Value*, 9.
64. Weininger 1906, 158; Weininger 1980, 205.
65. Russell 1951, 143. See also Monk 1990, 64; McGuinness 1988, 156.
66. Wittgenstein 1953, s.131.
67. Weininger, 1997, 148; 2001, 118–19.

68. Weininger, 2001, 96.
69. Wittgenstein 1980, 40; 1998, 46.

References

Anscombe, Elizabeth (1991). "Wittgenstein: Whose Philosopher?" In A. Phillips Griffiths, ed., *Wittgenstein Centenary Essays.* Cambridge: Cambridge University Press, 1–10.

Bouveresse, Jacques (1995). *Wittgenstein Reads Freud: The Myth of the Unconscious.* Translated by Carol Cosman; first published in French in 1991. Princeton: Princeton University Press.

Bouwsma, Oets (1986). *Wittgenstein Conversations, 1949–1951.* Indianapolis, IN: Hackett.

Flowers, F. A. III, ed. (1999). *Portraits of Wittgenstein, Volume II.* Bristol: Thoemmes Press.

Goodman, Russell (2002). *Wittgenstein and William James.* Cambridge: Cambridge University Press.

Haller, Rudolf (1988). "What Do Wittgenstein and Weininger Have in Common?" In Haller, *Questions on Wittgenstein.* Lincoln: University of Nebraska Press, 90–9.

Hallett, Garth (1977). *A Companion to Wittgenstein's "Philosophical Investigations."* Ithaca, NY: Cornell University Press.

Harrowitz, Nancy A., and Barbara Hyams, eds. (1995). *Jews and Gender: Responses to Otto Weininger.* Philadelphia: Temple University Press.

Janik, Allan (1980). "Philosophical Sources of Wittgenstein's Ethics." *Telos* 44: 131–44. Reprinted in Janik (1985), 74–95.

——— (1981). "Therapeutic Nihilism: How not to write about Otto Weininger." In Barry Smith, ed. *Structure and Gestalt: Philosophy and Literature in Austria-Hungary and her successor states.* Amsterdam: John Benjamins B. V., 263–92.

——— (1985). *Essays on Wittgenstein and Weininger.* Amsterdam: Rodopi.

——— (1995). "How Did Weininger Influence Wittgenstein?" In Nancy A. Harrowitz and Barbara Hyams, eds., *Jews and Gender: Responses to Otto Weininger.* Philadelphia: Temple University Press, 61–72.

——— (2001). *Wittgenstein's Vienna Revisited.* New Brunswick and London: Transaction Publishers.

——— (2002). "From Logic to Animality or How Wittgenstein Used Otto Weininger." *Nomadas* 4. *http://www.ucm.es/info/eurotheo/nomadas/n4-ajanik1.htm*

——— (2002). "The Dionysian Element in Kant or How Friedrich Nietzsche Influenced Otto Weininger." Paper presented at the Nietzsche and Central Europe symposium held in Vienna, 2002. (Proceedings forthcoming, edited by Jacob Gomomb, published by Wiener Universitaets Verlag.)

Janik, Allan, and Stephen Toulmin (1973). *Wittgenstein's Vienna.* New York: Simon & Schuster. (1996, revised second edition, Chicago: Ivan Dee.)

Kitching, Gavin, and Nigel Pleasants, eds. (2002). *Marx and Wittgenstein: Knowledge, morality and politics.* London: Routledge.

Klagge, James, ed. (2001). *Wittgenstein: Biography and Philosophy.* Cambridge: Cambridge University Press.

Le Rider, Jacques (1982). *Le Cas Otto Weininger: Racines de l'antiféminisme et l'antisémitisme.* Paris: Presses Universitaires de France.

——— (1985). *Der Fall Otto Weininger: Wurzeln des Antifeminismus und Antisemitismus.* Translated by Dieter Hornig. Revised edition of Le Rider (1982). Vienna and Munich: Löcker.

——— (1993). *Modernity and Crises of Identity: Culture and Society in Fin-de-Siècle Vienna.* Translated by Rosemary Morris (first published in French in 1990). New York: Continuum.

——— (1995). "The Otto Weininger Case Revisited." In Nancy A. Harrowitz and Barbara Hyams, eds., *Jews and Gender: Responses to Otto Weininger.* Philadelphia: Temple University Press, 21–33.

McGuinness, Brian (1982). "Freud and Wittgenstein." In McGuinness, ed., *Wittgenstein and his Times.* Chicago: University of Chicago Press, 27–43.

——— (1988). *Wittgenstein: A Life. Young Ludwig (1889–1921).* London: Duckworth.

——— (2002). *Approaches to Wittgenstein: Collected Papers.* London: Routledge.

Malcolm, Norman (1984). *Ludwig Wittgenstein: A Memoir.* Second edition. Oxford: Oxford University Press.

Monk, Ray (1990). *Ludwig Wittgenstein: The Duty of Genius.* New York: Free Press.

Rhees, Rush (1967). "Conversations on Freud." In Ludwig Wittgenstein, *Lectures and Conversations on Aesthetics, Psychology and Religious Belief,* edited by Cyril Barrett. Berkeley: University of California Press, 41–2.

——— ed. (1981). *Ludwig Wittgenstein: Personal Recollections.* Oxford: Basil Blackwell.

——— ed. (1984). *Recollections of Wittgenstein.* Oxford: Oxford University Press.

Sengoopta, Chandak (1992) "Science, Sexuality and Gender in the Fin de Siècle: Otto Weininger as Baedeker." *History of Science* 30, (88): 249–79.

——— (2000). *Otto Weininger: Sex, Science and Self in Imperial Vienna.* Chicago: Chicago University Press.

Smith, Barry, ed. (1981). *Structure and Gestalt: Philosophy and Literature in Austria-Hungary and her successor states.* Amsterdam: John Benjamins B. V.

Stern, David G. (1995). *Wittgenstein on Mind and Language.* Oxford: Oxford University Press.

——— (2000). "The Significance of Jewishness for Wittgenstein's Philosophy." *Inquiry* 43: 383–402. Reprinted in Stanford M. Lyman, ed., *Essential Readings on Jewish Identities, Lifestyles and Beliefs: Analyses of the Personal and Social Diversity of Jews by Modern Scholars.* New York: Gordian Knot Press, 2003, 132–51.

——— (2001). "Was Wittgenstein a Jew?" In James Klagge, ed., *Wittgenstein: Biography and Philosophy*. Cambridge: Cambridge University Press, 237–72.

Szabados, Béla (1992). "Autobiography after Wittgenstein." *Journal of Aesthetics and Art Criticism* 50 (1): 1–12.

——— (1995). "Autobiography and Philosophy: Variations on a Theme of Wittgenstein." *Metaphilosophy* 26: 63–80.

——— (1997). "Wittgenstein's Women: The Philosophical Significance of Wittgenstein's Misogyny." *Journal of Philosophical Research* 22: 483–508.

——— (1999). "Was Wittgenstein an Anti-Semite? The Significance of Anti-Semitism for Wittgenstein's Philosophy." *Canadian Journal of Philosophy* 29: 1–28.

von Wright, G. H. (1982). *Wittgenstein*. Oxford: Basil Blackwell.

Weininger, Otto (1906). *Sex and Character.* New York: Heinemann. Reprinted in 2003 by Howard Fertig, New York.

——— (1980). *Geschlecht und Charakter: Eine prinzipielle Untersuchung.* Munich: Matthes & Seitz. First published in 1903.

——— (1997). *Über die letzten Dinge.* Munich: Matthes & Seitz. First published in 1904.

——— (2001). *A Translation of Weininger's Über die letzten Dinge (1904/1907)/ On Last Things*. Translated by Steven Burns. Lewiston, NY: Edwin Mellen Press.

——— (2004). *Sex and Character.* Translated by Ladislaus Löb, edited by Daniel Steuer and Laura Marcus, with an introduction by Daniel Steuer. Bloomington: Indiana University Press.

Wittgenstein, Ludwig (1922). *Tractatus Logico-Philosophicus.* Translation on facing pages by C. K. Ogden. London: Routledge & Kegan Paul. Second edition, 1933.

——— (1953). *Philosophical Investigations.* Edited by G. E. M. Anscombe and R. Rhees. Translation on facing pages by G. E. M. Anscombe. Oxford: Blackwell.

——— (1967). *Lectures and Conversations on Aesthetics, Psychology and Religious Belief.* Edited by Cyril Barrett. Berkeley: University of California Press.

——— (1969). *Philosophical Grammar.* First published as *Philosophische Grammatik,* German text only, edited by Rush Rhees, Oxford: Blackwell. English translation by A. Kenny, 1974, Oxford: Blackwell.

——— (1980/1998). *Culture and Value.* First published in 1977 as *Vermischte Bemerkungen,* German text only, edited by G. H. von Wright and Heikki Nyman, Frankfurt: Suhrkamp. Amended second edition, with translation by P. Winch, 1980, Oxford: Blackwell. Revised second edition, German text only, edited by G. H. von Wright and Heikki Nyman, with revisions by Alois Pichler, 1994, Frankfurt: Suhrkamp. Revised second edition, with new translation by P. Winch, 1998, Oxford: Blackwell. Pagination given in the Notes is for the 1980 and 1998 editions of the book; translations are taken from the 1998 edition.

——— (1995). *Ludwig Wittgenstein, Cambridge Letters: Correspondence with Russell, Keynes, Moore, Ramsey and Sraffa.* Edited by Brian McGuinness and G. H. von Wright. Oxford: Blackwell.

——— (1997). *Denkbewegungen: Tagebücher 1930–1932, 1936–1937 (MS 183).* Edited by Ilse Somavilla. Innsbruck, Austria: Haymon Verlag.

——— (2000). *Wittgenstein's Nachlass: The Bergen Electronic Edition.* Oxford: Oxford University Press. References are to the von Wright (1982) numbering system.

——— (2003). *Ludwig Wittgenstein: Public and Private Occasions.* Edited and translated by James Klagge and Alfred Nordmann. Lanham, Maryland: Rowman and Littlefield.

1

Eggshells or Nourishing Yolk?

A Portrait of Wittgenstein as a Weiningerian

Béla Szabados

> Every artist has been influenced by others & shows (the) traces of that influence in his works; but what we get from him is all the same only his own personality.(but what he means to us is all the same only *his* personality) What is inherited from others can be nothing but egg shells. We should treat the fact of their presence with indulgence, but they will not give us Spiritual nourishment
>
> (CV, 27).

> Influence, properly understood, refers to nothing less than the reconstruction of genesis of outstanding achievement . . . rather than to mere intellectual pushing and pulling
>
> (Janik 1995, 62).

Did Weininger Influence the Later Wittgenstein?

In 1931 Wittgenstein listed the names of ten thinkers who had influenced him. Here is what he wrote: "I think I have never *invented* a line of thinking but that it was always provided for me by someone else & I have done no more than passionately take it up for my work of clarification. That is how Boltzmann Hertz Schopenhauer Frege, Russell, Kraus, Loos Weininger Spengler, Sraffa have influenced me" (CV, 16). Commenting on Wittgenstein's list of influences, Georg von Wright writes that the list presents a chronological account, and that it is unlikely that Wittgenstein would have added to it later on in life (von Wright 1982, 213).

Let us revisit the list then. It is clear that the first seven thinkers named, Boltzmann, Hertz, Schopenhauer, Frege, Russell, Kraus, and Loos, were influences on the early work of the *Tractatus*, while the last two, Spengler and Sraffa, clearly influenced Wittgenstein's later work eventually culminating in the *Philosophical Investigations*. This raises the question: where does Weininger fit in? This is an especially intriguing question given the position of Weininger's name between the two groups. If von Wright is correct in suggesting that the list presents a chronological accounting of Wittgenstein's influences, then Weininger's name is placed in a way which leaves it ambiguous whether Weininger influenced Wittgenstein's early or later work. Thereby the possibility is left open that Weininger not only influenced the *Tractatus*, as has been argued by Rudolf Haller, Ray Monk and Brian McGuinness (Haller 1988, 90–9; McGuinness 1988, 40–3; Monk 1990), but that he also influenced Wittgenstein's transition period and the mature philosophy. If so, then part of the Wittgenstein/Weininger riddle, namely how, if at all, did Weininger influence the later Wittgenstein, is still to be solved. I aim to provide some answers to this question.

Externalist-Negative Approaches

Among the significant scholars who take up the question of how Weininger may have influenced the later Wittgenstein are Brian McGuinness, Ray Monk, Jacques Le Rider and Allan Janik. However, they all seem to be impatient with or despair of the task of tracing textual connections and seek to locate, in their different ways, Weininger's influence in the category of the personal, in something external to and deeper than the texts.

To begin with, Wittgenstein's biographers, Brian McGuinness and Ray Monk, touch on the riddle. In his biography of *Young Ludwig* McGuinness lists details of Wittgenstein's early Tractarian philosophical indebtedness to Weininger, such as the theory of elements, the placing of logic and ethics on the same level, and the idea that a man's character is a microcosm of the world (TLP 5.62–5.63; 6.13; 6.421–6.43). But what McGuinness goes on to say has implications for a view on Weininger's later influence. What is of utmost importance, McGuinness suggests, is the *personal aspect* of the influence: "Weininger's thought about character, superficial and half-baked at times, came from a deep concern with ethical problems of his own life," and for that reason alone *Sex and Character* remained an important book for him (McGuinness 1988, 40).

Ray Monk thinks that there is reason to believe that of all the books Wittgenstein read in his adolescence, Weininger's *Sex and Character* "had the greatest and most lasting impact on his outlook" (Monk 1990, 25). Yet Monk is perplexed and wonders out loud:

> Why did Wittgenstein admire the book so much? Indeed, given that its claims to scientific biology are transparently spurious, its epistemology obvious nonsense, its psychology primitive, and its ethical prescriptions odious, what could he possibly have learnt from it? (Monk 1990, 23)

Monk's answer also runs along personal and ethical lines. What Wittgenstein admired in *Sex and Character* was the sharp distinction between love and sexuality, the valorization of the figure and works of the male genius, the passionate commitment to the pursuit of honesty, self-knowledge and the genius in oneself. The conclusion that Monk draws is that these themes in Weininger's work chime with attitudes expressed by Wittgenstein time and again throughout his life (Monk 1990, 25).

In his book *Le Cas Weininger* Jacques Le Rider briefly expresses the view that it is "futile to seek precise traces of Weininger's influence in Wittgenstein's writings, since to admire Weininger through Wittgenstein's eyes does not mean agreement with his ideas." What they had in common, Le Rider writes, is a shared ethical preoccupation, an existential disquietude, an inclination to homosexuality, and being haunted by recurring thoughts of suicide. What Wittgenstein admired is Weininger's passionate sincerity and his absolute demand to make explicit in his own life all the consequences of his theory. In effect Le Rider's conclusion is that Weininger had no philosophical impact on the later philosophy, since Wittgenstein rejected his views and ideas, yet the personal admiration for Weininger's authenticity and courage was lifelong (Le Rider 1982, 225).

The claim that Wittgenstein rejected Weininger's views and ideas is based on a letter to G. E. Moore, who had dismissed Weininger's *Sex and Character* as "fantastic," meaning by that "a product of fantasy." In the letter Wittgenstein explains:

It is true that he is fantastic, but he is *great* and fantastic. It isn't necessary or rather not possible to agree with him, but the greatness lies in that with which we disagree. It is his enormous mistake which is great. I.e. roughly speaking if you add a "∼" to the whole book it says an important truth. (LRKM, 159)

Using the same letter as evidence, Allan Janik has recently argued in a similar vein that Weininger's influence cannot be the appropriation of content, since Wittgenstein recognized a monumental mistake at the core of *Sex and Character* and disavowed its specific theses. Hence "influence" in this case is not to be construed "in the push and pull way that textbook histories suggest," but should be seen as perspectival. According to Janik,

What Wittgenstein and Weininger have in common in their otherwise very different undertakings is the notion that there is a deep and ineliminable source of our tendency to self-deception in precisely those matters that are of the greatest importance to us. In Weininger this is connected with our sexuality... in Wittgenstein with our tendency to be dazzled by grammar (Janik 1995, 65).

For both, philosophical problems are deep disquietudes rooted in our forms of life as constituted by language, and not merely matters of the intellect. Their resolution requires "a change of heart, a transition from a theoretical to a practical perspective" (Janik 1995, 71).

Janik and Le Rider are at one then in that Weininger's influence on the later Wittgenstein is not a textual or surface similarity that can be taken in at a glance, but a deep impact to be discerned in their joint emphasis on practice over theory. Both struggle against our tendency to self-deception and try to find a way of living authentically, insisting that honesty in theorizing has an existential dimension. Janik and Le Rider also agree that Weininger's influence on the mature philosophy of Wittgenstein is best traced through negations or perspectival affinities. Janik even cautions us to take his proposals as "conjectural," since "there is no direct evidence" from Wittgenstein himself as to what he found so impressive in Weininger (Janik 1995, 61).

Suffice it to say that in general these interpreters proceed by first drawing a sharp distinction between the personal and the philosophical; then they claim that Weininger had a lifelong personal/ethical influence on Wittgenstein's attitudes; and that while he had some philosophical influence on the early work of the *Tractatus*, he had no philosophical influence at all on the later works of the mature Wittgenstein. Weininger's influence on the mature Wittgenstein then is restricted to the category of the *personal*, to matters external to the texts of the later *philosophical* works, or to a more negative impact expressed by a repudiation of *Sex and Character* in its entirety. Even Janik's insightful and promising observation about their shared perspective that our very own concepts impose self-deception on us as we philosophize is textually unsupported and is considered to be "a conjecture."

Direct Evidence

How does this externalist-negative approach stand up to whatever hard evidence we possess linking the two thinkers? If "direct evidence" means texts in which Wittgenstein explicitly mentions or refers to Weininger, then the fact is that there is more direct evidence of such a link than Janik and Le Rider care to produce. There are at least five pieces of direct evidence, and they are worth putting right up front.

First, there is the already quoted letter to G. E. Moore in which Wittgenstein tries to explain why he admires Weininger. We have seen that it is this letter that largely motivates the externalist-negative approach.

The second piece of direct evidence is a conversation recorded by Drury. Wittgenstein advised Drury, a student and friend, to read *Sex and Character*, describing its author as "a great genius." After having read the book, Drury complained: "Weininger seems to me to be full of prejudices." Wittgenstein replied: "Yes, he is full of prejudices, only a young man would be so prejudiced." And then with regard to Weininger's theme that women and the female element in men was the source of all evil, he exclaimed: "How wrong he was, my God he was wrong" (Drury 1981, 106).

It is clear from these passages that Wittgenstein rejects Weininger's central thesis about femininity and the misogyny and racism that go hand in hand with it. He also speaks of Weininger's "enormous mistake" and the need to negate the whole book. To this extent then the negative-externalist approach of Janik and Le Rider is justified.

The third piece of hard evidence comes from a personal journal, dated as late as 1950. Wittgenstein writes:

> It is not unheard of (<There is> nothing unheard of in the idea) that someone's character may be influenced by the external world (Weininger). For that only means that, as we know from experience, people change with circumstances. If someone asks: How *could* the environment *coerce* someone, the ethical in someone? – the answer is that he may indeed say, "No human being has to give way to coercion," but all the same under such circumstances (<circumstances> of this nature) someone *will* do such & such. "You don't HAVE to, I can show you a (different) way out, – but you won't take it" (CV, 95).

This overlooked passage is a response to, and rejection of, Weininger's characterology, which makes possible a priori and dogmatic generalizations about sexual, racial, and national characters. (For a somewhat more complex way of reading the fragment, see Stern 2001, 250.) According to Weininger,

> in characterology we must seek the permanent, existing something through the fleeting changes.... The character, however, is not something seated behind the thoughts and feelings of the individual, but something revealing itself in every thought and feeling.... so the whole man is manifest in every moment of the psychical life, although, now one side, now another, is more visible (S&C, 83).

Furthermore, and directly bearing on Wittgenstein's remarks, Weininger not only denies but finds it outrageous that a man's character may be influenced by the world outside him. "Outward circumstances," he asserts, "do not mould a race in one direction, unless there is in the race the inner tendency to respond to the moulding forces.... It is certain that individual and racial characters persist in spite of all adaptive moulding" (S&C, 308).

Even though the construal of Weininger's influence as negative is so far supported by these texts, I disagree with the proposals that Weininger's "enormous mistake" is his desire to transcend our animality (Janik) or to have charged Woman as the source of all evil when he should have charged Man (Monk). It seems to me that the enormous mistake that Wittgenstein discerned cannot be a particular substantive disagreement, but it has to be the core source from which most other particular errors, prejudices, and illusions in *Sex and Character* can be derived. Weininger's desire to transcend our animality and his antifeminism are indeed prejudices, but do not qualify for the status of a philosophically instructive "enormous mistake," even though they may be its products.

I believe that Wittgenstein saw Weininger's enormous mistake to be *methodological*, locating it in his Platonising, essentialist way of thinking about the role of the "ideal" or the prototype – whether it be of Woman, Man or Game – which is applied in an extreme and inappropriate manner in every nook and cranny of our lives. Weininger declares that "such types not only can be constructed, but must be constructed. As in art so in science, the real purpose is to reach the type, the Platonic Idea" (S&C, 7). It is this way of thinking that is presupposed by and explains Weininger's bizarre project of characterology. What Wittgenstein negates is Weininger's essentialism and project of characterology, since such a way of thinking is alien to the resolute anti-essentialism of Wittgenstein's later work. The important truth that the negation of Weininger's book yields is a method that dispenses with essentialist prototypes, which are the sources of dogmatism and prejudice, a method that urges us to look and see how persons and things really are.

Another passage where Wittgenstein mentions Weininger explicitly is in the first part of what has been published as *Philosophical Grammar* and can be roughly dated as contemporaneous with the dictation of the *Blue and Brown Books* around the early 1930s.

> If I say that this face has an expression of gentleness, or kindness, or cowardice, I don't seem just to mean that we associate such and such feelings with the look of the face, I'm tempted to say that the face is itself one aspect of the cowardice, kindness, etc. (Compare e.g. Weininger). It is possible to say: I see cowardice in this face (and might see it in another too) but at all events it doesn't seem to be merely associated, outwardly connected, with the face; the fear has the multiplicity of the facial features (PG, 176–7).

There are also multiple versions of this passage from *Philosophical Grammar* in the *Nachlass*, most of them including the Weininger reference (Wittgenstein, 2000). It is important to notice that the extensive discussions of the topic of familiarity, "reading" a face, and so forth, in the *Brown Book* seem to be creative variations on, and elaborations of, the above fragment, yet Weininger's name goes unmentioned there

(BB 162–8). Again, when the fragment from *Philosophical Grammar* appears in a somewhat revised form in the *Philosophical Investigations* (see pars. 536 and 537), the reference to Weininger is no longer present. This move of mentioning, working with and against, and then erasing Weininger may be characteristic of Wittgenstein's ways of rewriting.

What part of Weininger's book *Sex and Character* is Wittgenstein asking us to compare his own reflections with? I suggest the following as a promising fit:

> In the association psychology, which first splits up the psychic life, and then vainly imagines that it can weld the re-assorted pieces together again, there is another confusion.... The recognition of a circumstance does not necessarily involve the special reproduction of the former impression, even although there seems to be a tendency for the new impression, at least, partly to recall the old one. But there is another kind of recognition, perhaps as common, in which the new impression does not appear to be directly linked with an association, but in which it comes, so to speak, "coloured" (James would say "tinged") with that character that would be called ... the "familiarity quality".... To him who returns to his native place the roads and the streets seem familiar, even although he has forgotten their names, has to ask his way, and can think of no special occasion on which he went along them. A melody may seem "familiar" and yet I may be unable to say where I heard it. The "character" ... of familiarity, of intimacy, hovers over the sense-impression itself, and analysis can detect no associations, none of the fusing of the old and new, which, according to the assertion of a presumptuous pseudo-psychology, produces the feeling (S&C, 144).

While these passages deserve careful study, what is noteworthy for the present purpose is the common rejection, in strikingly similar terms, of the associationist picture of recognising a familiar-looking place or recalling a familiar-sounding melody in Weininger on the one hand, and of seeing a fearful face in Wittgenstein on the other. There is also a joint turning toward the idea of aspect seeing and hearing, which is treated more extensively in Part II of the *Investigations.* And notice again the rare explicit reference to Weininger, although it is parenthetical, and later erased.

Finally, Wittgenstein specifically mentions Weininger in connection with the question of understanding other cultures. Observing that since we are inclined to take the words of our language as the only possible standards for classification and evaluation of people and the contributions of other cultures in general, Wittgenstein claims that as a result "we are always doing [them] injustice" (CV, 23). In particular he alludes to the history of European failures to do justice to Jews and to properly estimate their contributions (Stern 2001; Szabados 1999). Different standards are applicable to the activities of people in different cultural forms of life, and, using the appropriate scale, we can appreciate without at one time overestimating, and at another underestimating. Such a misestimation seems to have plagued Weininger who was at first seen as an intellectual comet and later dismissed or ignored. For these reasons Wittgenstein agrees that, "in this context Spengler is quite right not to classify Weininger with the western philosophers (thinkers)" (CV, 23). The inclination to regard these remarks as having no philosophical relevance needs to be resisted in light of a passage from the Big Typescript: "Our only task is to be just. That is, we must only point out and resolve the injustices of philosophy, and not posit new parties – and creeds" (PO, 181).

The following points need to be underscored: There is, as we have seen, much more direct evidence linking the two thinkers than is treated in the literature; Wittgenstein was a lifelong reader of Weininger who was probably the first philosopher read by him in early adolescence, preoccupying him even in 1950, a year before he died; Wittgenstein is concerned to do Weininger justice; furthermore, and most significantly, apart from the outright rejections of specific sensationalist Weiningerian positions, there appears to be a promise of a positive textual influence that can be traced to their works, despite received views to the contrary.

A Positive Textual Approach: Wittgenstein Rereads Weininger

I suggested that even the strongest version of the externalist-negative approach, which construes Weininger's monumental mistake as methodological, does not go far enough to shed light on the extent of Weininger's influence on the mature Wittgenstein. Let us recall the way Wittgenstein acknowledges that influence: "I think I have never *invented* a line of thinking but that it was always provided for me by someone else & I have done no more than passionately take it up for my work of clarification" (CV, 16). And then comes the list of influences, including Weininger. It is evident from a careful reading of this passage that Wittgenstein did not regard Weininger merely as a repository of dangerous, ground-floor philosophical errors. It is not as if one could say, "I'll give another reading to Weininger's *Sex and Character* just to remind myself of what a really big philosophical mistake looks like." It is natural to think that Wittgenstein gave us a list of those authors from whom he received nourishing ideas and resources for his philosophy. As he says, it is "a line of thinking" ("*Gedankenbewegung*") that he found in Weininger, that he took up and clarified in his own work.

Most scholars have looked for the "one big answer" to the question of influence. In contrast to that approach, I argue for the thesis that there are multiple and interrelated lines of influence between Weininger and Wittgenstein. The argument does not only rely on the explicit connections so far traced. Anticipating my later results, my real point is that there are other, much more basic but less easily recognized, discussions of Weiningerian themes in the later Wittgenstein.

My working hypothesis is that upon his return to philosophy in 1929, Wittgenstein reread Weininger's works again and again. This claim is supported by the fact that many of his journal entries, in 1929 and throughout the 1930s, are concerned with such salient Weiningerian themes as the nature of genius, of originality and creativity, of culture, and even of influence. Consider Wittgenstein's 1929 exclamation printed as one of the first remarks in *Culture and Value*: "It is a good thing I don't let myself be influenced!" (CV, 3) Ironically, this resistance to influence may itself be influenced by his reflections on Weininger's passage on influence and genius: "a great man . . . will not allow alien views to be imposed on him, so obscuring the judgment of his own ego; he will not passively accept the interpretation of another, of an alien ego, quite different from his own, and if ever he has allowed himself to be influenced, the thought will always be painful to him" (S&C, 174). The juxtaposition of such parallel reflections from Wittgenstein and Weininger enables us to see Weininger as an important source and conversation partner for Wittgenstein during his transition period from the early to the later philosophy.

But how does Wittgenstein's resistance to influence square with his giving us, in 1931, only two years later, a list of influences on his work? The passage from Weininger helps to resolve the apparent conflict: the people named in the list are not "foreign" to Wittgenstein but form his "cultural circle" and are "as it were [his] fellow countrymen" (CV, 12–13). Nevertheless the remark, "It is a good thing I don't let myself be influenced!" seems to reveal a frame of mind that Harold Bloom called "the anxiety of influence": "Strong poets ... wrestle with their strong precursors, even to the death. Weaker talents idealize; figures of capable imagination appropriate for themselves. But nothing is got for nothing, and self-approbation involves the immense anxieties of indebtedness, for what strong maker desires the realization that he has failed to create himself?" (Bloom 1975, 5) While Bloom talks about poets, not philosophers, it is not to be forgotten that Wittgenstein remarked: "I believe I summed up where I stand in relation to philosophy when I said: really one should write philosophy only as *one writes a poem*" ("*Philosophie dürfte man eigentlich nur* dichten") (CV, 28).

It might be argued that, *pace* Peter Winch, "*Dichter*" and "*dichten*" are definitely not to be translated as "poet" and "poetry," because then the point is lost that Wittgenstein should be compared with, say, James Joyce (*Dichter*), and not William Butler Yeats (*Lyriker*). The suggestion then is to translate *dichten* as a matter of writing fiction or, better perhaps, writing creatively (Janik and Stern, Personal Correspondence, 2002). This suggestion has merits: it widens the connotation of *dichten* and *Dichter*, thereby offering the possibility of drawing more fertile comparisons as well as avoiding those that are misleading. And insofar as creative writers come up with new similes, the suggestion is also compatible with Wittgenstein's characterization of his own achievement as "inventing new similes" and making fresh comparisons.

However, "poet" and "poetry" seem to fit that characterization equally, if not better, since part of the poet's art involves the invention of strikingly fresh similes and metaphors to look at things differently. Let us also remember that Wittgenstein in fact refers to Shakespeare as *Dichter* and genius, in a rather Weiningerian way: "I do not think that Shakespeare can be set alongside any other poet [*andern Dichter*]. Was he perhaps a *creator of language* [*Sprachschöpfer*] rather than a poet?" (CV, 95) Recall Weininger's remark that the genius is not a critic of language, but its creator (S&C, 138). Furthermore, the suggested translation has the unfortunate consequence of blurring a contrast that Wittgenstein is keen to make elsewhere, namely, the contrast of *dichten* with his ability to write prose. Consider: "Just as I cannot write verse (Verse), so too I can write prose only *up to a certain point*, & no further. There is quite a definite limit to my prose, & I can no more overstep it, than I would be able to write a poem [*ein Gedicht*]. *This* is how my equipment is constituted; it is the only equipment available to me. It is like someone's saying: In this game I can attain only *this* level of perfection, & not *that*" (CV, 67). Add to this Wittgenstein's composition of "A Poem" (*Ein Gedicht*), which appears in *Culture and Value* at page 100, as well as his previous acknowledgment in this context that he is "someone who cannot quite do what he would like to be able to do"(CV, 28), and then the case for translating *Dichter* as poet and *dichten* as poetry seems somewhat stronger (CV, 28). Finally, we might observe that German and Austrian intellectuals, at least from the time of the First World War, made a general distinction between *Dichter* and *Schriftsteller* (the latter would be "writer," or "littérateur" in French) to indicate a rank ordering, which was intended to mark off the *deep* from the somewhat *shallow.* So if Wittgenstein had meant "creative writer" or "fiction writer," he probably would not have used *Dichter.* In my view, then, Peter Winch's translation of *Dichter* as poet is just right.

In any event, Bloom's thesis applies to all literary production, not just poetry – at least that is how literary critics speak of it. Hence his observation may have a bearing on Wittgenstein's attitude to Weininger as well as to his other influences, and may partly explain his failure to acknowledge the details and extent of his intellectual debts by way of footnotes, quotations or references. What is more, even though poets do not footnote, they make allusions which, *pace* Bloom, may be friendly or hostile – but nevertheless difficult to discern.

In the prefaces to his two master works, Wittgenstein shows an awareness of this problem and gives us two sorts of reasons, better still, excuses, for such culpable negligence. One is "indifference" to originality; the other is that his remarks "bear his stamp." In the preface to the *Tractatus* he says, "Indeed, what I have written here makes no claim to novelty in detail, and the reason why I give no sources is that it is a matter of indifference to me whether the thoughts that I have had have been anticipated by someone else" (TLP, 3). In the preface to the *Investigations* he sounds a somewhat different note: "If my remarks do not bear a stamp which marks them as mine, – I do not wish to lay any further claim to them as my property" (PI, x). Indeed his characteristic stamp is on all of the thoughts expressed, even though his claim to indifference to originality is belied by his anxious reflections on the topic in his journal entries. These reflections are in tune with Weininger's dark description of the age as "a time when genius is supposed to be a form of madness; a time with no great artists and no great philosophers; a time without originality and yet with the most foolish craving for originality" (S&C, 329). Perhaps Wittgenstein aims to resist such a "foolish craving," albeit differently from Weininger. For the latter's book in its original Austrian edition has an abundance of scholarly notes and references; these are omitted from the anonymous 1906 English translation, which is described by Wittgenstein as "that beastly translation" (LRKM, 159).

In any case, what is important is that Wittgenstein's general acknowledgment of Weininger's influence and his unacknowledged specific engagements with Weininger during the crucial transition period to the mature philosophy leave open the possibility of unrecognized substantial and positive philosophical indebtedness. My task then is to retrieve and elaborate some features of "the line of thinking" that Wittgenstein found in Weininger and in doing this I adopt a resolutely textual approach. Considering numerous themes, I suggest and argue that Wittgenstein's later philosophical procedures and ideas, as well as the more general direction of his philosophy, are interestingly and pointedly Weiningerian. Perhaps the best way to accomplish this task is to put, side by side, passages from Weininger's book that express his little noticed and more fertile ideas, and passages from Wittgenstein's *Blue and Brown Books*, the *Philosophical Investigations*, and the later work in general. This helps us to remember the actual Weininger in connection with Wittgenstein, rather than the popular/mythological caricature of hatred that he has become.

Clarification

Both Weininger and Wittgenstein are centrally concerned with clarification, description, and attention to detail. For Weininger, "The whole history of thought is a continuous 'clarification,' a more and more accurate description or realisation of details." "The process of clarification," he holds, "is spread over many generations . . . [and] every scientific discovery, every technical invention, every artistic creation passes through a preliminary phase of indistinctness" (S&C, 97). Weininger likens the process "to the series of impressions that would be got [if] a statue were gradually unwrapped from a series of swathings. The same kind of sequence occurs, although, perhaps, in a very brief space of time, when one is trying to recall a piece of music" (S&C, 97). Then he asserts:

> Every thought is preceded by a kind of half-thought, a condition in which vague geometric figures, shifting masks, a swaying and indistinct background hover in the mind. The beginning and the end of the whole process, which I may term "clarification" are what take place when a short-sighted person proceeds to look through properly adapted lenses (S&C, 97).

Now Wittgenstein himself characterizes his own task as "my work of clarification" (CV, 16). He is "not interested in erecting a building but in having the foundations of possible buildings transparently before" him (CV, 9). Now, according to him, for the traditional Western thinker engaged in theory construction, "even clarity is only a means to this end & not an end in itself" (CV, 9). By contrast, for both Weininger and Wittgenstein clarity and perspicuity are intrinsically valuable. As Wittgenstein says: "For me on the contrary clarity, transparency, is an end in itself" (CV, 9). Similarly, Weininger rejects a "social utilitarian," instrumentalist conception of such values: "Truth, purity, faithfulness, uprightness . . . are the only conceivable ethics. . . . Not only virtue, but also insight, not only sanctity but also wisdom are the duties and tasks of mankind" (S&C, 159).

This primacy of clarity and perspicuity is intimately connected with Wittgenstein's aim in philosophy and his conception of a philosophical problem: "For the clarity that we are aiming at is indeed *complete* clarity. But this simply means that the philosophical problems should *completely* disappear" (PI, 133), precisely because they are due to confusion. What is a main source of our failure to understand? "[W]e do not *command a clear view* of the use of our words. – Our grammar is lacking in this sort of perspicuity" (PI, 122). The work of clarification is pursued in the later philosophy by abandoning the Tractarian picture of a singular conception of philosophical problems, together with "the strictly correct method of philosophy." The mature Wittgenstein opens windows to a pluralistic conception of problem and method: "Problems are solved (difficulties eliminated), not a *single* problem. There is not *a* philosophical method, though there are indeed methods, like different therapies" (PI, 133). In the later work the transcendent conception of logic and the idea of the essence as providers of "ultimate clarity about something incomparable" drop out, and Wittgenstein turns to the exploration of human forms of life and the clarification of language games connected with them. As words become deeds, the arrogance and dogmatism associated with the transcendent conception of logic and the "ideal" are shed and a humbler attitude emerges.

Reverence, Language, Similes, and Projection

This humbler, unpretentious attitude, has a Weiningerian ring to it inasmuch as Weininger insists that *reverence* is a moral virtue and a mark of genius. Reverence extends to the past, which is the source of value (S&C, 135), to forms of life, and it includes respect for everyday language. "A man is first reverent about himself, and self-respect is the first stage in reverence for all things.... A man is himself important precisely in proportion that all things are important to him" (S&C, 127). Weininger sees this spirit of inquiry "to have a deep significance... bearing on the universality, comprehension and comparison exhibited by the genius" (S&C, 127). Reverence in this sense excludes a forcing, reformative attitude and is a precondition of insight, understanding, and a respect for difference.

Careful readers may notice the Weiningerian reverence shown to the language of the everyday in passages such as this: "The most extraordinary wisdom is concealed in [common speech], a wisdom which reveals itself to a few ardent explorers but which is usually overlooked by the stupid professional philologists" (S&C, 138). The implication seems to be that language does not wear its wisdom on its sleeve, as it were, but the wisdom lies in understanding its workings, which tend to escape those who are preoccupied with abstractions and yearn for simplistic generalizations about its nature or meaning.

The tone and content of these passages are in striking agreement with the fundamental shift in Wittgenstein's philosophical orientation during the transition period. This shift involves rejecting not only the imposition of an ideal language on our actual language use, but also the reformative impulse of logical analysis. Consider some early formulations of this. In the Big Typescript we are given a clear signal of the new attitude to everyday language: "All my reflections can be carried out in a much more homespun manner than I used to do. And therefore no new words have to be used in philosophy, but rather the old common words of language are sufficient" (PO, 181). In *The Blue and Brown Book* the new attitude is more pointed: "It is wrong to say that in philosophy we consider an ideal language as opposed to our ordinary one. For this makes it appear as though we could improve on ordinary language. But ordinary language is all right" (BB, 28). Later expressions of this thought are no less adamant: "Philosophy may in no way interfere with the actual use of language; it can in the end only describe it" (PI, 124). Again, "When I talk about language (words, sentences, etc.) I must speak the language of every day" (PI, 120). As Wittgenstein continues to unpack this theme, he asks rhetorically: "Is this language somehow too coarse and material for what we want to say? *Then how is another one to be constructed?* – And how strange that we should be able to do anything at all with the one we have!" (PI, 120) Even though "Philosophy is a battle against the bewitchment of our intelligence by means of language" (PI, 109), its problems are solved "by looking into the workings of our language, and that in such a way as to make us recognize those workings: *in despite of* an urge to misunderstand them" (PI, 109).

There may appear to be a tension between this diagnosis of the etiology of philosophical problems and the prescribed remedy. The felt tension is dissolved, however, once we consider the ambiguity in "by means of." Language is both the means of bewitchment through the misleading pictures surface grammar suggests to us, and our tool in the battle against bewitchment through the careful examination of the actual use of words or the actual employment of such pictures. In this connection, I find a simile Wittgenstein proposes in 1931 illuminating: "Compare the solution of philosophical problems with the fairy tale gift that seems magical in the enchanted castle and if it is looked at in daylight is nothing but an ordinary bit of iron (or something of the sort)" (CV, 13–14). Perhaps when we are disenchanted, we realize that the ordinary bit of iron is a handy tool for getting a job done.

In any event, the traditional philosophical impulse to reform language is resisted, along with the violent revolutionary impulse to change the world through ideology: "Philosophy leaves everything as it is," we are told, and, "What has to be accepted, the given, is – so one could say – *forms of life*" (PI, 192). If reverence is a basic religious/ethical attitude, then Wittgenstein's remark, "I am not a religious man but I cannot help seeing every problem from a religious point of view" (Drury 1981, 94), acquires deep philosophical relevance. For Weininger, reverence is diametrically opposed to criminality: the criminal displays a forcing, compelling attitude. The criminal wants to leave nothing free, does not respect autonomy, boundaries and limits: "he cannot tolerate the idea of barriers, of limits (including limits to knowledge)" (LT, 101); "he wilfully treats the facts without ceremony. . . . It is he who *scorns the object,* which he does not behold and revere in its great and solemn majesty, but wants to master and enslave" (LT, 142). This characterization enables us to see Wittgenstein's later works partly as a form of resistance against the philosopher as criminal, as having justice as its goal.

Now Weininger is quite emphatic in his claim that "The genius is not a critic of language, but its creator" (S&C, 138). "Every single word," he asserts,

> has been the invention of a single man, as indeed we still see if we leave out of consideration the merely technical terms. . . . The earlier words were "onomatopoeic"; a sound similar to the exciting cause was evolved almost without the will of the speaker, in direct response to the sensuous stimulation. All the other words were originally metaphors, or comparisons, a kind of primitive poetry, for all prose has come from poetry. Think of the proverbs, now almost commonplaces, such as "one good turn deserves another." These were said for the first time by some great man. . . . Language is as little the work of the multitude as our ballads. Every form of speech owes much that is not acknowledged to individuals of another language (S&C, 137–8).

It is not difficult to recognize in these passages stimulating sources for Wittgenstein's later philosophy. Although Wittgenstein drops Weininger's idea of the individual as the creator of language in general, he picks out, in a notably Weiningerian way, his own achievement as a creator of metaphors, similes, as an inventor of "new *comparisons*" (CV, 16). The Weiningerian context makes it clear that in saying this Wittgenstein identifies his own achievement positively rather than denigrating his own work, since the creation of new metaphors and similes is regarded as a mark of genius. For Wittgenstein it is not only that a good simile "refreshes the intellect" (CV, 3), but that far more philosophical disagreements rest on a "preference for certain comparisons . . . than appears at first sight" (CV, 17–18). One common way that philosophical problems arise is that we are misled by certain grammatical analogies: "A simile that has been absorbed into the forms of our language produces a false appearance, and this disquiets us. 'But *this* isn't how it is!' – we say. 'Yet *this* is how it has to *be*!' " (PI, 112) Fresh metaphors and similes, then, have an unexpected philosophical relevance in that they provide new ways of looking at and seeing phenomena. Thus they may liberate us from the prison of philosophical tradition, which sees things from the same old point of view and which has been shaped by dead metaphors, figures of speech by now ossified or misunderstood. Fresh similes may help the striving philosopher "to find the liberating word, that is, the word that finally permits us to grasp what up until now has intangibly weighed down our consciousness" (PO, 165). Philosophical problems, according to Wittgenstein, are partly due to our inclination to be dazzled by grammatical pictures and illusions that we project on language, since we lack a perspicuous overview of its workings. To resist these misleading inclinations, we need to look into the actual uses of language and survey the applications of the pictures.

In the *Tractatus* the early Wittgenstein himself adopted the method of projection: "In a proposition a thought finds an expression that can be perceived by the senses. We use the perceptible sign of a proposition (spoken or written, etc.) as a projection of a possible situation. The method of projection is to think of the sense of the proposition" (TLP, 3.1–3.11). The later Wittgenstein sees this as a grave error on two counts. The *Tractatus* not only projects a general picture of meaning as reference on all language, but it also suggests that to understand a proposition is a matter of having before one's mind a mental image, or a matter of undergoing a psychological process. Reflecting on the earlier work, the later Wittgenstein observes: "I had used a metaphor (of the projection method, etc.) but through the grammatical illusion of homogeneous ideas it didn't seem to be a metaphor" (Wittgenstein 2000, MS 157b, 10–12). The life of the sign for the later Wittgenstein is not in the mind but in its use.

How does this connect with Weininger? In conversation, Wittgenstein pointed out to Drury that "Weininger at the age of twenty-one had recognized, before anyone else had taken much notice, the future importance of the ideas Freud was putting forward in his first book, the one in which he had collaborated with Breuer, *Studies in*

Hysteria" (Drury 1981, 106). I suggest that the idea of projection is one such idea, and Weininger makes striking and imaginative applications of it in his book *Sex and Character.* Weininger argues that our distorted and clichéd pictures of Man and Woman are largely due to the phenomenon of projection as we project our lack and desires on one another; hence a major source of misunderstanding between the sexes. Consider:

> This one thing, however, remains none the less certain: whoever detests a disposition detests it first of all in himself; that he should persecute it in others is merely his endeavour to separate himself in this way from it; he strives to shake it off and to localise it in his fellow-creatures, and so for a moment to dream himself free of it (S&C, 304).

Both love and hate are forms of projection for Weininger: "In hate we picture to ourselves that our own hateful qualities exist in another, and by so doing we feel ourselves partly freed from them. In love we project what is good in us, and so having created a good and an evil image we are more able to compare and value them" (S&C, 247). Weininger uses the idea of projection to explain the prevalent forms of social malaise, such as misogyny, homophobia, and anti-Semitism ("Woman is nothing but man's expression and projection of his own sexuality") (S&C, 300).

Wittgenstein seems to have adopted and modified Weininger's perceptive application of projection to deal with his own concerns about language and philosophical malaise. In Wittgenstein we are philosophically self-deceived when we are dazzled by the seductive grammatical pictures we project on language, thus ignoring the realities of its uses. Our task is "to bring words back from their metaphysical to their correct (normal) use in language" (PO, 167). In Weininger we are sexually self-deceived or gender-biased when we are dazzled by our projections of distorted, stereotypical pictures of Man and Woman on actual individual persons. We might say then that our task is to bring the words "Man" and "Woman" back from their metaphysical/projective meanings to uses that do not distort the realities of particular men and women.

Apart from sharing with Weininger a general emphasis on the importance for our thinking of metaphors and similes, Wittgenstein also appropriates, and applies in illuminating ways to his own concerns with language, some of Weininger's arresting metaphors, such as those of "a short-sighted person looking through properly adapted lenses" (S&C, 97), and "shoemakers, who makes shoes to measure" (S&C, 57). These metaphors are employed in a discussion of the role of the "ideal" or the "prototype," and in anti-essentialist remarks, to which I now turn.

Anti-essentialism

In introducing *Sex and Character* Weininger announces and promises to develop crucial themes that readily resonate with prominent features of Wittgenstein's later philosophy: anti-essentialism, a heuristic role of the ideal, and attention to individual differences. Weininger's focus is Man and Woman, "two general conceptions [that] have come down to us from primitive mankind, and from the earliest times have held our mental processes in their leash" (S&C, 1). Even though they have been sent back to the workshop for periodic alterations and adjustments of a minor sort, none the less these primitive conceptions of male and female still "stand between us and reality" (S&C, 1–2) and distort our perspective.

Weininger claims that the assumption of this rigid dualism between Man and Woman leads to the erroneous common view that "all women and men are marked off sharply from each other, the women on the one hand alike in all points, the men on the other" (S&C, 2). He remarks on the "pitiful monotony in the fashion according to which . . . 'men' and 'women' have been treated as if, like red and white balls, they were alike in all respects save colour" (S&C, 2). These primitive conceptions produce "a complete disharmony between language and ideas" (S&C, 3). If we look, "nowhere else in nature is there such a yawning discontinuity. . . . We know, in fact, that there are unwomanly women, man-like women, and unmanly, womanish, woman-like men" (S&C, 2). Then Weininger adds that:

> among human beings, the state of the case is that there exist all sorts of intermediate conditions between male and female – sexually transitional forms. . . . So, there exist only the intermediate stages between absolute males and females, the absolute conditions never presenting themselves. . . . The task of science is to define the position of any individual between these two points, and to throw light on . . . the differences between different individuals (S&C, 7).

In these passages Weininger in effect targets a form of essentialism about our concepts of Man/Masculine and Woman/Feminine, and deconstructs the conventional dichotomy by asking us to look at the many particular cases that fall in between such sharp extremes. He suggests that: "It is only in obedience to the most general, practical demand for a superficial view that we classify, make sharp divisions, pick out a single tune from the continuous melody of nature. But the old conceptions of the mind, like the customs of primitive commerce, become foolish in a new age" (S&C, 3). We can take for granted "the improbability . . . of finding in nature a sharp cleavage between all that is masculine on the one side and all that is feminine on the other. . . . Matters are not so clear" (S&C, 3).

Weininger seems to be an anti-essentialist in the sense that he rejects a Platonist conception of the "ideal" or the "prototype," saying that the absolute conditions at the extremes (the ideal types) are "not metaphysical abstractions above or outside the world of experience," nor are they given. Yet he insists on a heuristic role of the ideal types claiming that "their construction is necessary as a philosophical and practical mode of describing the actual world" (S&C, 9). Nor is the ideal type to be used as a basis for evaluation, since its use is meant "to exclude judgment as to value" (S&C, 9). These quotes from Weininger sound somewhat like what Goethe says on *Urphaenomene* in paragraph 174 of his *Theory of Colour.* Goethe claimed that his *Urphaenomene,* for example, the Ur-plant, were on the one hand not to be found among the empirically given phenomena, and therefore were similar to ideas; but on the other hand, the *Urphaenomen* is not just an abstract concept either, but a phenomenon, and therefore not at all like an idea. It is neither behind nor above the phenomena, as he likes to put it (Rueger, Personal Correspondence 2002). So there is good reason to think that Weininger, as well as Wittgenstein, was influenced by Goethe's methodology. This claim is further supported by the many references to Goethe in Weininger (S&C, 40, 41, 43 and passim) and in Wittgenstein (CV, 11, 20, 26 and passim). The latter's reflections on Goethe's theory of colour are to be found in his *Remarks on Colour.*

In any event, the Weiningerian fragments just quoted have a content and direction similar to Wittgenstein's most characteristic thought maneuvers in the later philosophy. The Weiningerian approach is adopted, and adapted, to Wittgenstein's concerns about language:

> A principle of our investigation: describe in practical details and objectively how a reality looks which corresponds to the general world-description of the philosophers. You then at the same time clearly see that the world doesn't look like that and which part of the world actually does look like that. Take the general (vague) talk of philosophers seriously and make a practical application of it (Wittgenstein 2002, MS 131, 51).

Weininger reduces to absurdity the primitive conceptions about Man and Woman by looking at how they fail to apply to, distort, and impoverish individual sexual realities. Extending the investigation's scope, Wittgenstein reduces to absurdity our preconceived ideas or pictures about language, meaning, knowledge, and psychological concepts such as thinking, wishing, expecting, intending, and hope by looking to see how they fail to do justice to the multiplicity and richness of our actual uses of language.

Weininger deplores the essentialist position concerning Man and Woman, which makes it appear as if individual men all have a common essence or set of properties, as do individual women. Similarly, Wittgenstein urges us to resist the philosophical "tendency to look for something in common to all the entities which we commonly subsume under a general term. – We are inclined to think that there must be something in common to all games, say, and that this common property is the justification for applying the general term 'game' to the various games" (BB, 17). But, as he bluntly says later: "Don't think, but look!" (PI, 66) Wittgenstein observes that

> The idea that in order to get clear about the meaning of a general term one had to find the common element in all its applications has shackled philosophical investigation; for it has not only led to no result, but also made the philosopher dismiss as irrelevant the concrete cases, which alone could have helped him to understand the usage of the general term. When Socrates asks the question, "What is knowledge?" he does not even regard it as a *preliminary* answer to enumerate cases of knowledge (BB, 19–20).

In the *Philosophical Investigations* Wittgenstein is even more specific:

> When philosophers use a word – "knowledge," "being," "object," "I," "proposition," "name" – and try to grasp the *essence* of the thing, one must always ask oneself: is the word ever actually used in this way in the language which is its

original home? – What *we* do is to bring words back from their metaphysical to their everyday use (PI, 116).

Attention to Particulars

Weininger and Wittgenstein also agree in their diagnosis of the malaise of essentialism, one aspect of which is disregard for and regimentation of "the individual," "the particular," "the concrete." Weininger laments the fact that the general conceptions of Man and Woman that constitute our "present system stamp out much that is original, uproot much that is truly natural, and distort much into artificial and unnatural forms" (S&C, 57). What is wanted, Weininger proposes, is an "'orthopaedic' treatment of the soul":

> At the present time shoemakers, who make shoes to measure, deal more rationally with individuals than our teachers and schoolmasters in their application of moral principles. At present the sexually intermediate forms of individuals (especially on the female side) are treated as if they were good examples of the ideal male or female types. There is wanted an "orthopaedic" treatment of the soul instead of the torture caused by the application of ready-made conventional shapes (S&C, 57).

Weininger continues to complain that our conceptual framework, system of education, and "the different laws and customs to which the so-called sexes are subjected press them as by a vice into distinctive moulds" (S&C, 58). Weininger aims to resist such limiting stereotypes and resolves "to pursue a psychology of individual differences" (S&C, 59), and to contribute "towards the definite description of the individual" (S&C, 53), of "concrete cases": "In principle ... the conception of sexually intermediate forms makes possible a more accurate description of individual characters in so far as it aids in determining the proportion of male and female in each individual, and of measuring the oscillations to each side of which any individual is capable" (S&C, 55).

The above fragments from Weininger resonate, in attitude, content, and vocabulary, with treatments Wittgenstein accords to preconceived ideas, grammatical pictures and philosophical theories: "A *picture* held us captive. And we could not get outside it, for it lay in our language and language seemed to repeat it to us inexorably" (PI, 115). "Our craving for generality," manifest in essentialist ways of thinking, tends to produce "the contemptuous attitude towards the particular case" (BB, 18), "the concrete cases" (BB, 19), which are necessary as aids for understanding the usage of the term. Our investigation of the uses of language "weakens the position of certain fixed standards of our expression which had prevented us from seeing facts with unbiased eyes... [and] removes this bias, which forces us to think that the facts *must* conform to certain pictures embedded in our language" (BB, 43). When we are engaged in philosophical activity, the salience of these fixed standards, together with the rich diversity of linguistic phenomena, induces a "mental cramp" in us. The Weiningerian echo of "the shoemaker" and the need for an "orthopaedic treatment" can be heard in Wittgenstein's elegant forging of the "tight shoes" metaphor: "The language used by philosophers is already deformed, as though by shoes that are too tight" (CV, 47).

A Heuristic Role for the Ideal

It is possible to discern in Weininger's remarks a perspective on the proper role of the "ideal." The negative injunction is: do not use the ideal types for pigeonholing individual cases, since such a move results in violence, injustice and misunderstanding. Individuals are not to be treated as if they conformed to fixed standards, for thereby their differences are ignored and what is natural and original in them is stamped out. Nor are such ideal types to be used normatively as a basis for evaluation. Such an employment of the "ideal" is "criminal." Weininger's positive proposal amounts to a "heuristic" role for the ideal types in the *description* of individual cases: we make comparisons, draw out the similarities and differences between a person and the ideal male and female types. This way we throw light on individual differences and, at the same time, avoid a priorism and violence.

It is not difficult to see how these themes from Weininger may have been one powerful source for Wittgenstein's radical shift in his conception of the role of the "ideal." Wittgenstein found Weininger's line of thinking (*Gedankenbewegung*) suggestive and applicable to his own concerns with concepts and language. The Tractarian picture theory of language assumes an ideal order of language – a sublime, crystalline essence – the *real* words, the *real* propositions, which are the fixed standards for what makes sense in our vague and confused ordinary discourse. The early Wittgenstein laid down the rule that "every sentence must be a picture, for they must all be essentially the same. Every sentence says: this is how things are" (Wittgenstein 2002, MS 157a, 112). The later Wittgenstein recognizes and rejects the dogmatic, arrogant role that this ideal of language played in his earlier philosophy, much like Weininger who warned against the inclination to misuse the ideal male and female types to pigeonhole, torture, and denigrate individuals. The picture theory of meaning as an "ideal . . . forces its way on the phenomena" (Wittgenstein 2002, MS 157a, 112), as Wittgenstein observed later. Weininger's focus is on the recognition of the multiplicity of sexual differences among individuals, while the later Wittgenstein is concerned with the multiplicity of the different games we play with language.

Both thinkers then combat the tendency to homogenize – sexuality or language respectively. To homogenize in philosophy or cultural reflection is in effect to succumb to scientism (LT, 138). Rather than shedding light on sexual diversity, the abuse of the ideal male and female types blinds us to the facts. Similarly, rather than illuminating the realities of language use, the picture theory as an ideal blinds us to the actual multiplicity of the workings of language. Consider the following passage (an early version of PI, 103): "How have you come by this ideal? The ideal is unshakeable. You can never get outside it. You must always turn back. There is no outside; outside you cannot breathe. Where does this come from? Where does this feeling come from? . . . It is as if we don't recognize a form of expression as a form of expression" (Wittgenstein 2000, MS 157a, 114–16). To explain this blind spot Wittgenstein in the same text effectively brings in the Weiningerian metaphor of "the lenses" (S&C, 97): it is "almost as if we took the colour of the glasses, or a mark on the glasses through which we see, for the colour or characteristic of the thing we look at. For example, Every proposition after all says: 'This is how things are.' That is such a pair of glasses." The metaphor recurs, even though more cryptically, in the *Philosophical Investigations.* "The ideal . . . is like a pair of glasses on our nose through which we see whatever we look at. It never occurs to us to take them off" (PI, 103).

Wittgenstein's heuristic role for the ideal is already firmly in place by the early 1930s. In a 1931 journal entry, he speaks of the ideal or the prototype as an "object of comparison" (*Vergleichsobject*) (CV, 21). In the *Blue and Brown Book* he is more forthcoming:

> Whenever we make up "ideal languages" it is not in order to replace our ordinary language by them; but just to remove some trouble caused in someone's mind by thinking that he has got hold of the exact use of a common word. That is also why our method is not merely to enumerate actual usages of words, but rather deliberately to invent new ones, some of them because of their absurd appearance (BB, 28).

Two years later, in 1933, he speaks of setting up the language games simply "to shed their light on the particular problems" (Wittgenstein 2000, MS 115, 81). Finally, in the *Philosophical Investigations* he explicitly speaks of "*constructing* ideal languages" (konstruierten *ideale Sprachen*) with which we can "compare our use of words" (PI, 81). Analogously, Weininger spoke of the *heuristic* necessity of the *construction* of ideal types (*ihre konstruktion ist notwendig aus dem heuiristischen*) to throw light on the differences between different individuals by way of comparison and contrast to these ideal types (S&C, 9).

Philosophical Error and the Teaching of Difference

There is another Weiningerian theme that crops up in the mature works of Wittgenstein. This theme is the crucial methodological role that *comparisons* play in the acquisition of knowledge and understanding, and how the discernment of similarities and differences connects to memory. Weininger thinks that

> the extent to which a man can detect differences and resemblances must depend on his memories. This faculty will be best developed in those whose past permeates their present, all the moments of the life of whom are amalgamated. Such persons will have the greatest opportunity of detecting resemblances and so finding the material for *comparisons* [my italics]. They will always seize hold of that from the past which has the greatest resemblance to the present experience, and the two experiences will be combined in such a way that no *similarities or differences* [my italics] will be concealed (S&C, 117–18).

Now the improper use of the ideal sexual types forces, according to Weininger, the particular individual, as by a vice, into a priori molds. We are so dazzled by the ideal types that we are inclined to forget to describe the individual case as *intermediate* and instead treat him or her "as if they were good examples of the ideal male or female types" (S&C, 57). Such a fixation on the prototype cuts off or undermines the possibility of an adequate range of comparisons and contrasts between the individual case and the ideal types. The proper use of the ideal is as an aid in "determining the proportion of male and female in each individual, and of measuring the oscillations to each side of which any individual is capable" (S&C, 55).

Wittgenstein's later work is sprinkled with such exhortations as "compare" and "contrast." As we have seen, he shares Weininger's heuristic view of the ideal, and cautions us not to mistake a means of representation for a representation. "The language-games are rather set up as *objects of comparison* which are meant to throw light on the facts of language by way not only of similarities, but also of dissimilarities" (PI, 130). The possibility of unearthing relevant similarities and differences is undercut by our dazzlement with certain grammatical pictures or analogies. As an antidote, Wittgenstein prescribes "a clearly arranged presentation," "a perspicuous overview" of our uses of words, which "allow us to see connections. Hence the importance of finding connecting links." A later articulation of this appears in the *Philosophical Investigations* as: "A perspicuous presentation produces just that understanding which consists of 'seeing connexions.' Hence the importance of finding and inventing *intermediate cases.* The concept of a perspicuous presentation is of fundamental significance for us. It earmarks the form of account we give, the way we look at things" (PI, 122). These themes of comparison, intermediate cases and the proper use of the ideal as an object of comparison have a familiar Weiningerian ring.

Let me now link this issue of an impoverished capacity for making proper comparisons to Wittgenstein's and Weininger's diagnosis of a central source of error. I put their views side by side for ready inspection. For Wittgenstein of the *Philosophical Investigations,* "the main cause of a philosophical disease – is a one-sided diet: one nourishes one's thinking with only one kind of example" (PI, 593). There is in Weininger a close sexual parallel to this. What, he asks, is the source of the common illusion that "all women are alike," that "no individuals exist among women," in spite of the fact that stares us in the face that "there are plenty of differences among women"? Weininger suggests that "the psychological origin of this common error depends chiefly on . . . the fact that every man in his life becomes intimate only with a group of women defined by his own constitution, and so naturally he finds them much alike" (S&C, 58). So a one-sided view of women is a main cause of the fallacy of sexual stereotyping.

Weininger goes on to say, taking as his target of criticism the fin-de-siècle feminism of his age: "For the same reason, and in the same way, one may often hear a woman say that all men are alike. And the *narrow uniform* view about men, displayed by most of the leaders of the women's movement depends on precisely the same cause" (S&C, 58–9). It is not hard to hear this resonance in Wittgenstein's own etiology of a central sort of philosophical disease as caused by a one-sided diet of examples.

Wittgenstein, Weininger, and Spengler on the Prototype

Wittgenstein's turn to the later view of the ideal (or prototype) as a "comparison-object" (*Vergleichsobject*) is dated by scholars with reference to a 1931 journal entry that discusses Spengler:

> Spengler could be better understood if he said: "I am *comparing* different periods of culture with the lives of families; within the family there is a family resemblance, while you will also find a resemblance between members of different families; family resemblance differs from the other sort of resemblance in such & such ways etc." What I mean is: We have to be told the object of comparison, the object from which this approach is derived, so that prejudices do not constantly slip into the discussion. Because then we shall willy-nilly ascribe what is true (holds) of the prototype of the approach (of the comparison) to the object to which we are applying the approach as well; & we claim "*it must always be* . . . " This comes about because we want to give the prototype's characteristics a foothold in the approach. But since we confuse prototype & object, we find ourselves dogmatically conferring on the object properties which only the prototype necessarily possesses (CV, 21).

This allusion to Spengler is helpful in dating Wittgenstein's turn to a new conception of the role of the ideal, but it would be a serious mistake to infer from it that Spengler is an exclusive stimulus for it or that Wittgenstein agrees with Spengler's use of the ideal. Now there is no doubt that Spengler was an important influence on Wittgenstein's later philosophy. He admired Spengler's rejection of that "drydust scheme . . . that empty picture of one linear world-history which can only be kept up by shutting one's eyes to the overwhelming multitude of facts, the drama of a multiplicity of cultures . . . ; each stamping its material, its mankind, its own form, each having its own idea, its own passions, its own life, will and feeling, its own death" (Spengler 1926, 21). Besides this, the method of analogy implicit in Spengler's project of investigating history as a comparative morphology of cultures is likely to have appealed to Wittgenstein and reinforced the Weiningerian direction of the method of comparisons. What Weininger had done for sexual diversity, Spengler did for the "astonishing wealth of actual forms" of history, and Wittgenstein does, in a shared spirit of respect for difference, for the multiplicity in our actual uses of language and language games.

It is important to notice, however, that even as Wittgenstein acknowledges Spengler's insights when he says, "Spengler could be better understood if he said . . . ," in what follows Wittgenstein actually goes on to criticize Spengler in a rather Weiningerian way as still failing to see clearly the proper role of the ideal as an object of comparison, rather than the essence of the phenomenon under investigation. Spengler, who sees Rome as the prototype for understanding Western European/American culture, does not regard Rome merely as a comparison-object, but perceives it as revealing the underlying essence of Western European/American culture. Hence, he dogmatically confers on the latter what only Rome necessarily had. Small wonder then that Spengler reaches such a dramatic conclusion about the decline of the West. It is precisely this distorting use of the ideal, this forcing or pressing into molds that Weininger warned us against in the first place. Clarifying the proper role of the ideal helps to refine the method of comparison and aids in the avoidance of philosophical error.

Conclusion

I have aimed to solve the new Wittgenstein/Weininger riddle as crystallized in the twin questions, "How did Weininger influence Wittgenstein's transition from the early work of the *Tractatus* to the later work of the *Investigations*?" and "What are the discernible textual traces of the Weiningerian influence in Wittgenstein's later works?" I suggested that Wittgenstein reread and closely studied Weininger during the crucial transition period and beyond as evidenced by his journal entries in the late twenties and throughout the thirties. He found in Weininger a line of thinking (*Gedankenbewegung*), a spirit of inquiry, methodological directions, and substantive themes, which he clarified and applied in striking new ways to his particular concerns with language. What Wittgenstein inherited from Weininger and made his own were no "mere eggshells" but nourishing yolk.

Using a method of juxtaposition, I put side by side passages on significant philosophical themes from Weininger's *Sex and Character* and *On Last Things* on the one hand, and Wittgenstein's later works (*The Blue and Brown Books, Philosophical Grammar, The Big Typescript* (*Wittgenstein's Nachlass*), and the *Philosophical Investigations*) on the other. When compared, these passages show Wittgenstein's later philosophical procedures to be in notable accordance with a consistent practice of Weininger's recommendations to acknowledge and attend to multiplicity, respect difference, employ the notion of the ideal heuristically (without dogmatism or bias), make use of a comparative method, and be aware of the power of similes and metaphors. I hope to have made it plain that, contrary to received views among Wittgenstein scholars, there are important textual traces of the Weiningerian influence in Wittgenstein's later works, and what he took over from Weininger and made his own was no mere admiration of existential authenticity or the platitude that philosophical problems can only be solved by a change of heart.

And now for three caveats. *Of course*, notwithstanding the Weiningerian "footnotes" I have provided, Wittgenstein's significance and achievement for us remain unique, his originality and genius peculiarly his own. Weininger's seed, though now fully noticeable, still seems quite tiny in Wittgenstein's fertile soil, as are Spengler's and Sraffa's, who were also contributors to his powerful later line of thinking. *Of course*, it is wrong to jump from Wittgenstein's acknowledgment of an intellectual debt to Weininger and my "footnotes" to the view that whatever is true of Weininger's thinking also applies to Wittgenstein's. Apart from being contradicted by Wittgenstein's own explicit repudiations of some of Weininger's tenets, and his implicit repudiations of Weininger's inconsistencies, such a move would involve precisely the sort of error Wittgenstein warns us against: do not mistake the "object of comparison" for the object viewed in its light. And finally, *of course*, as Allan Janik says, "influence is not to be construed in the push and pull way that textbook histories suggest... but is properly understood as nothing less than the reconstruction of outstanding achievement."

Postscript

As I reread my contribution to show how Weininger influenced the later Wittgenstein, I am embarrassed by the realization that I may (seem to) have produced, to put it politely, a new riddle, or, to put it bluntly, an inconsistency. How could it be true that Weininger was both a source of the later Wittgenstein's anti-essentialism, as I have argued, as well as Wittgenstein's paradigm of an arch-essentialist, as evidenced by his rejection of Weininger's enormous methodological mistake?

I do not pretend to have an entirely satisfactory answer to this question, except to say that indeed Weininger was both. Here is how I see it. On the one hand, there is the notorious Weininger whose sole purpose of investigation in science as well as in the arts was "to reach the type, the Platonic idea" and whose dead ends are stereotype, prejudice, and absurdity. This is Weininger as *eggshells*: the doctrinaire, essentializing, scientistic Weininger, iconic of the theoretical urge run amok, who presents us with seductive pictures, and whose being consists in "what is inherited from others." On the other hand, there is the little-known but deep Weininger: antiscientistic, anti-essentialist, whose actual work shows a struggle to attend and do justice to particularity and difference. This is the Weininger who subverts the essentialist pictures by noticing that their applications result in harmful distortions and injustice. This is the Weininger of new similes and metaphor looking at things differently. This is Weininger as *Dichter*, as *nourishing yolk*.

Now this makes it *appear* that there are two Weiningers. Wittgenstein identifies this tension, waking up to the fact that Weininger's aim to do justice does not square with his (Weininger's) own professed method. Returning to the quotation I began with: Weininger as "eggshells" is to be "treated with indulgence," "but what he means to us is all the same only *his* personality" – this is what gives us "Spiritual nourishment." Adopting this perspective, we can see that Wittgenstein not only provides a critique of Weininger from the inside, but clarifies and reconceives Weininger's anti-essentialist line of thought by ridding it of its essentialist elements, and thereby making it his own. Thus, for Wittgenstein, Otto Weininger was, like language, both a means of philosophical bewitchment and involved in the struggle against it.

Notes

Ancestral versions of this essay were presented at the Philosophy Colloquium of the University of Alberta in March 2000, and at the Wittgenstein/Weininger symposium at the May 2001 meetings of the Canadian Philosophical Association in Quebec City. I am grateful to Alex Rueger, David Stern, Heather Hodgson, and Martin Tweedale for incisive comments and encouragement.

References

Often-cited works by Weininger and Wittgenstein are listed under the abbreviations used in the text references.

BB: Wittgenstein, Ludwig (1958/1964). *The Blue and Brown Books.* Edited by Rush Rhees. Oxford: Basil Blackwell.

Bloom, Harold (1975). *The Anxiety of Influence.* New York: Oxford University Press.

CV: Wittgenstein, Ludwig (1980/1998). *Culture and Value.* Edited by G. H. von Wright in collaboration with Heikki Nyman. Translated by Peter Winch. Oxford: Basil Blackwell. Cited translations are taken from the revised second edition (1998) with a new English translation by Peter Winch. Oddly enough, the main text of this translation shows Wittgenstein's first drafts of his thoughts and footnotes the variant final drafts. In my quotations I show both variants by including the final drafts in parentheses.

Drury, M. O'C (1981). "Some Notes on Conversations with Wittgenstein." In Rush Rhees, ed., *Ludwig Wittgenstein: Personal Recollections,* 87–110. Oxford: Basil Blackwell.

Haller, Rudolf (1988). "What Do Wittgenstein and Weininger Have in Common?" In Haller, *Questions on Wittgenstein,* 90–9. Lincoln: University of Nebraska Press.

Harrowitz, Nancy A., and Barbara Hyams, eds., (1995). *Jews and Gender: Responses to Otto Weininger.* Philadelphia: Temple University Press.

Janik, Allan (1995). "How Did Weininger Influence Wittgenstein?" In Nancy A. Harrowitz and Barbara Hyams, eds., *Jews and Gender: Responses to Otto Weininger,* 61–72. Philadelphia: Temple University Press.

Janik, Allan, and David G. Stern (2002). Personal Correspondence.

Klagge, James, ed. (2001). *Wittgenstein: Biography and Philosophy.* Cambridge: Cambridge University Press.

Le Rider, Jacques (1982). *Le Cas Otto Weininger: Racines de l'antiféminisme et l'antisémitisme.* Paris: Presses Universitaires de France.

LRKM: Wittgenstein, Ludwig (1974). *Letters to Russell, Keynes and Moore.* Edited by G. H. von Wright. Oxford: Basil Blackwell.

LT: Weininger, Otto (1904). *Über Die Letzten Dinge.* Vienna & Leipzig: W. Braumüller. Translated by Steven Burns as *On Last Things.* Lewiston, NY: Edwin Mellen Press, 2001.

McGuinness, Brian (1988). *Wittgenstein: A Life. Young Ludwig (1889–1921).* Berkeley: University of California Press.

Monk, Ray (1990). *Ludwig Wittgenstein: The Duty of Genius.* New York: Free Press.

PG: Wittgenstein, Ludwig (1974). *Philosophical Grammar.* Edited by Rush Rhees. Translated by Anthony Kenny. Oxford: Blackwell.

PI: Wittgenstein, Ludwig (1953). *Philosophical Investigations.* Edited by G. E. M. Anscombe and Rush Rhees. Translated by G. E. M. Anscombe. Oxford: Basil Blackwell. Second edition, 1958; third edition, 1973; fourth edition, 2001. Translations are taken from the fourth edition.

PO: Wittgenstein, Ludwig (1993). *Philosophical Occasions, 1912–1951.* Edited by James Klagge and Alfred Nordmann. Indianapolis, IN: Hackett.

Rhees, Rush, ed. (1981). Ludwig *Wittgenstein: Personal Recollections.* Oxford: Basil Blackwell.

Rueger, Alexander (2002). Personal Correspondence.

S&C: Weininger, Otto (1903/1906). *Geschlecht und Character: Eine prinzipielle Untersuchung.* Munich: Matthes & Seitz. Translated, anonymously and without footnotes, as *Sex and Character.* New York: Heinemann, 1906. Page references in the text are to the 1906 edition.

Spengler, Oswald (1926). *The Decline of the West.* Translated by C. F. Atkinson. London: George Allen & Unwin.

Stern, David G. (2001). "Was Wittgenstein a Jew?" In James Klagge, ed., *Wittgenstein: Biography and Philosophy,* 237–72. Cambridge: Cambridge University Press.

Szabados, Béla (1999). "Was Wittgenstein an Anti-Semite? The Significance of Anti-Semitism for Wittgenstein's Philosophy." *Canadian Journal of Philosophy* 29: 1–28.

TLP: Wittgenstein, Ludwig (1922). *Tractatus Logico-Philosophicus.* Translated by D. F. Pears & B. F. McGuinness. London: Routledge & Kegan Paul, 1961.

von Wright, Georg Henrik (1982). "Wittgenstein in Relation to his Times." In von Wright, *Wittgenstein.* Oxford: Basil Blackwell, 108–20.

Wittgenstein, Ludwig (1978). *Remarks on Colour.* Edited by G. E. M. Anscombe. Translated by Linda L. McAlister and Margarete Schättel. Berkeley and Los Angeles: University of California Press.

______ (2000). *Wittgenstein's Nachlass: The Bergen Electronic Edition.* Oxford: Oxford University Press. References are to the von Wright (1982) numbering system.

2

Weininger and the Two Wittgensteins

Allan Janik

The relationship between Wittgenstein's personal beliefs and his philosophical views is considerably closer than normally is the case with philosophers, especially analytic philosophers. In Wittgenstein's case we know that his personal values were intimately related to his philosophizing and even exactly when his personal and his philosophical concerns began to overlap in ways that have to be taken seriously.[1] In 1916 he writes, "Colossal strain in the last month. Have reflected much about everything but curiously incapable of producing the connection with my mathematical trains of thought. However, the connection will be produced! What cannot be said *cannot* be said!" (*GT*, 6–7.VII,16) It seems that he had attained clarity about his problems relating to logic and now was challenged to apply the same approach that had been fruitful in logic to his existential problems: those problems must "dissolve" of themselves on the basis of an alternative mode of formulating them (*GT*, 26.XI,14; and see *CV*, 27). It is precisely at the point where Wittgenstein begins to "produce" that connection, as we shall see, that Otto Weininger started to become philosophically important to him. What is more, it is precisely here that the points of contact between Wittgenstein and so-called "Continental philosophers"[2] such as Friedrich Nietzsche, Søren Kierkegaard, and Martin Heidegger emerge.

Wittgenstein was surely aware of Weininger long before the section from *Über die letzten Dinge* called "Animal Psychology" came to play a crucial role in his own understanding of the ethical implications of his elimination of logical theory in the *Tractatus*. The dust jacket of the French edition of *Geschlecht und Charakter* makes the claim that Wittgenstein attended Weininger's funeral.[3] At first glance this seems more than a little strange, since Wittgenstein was only fourteen years old when Weininger committed suicide in October 1903. However, given his older sister Margaret's interest in questions relating to sexual differences and her general curiosity about celebrities, it is entirely possible that she took the young Ludwig there.[4] In any case, it would have been well-nigh impossible for someone growing up in Vienna at the turn of the century to be unaware of *Geschlecht und Charakter* or its author.

Already before the war Wittgenstein was showing signs of what, after the fact, seems to be a Weiningerian moral intensity that would later become typical of him. Thus he would tell Russell that he was reading William James's *The Varieties of Religious Experience* in 1912 in the vain hope of becoming a saint.[5] A bit later in a much-discussed episode he insisted that his morose silent pacing back and forth in Russell's Cambridge quarters was occasioned by distressing thoughts about logic and his sins that might well be Weiningerian in nature. At the beginning of the war Ludwig viewed his very enlistment as a buck private as a trial by ordeal (*Feuerprobe*) of his character (*GT*, 10.VIII.14). This would seem to indicate that he saw himself challenged by a strict moral obligation of precisely the sort that Weininger sought to legitimate in *Geschlecht und Charakter*. Later Norman Malcolm would similarly report that he had fears for Wittgenstein's life in the later 1940s when Ludwig thought that he was no longer capable of doing philosophy. This seems clearly connected with Wittgenstein's concept of the value of work and with what it is to be "*anständig*," all of which taken together has a strongly Weiningerian ring to it.[6]

Be that as it may, Wittgenstein's seemingly self-deprecating remarks in 1931 about the "reproductive" character of Jewish thinkers, which has scandalized many readers of *Culture and Value* (*CV*, 18 and passim), are also clearly attributable to Weininger's influence. Anyone who knows Otto Weininger's works will recognize nearly everything Wittgenstein says there about Jews and Judaism as derivative from fin-de-siècle Vienna's most influential cultural critic. This in itself shocks many of Wittgenstein's admirers; for Weininger, contrary to his intentions,[7] has meanwhile become positively notorious as grist to the mill of anti-Semites and misogynists (*Geschlecht und Charakter*, vi, ix, 450).[8] It therefore requires a certain explanation.

These opinions, like most of Weininger's views on Jews and Judaism, are themselves derivative from Houston Stewart Chamberlain, as the notes to Weininger's work amply attest (*Geschlecht und Charakter*, 405ff.). In Chamberlain we find a common ancestor for both Hitler's and Wittgenstein's rhetoric. However, this in itself tells us little; for as philosophers such as C. S. Peirce and Wittgenstein himself tell us, the meaning of a picture or a sentence is not somehow in that picture or sentence but in the use to which it is put. One and the same sentence can function as a vehicle of prejudice or as a part of an exercise in self-criticism – a point that till now has been lost, for example, on many "intentionalist" intellectual historians of totalitarian movements with respect to the precursors of those movements.[9]

In Wittgenstein's case, for example, reflections about the "reproductive" character of Jewish intelligence are part of a rigorous exercise in self-assessment. Steven Beller has insightfully shown how such seemingly prejudiced allegations were part and parcel of a specifically Jewish form of Enlightenment, which rejected the ghetto along with the Jewish religion, often with scathing criticism, with a view to preserving the rational core of Jewish religious and social values in a secular humanism based upon science and art. Indeed both Weininger and Wittgenstein are paradigm cases illustrating Beller's main thesis about the values associated with "assimilation" in fin-de-siècle Vienna.[10]

Ray Monk has clarified the circumstances in which Wittgenstein made his remarks about Jews and Judaism. They are related to his "confession" of 1931, which was Wittgenstein's way of settling with his past before marrying Marguerite Respinger.[11] It was the service of the late Rush Rhees to provide an in-depth analysis of the deeper meaning of Wittgenstein's confrontation with his own Jewishness.[12] Reading Wittgenstein very carefully, Rhees distinguishes Wittgenstein's way of using Weininger's picture of the Jew from Weininger's own way of employing it. In short, Wittgenstein simply wanted to get straight about his own spiritual state in a Pascalian sense. He sought to examine himself by confronting his own tendency to self-deception. Unlike Weininger, he did not aspire to overcome himself. Coming to grips with his own weaknesses was difficult enough for him, in his own eyes at least. His vanity was always there to lead him astray. But let us return to Weininger's account of Judaism.

From the start Weininger insists, following Chamberlain, that Judaism is neither to be identified with a race, a nation, nor a confession, but with an intellectual and spiritual disposition to unreflective conformity and mediocrity (*Geschlecht und Charakter*, 406ff.). Weininger makes it clear that he considers this the equivalent to precisely the sort of self-deception that Socrates set out to challenge. Moreover, such self-deception is a possibility for every human being. Indeed, it is from this point of view that he defines enlightenment as overcoming this tendency to self-deception, which we all find in ourselves. Thus Socratic self-knowledge begins when we recognize the existence of a tendency to self-deception in ourselves; that recognition then becomes the basis for overcoming our instincts.

Finding this picture highly useful in deciphering his own spiritual life, Wittgenstein insisted upon the importance of such images for helping us to recognize ourselves as we actually are and not as we might like to see ourselves or want to be seen by others. However, he does not believe that we are likely to change ourselves very much. His efforts are at once an exercise in self-criticism that should issue in modesty, a way of deflating an inflated self-image – exactly what he would demand of serious philosophers as well.

The publication of the so-called "secret diaries" of 1914–16 bear Rhees out with respect to the idea that Wittgenstein was principally concerned with forming an accurate assessment of himself and not with self-transcendence. There we find Wittgenstein recording his innermost thoughts and fears, even his sexual impulses, neither morbidly nor pruriently but rather clinically, with a view to establishing insight into his own character. It is an exercise inspired by Weininger but not entirely Weiningerian in nature. So there is no question about Wittgenstein's personal concern for Weininger. The question we need to pose is what all this has to do with his philosophy. We know a good deal about the answers to those questions from his biographers but it is not possible to avoid speculation altogether.

What follows is an account of Weininger's impact on Wittgenstein at a crucial point in his thinking in 1916 and its consequences for Wittgenstein's mature philosophizing. It documents the dramatic emergence of the "mystical" in the early Wittgenstein and proceeds to reconstruct certain central features of the so-called later Wittgenstein on the basis of that development. Thus the title "Weininger and the Two Wittgensteins."[13] The impact of Weininger on Wittgenstein's so-called early philosophy can be reconstructed readily. His impact upon the mature Wittgenstein is a more ticklish matter.

In a celebrated passage in *Culture and Value* Wittgenstein admits that his philosophical work of clarification was influenced by ten figures, including Otto Weininger (*CV*, 19). On this list, which can be safely assumed to be chronological, Weininger comes between Adolf Loos and Oswald Spengler. Since we know that Wittgenstein met Loos on the eve of World War I and that Spengler's work only appeared after the war, it is only logical to conclude that the influence that Weininger exerted upon him came during the war. Further, it is not unreasonable to associate Weininger with the most dramatic development during that period, the emergence of the "mystical," first tentatively, later with full conviction, in his philosophical notebooks (that is, the ones that were not in cipher) during the summer of 1916. At that point issues about God, the world (construed in a decidedly Augustinian-Pascalian sense) and the meaning of life – which had clearly been on his mind from at least the point when he became a perfect target for enemy fire as a searchlight operator on the patrol ship *Goplana* in Galicia in 1914 – made their way into his philosophical reflections. It seems that by the summer of 1916 he had *established* the connection he had been seeking between the answer to his existential problems and his philosophical problems about the nature of propositions. It is important to emphasize that this connection was not something he discovered but a procedure he performed, a matter of "technique" as it were.[14]

Let us look at the development of the *Tractatus* from this point of view. The earliest surviving thought that went into "*Die Abhandlung*," as Wittgenstein himself was wont to call it, was that logic must take care of itself – as he puts it at the very beginning of the notebooks (*N*, 22.VIII.14). There is much to be said for the thesis that the published *Tractatus* represents working out how that should be understood. If we examine the seven propositions that constitute the *Tractatus* alone, as the all important numbering system suggests to us (*F*, 26, 5.XII.19), we discover that only the last two are properly Wittgensteinian.

1. *Die Welt ist alles, was der Fall ist.*
   The world is all that is the case.
2. *Was der Fall ist, die Tatsache, ist, das Bestehen von Sachverhalten.*
   What is the case, the fact, is the existence of states of affairs.
3. *Das logische Bild der Tatsachen ist der Gedanke.*
   The logical picture of facts is the thought.
4. *Der Gedanke ist der sinnvolle Satz.*
   The thought is the meaningful proposition.
5. *Der Satz ist eine Wahrheitsfunktion der Elementarsätze. (Der Elementarsatz ist einer Wahrheitsfunktion seiner selbst.)*
   The proposition is a truth function of elementary propositions. (The elementary proposition is a truth function of itself).
6. *Die allgemeine Form der Wahrheitsfunktion ist:* $[\bar{p}, \bar{\xi}, N, (\bar{\xi})]$.
   The general form of a truth function is: $[\bar{p}, \bar{\xi}, N, (\bar{\xi})]$.
7. *Wovon man nicht sprechen kann, darüber muss man schweigen.*
   Whereof one cannot speak, thereof one must be silent.

The first four are identity statements that can be read as stipulating how a series of expressions define each other. They could be attributed to more or less any philosopher concerned with logic from Aristotle on. Proposition 5 states Frege's revolutionary view of complex propositions as functions of the truth values of their components and his Leibnizian notion that where there are complexes, there must be simples. These notions would become programmatic for analytic philosophy. Propositions 1 to 5 are thus by no means unique to Wittgenstein. Propositions 6 and 7 alone are distinctively Wittgensteinian. That fact has largely been overlooked by readers of the *Tractatus.* Those propositions tell us in effect that all of the propositions of logic can be derived from the Sheffer stroke, that is, not both p and q, and that once we have grasped that point, we shall understand that it is completely unnecessary to develop a *theory* of the nature of the proposition.

As far as proposition 6 goes, proceeding from the idea of a truth-functional connective that can represent every dyadic relation between propositions, Wittgenstein created a purely mechanical technique, the truth table, for demonstrating, "showing," the logical status of propositions as tautologies, contradictions, or empirical statements. One simply needs to know how to represent propositions and how to apply them to represent states of affairs. Thus application shows what the truth table does not about the nature of a proposition (*TL-P*, 3.262). With that the whole idea of a philosophy of logic became superfluous in Wittgenstein's eyes. There is simply no need to talk about the matter, and certainly no sense in arguing about the status of specific propositions, when we have a purely mechanical, crystal-clear, sure-fire means for showing it at our disposal. This was Wittgenstein's sober position before Weininger entered his philosophizing.

It would be wise to reiterate that this is the view of the *Tractatus* we get if, as people normally do not, we simply consider its seven propositions apart from their elucidating remarks. On this view there was, as Wittgenstein himself insisted, nothing left for philosophers to do: we should simply get down to the scientific task of making models (*Bilder*) of what we take to be facts, from time to time showing the nonsensicality of metaphysical assertions that have slipped into our scientific enterprises. However, the *Tractatus* was not read that way when it first appeared nor, unfortunately, do people read it that way now. One (but only one) major difference was the matter between propositions 6 and 7, the "mystical" (God, the meaning of life, ethics etc.), which has colored the reception of the *Tractatus*, for better or for worse, down to our times. This turns out to be where Weininger's influence upon Wittgenstein is most direct. It comes in aid of answering the questions: How do I obtain the same sort of clarity about the problems of life? and How do I put myself into a position in which they simply do not arise? This became increasingly important to Wittgenstein between 1916 and the publication of the *Tractatus* in 1922. The question is to what extent is it integral to the *Tractatus*?

Brian McGuinness has suggested, on the basis of a close study of the text-genesis of the *Tractatus*, that there is but a weak link between the "mystical" part of the *Tractatus* and the "logical" part that precedes it; he suggests that Wittgenstein was less successful in the work than he thought. Thus McGuinness concludes a lecture on the theme, "Wittgenstein and the Unsayable," with the following reflections:

> It will be seen that I think the propositions about value and the mystical in the completed *Tractatus* were indeed extracted from Wittgenstein somewhat against his original intention. This can be interpreted in two ways – that they

were a questionable extension of his insights (this was the view of one wing of the Vienna Circle) or that they are all the more trustworthy because, metaphysical as they seem, they forced themselves upon him. Whether the choice between these two alternatives is a matter of logic or sympathy I find hard to decide.[15]

McGuinness bases his claim principally upon a philological argument. He conjectures plausibly that there is in fact a caesura on page 71 of the so-called *Prototractatus*, where we find a line drawn after propositions 6.3 "All propositions are of equal value" and 7 "Whereof one cannot speak, thereof one must remain silent." He suggests that the propositions that come before that line are the substance of Wittgenstein's original reflections on the problems he had taken over from Russell and Frege before the war, that is what he had developed *before* his encounter with Paul Engelmann in Olomouc (Olmütz), Moravia, in 1916 (in which Wittgenstein really does pass over matters beyond the scope of the nature of the proposition in silence). What comes after them in the *Tractatus*, including his remarks on value and the mystical, are basically an accretion stemming from intense personal reflections, but not necessarily of profound philosophical significance: "While his logical insights gave them an underpinning for their philosophy of life, he learnt from them how he could say something about his deepest convictions without running counter to those same insights."[16] Thus Brian McGuinness further suggests, first, that the mystical was a dubious extension of Wittgenstein's previous "mathematical" train of thought, and, second, that it is not a simple task to make a conclusive case for the logical coherence of the resulting book, which has come down to us as the *Tractatus Logico-Philosophicus*, on the basis of the textual considerations alone. On this view, it would not be absurd to speak of a predominantly Russellian-Fregean version of the *Tractatus* and a predominantly Wittgensteinian-Weiningerian version as well (whether it would be wise to do so is another question). In throwing away the proverbial ladder that is, rejecting the idea that there are limits to language, the so-called New Wittgensteinians would appear to be playing off the former against the latter and in fact throwing Wittgenstein away with the ladder; for this notion will be the basis of all of Wittgenstein's subsequent philosophizing.[17] But that is another matter.

This is not the place to examine these claims in detail, but it seems necessary to admit that they seem to have a prima facie validity. In 1916 Wittgenstein seems to have shifted gears as it were. The intensive fighting in the course of Brusilov's offensive, in which Austria-Hungary lost two-thirds of her 620,000 troops on the Eastern Front in one way or another, and in which Wittgenstein was conspicuous for his extraordinary valor in combat, seems to have brought with it clarity with respect to his existential problems (God, the world, the meaning of life), which were consonant with his project in logic of making the problems dissolve on the basis of a new technique for representing propositions and pseudo-propositions. Moreover, his transfer to Olomouc shortly thereafter brought him into contact with Paul Engelmann, who, as Brian McGuinness suggests, decisively reinforced this way of thinking.[18] Weininger was doubtlessly in the center of these developments.

Wittgenstein became the Wittgenstein we know as he struggled to produce a common solution to both his existential problems and his philosophical problems. He had learned from Heinrich Hertz that "showing" is the only strict way to resolve philosophical problems, that is, by dissolving them on the basis of a striking alternative representation of the problematic matter.[19] This is more a matter of invention than of discovery, which is why Wittgenstein could allege later that philosophy can only really be written as fiction. Moreover, the truth of that alternative way of thinking was less important to Wittgenstein than its ability to reorient his thinking from a conceptual impasse to a productive way of thinking. Thus he would employ those few pages in Weininger's *Über die letzten Dinge*[20] to intensify and encapsulate what he had already learned from Schopenhauer,[21] James,[22] and Tolstoy.[23] What, in fact, had he learned from James and Tolstoy?

The "Secret Diaries," those facing pages of his philosophical notebooks that Wittgenstein wrote in cipher to protect the privacy of his innermost thoughts, record Wittgenstein's efforts to lead what he took to be a philosophical life[24] in the face of death each night on the *Goplana*. His exercise in courage was certainly inspired by his prewar encounters with William James's *Varieties of Religious Experience*. The role of James as a background figure to Wittgenstein's philosophizing has been highly neglected. The influence of *The Varieties of Religious Experience* on his personal beliefs is clear from Wittgenstein's letter to

Russell (*RKM, R* 2, 22.VI.12), where he claims to be reading James to improve himself morally. His sister Hermine's letter of 15 April 1916,[25] in which she implores Ludwig to accept the opportunity of becoming an officer and put off his project to be a "James *Mensch*" until after the war, seems to indicate that his resolve to go to war to test his character had something to do with James.

In the early months of the war his discovery of Tolstoy's *The Gospel in Brief* certainly lent him strength in the face of fear by reminding him that we are weak in the body, but can become strong through the spirit by subordinating our will to the will of God. He would refer to this idea as the "saving word" (*das erlösende Wort, GT*, 21.XI.14), and regularly lament that he could not bring himself to pronounce it. For all his efforts, he could not entirely subordinate his Flesh to his Spirit. There was a limit here that he could not evade.

G. H. von Wright has called attention to Wittgenstein's profound interest in the section of Weininger's *Über die letzten Dinge* entitled "Animal Psychology," which was already referred to in connection with the "mystical" in the *Tractatus*.[26] It is only now that we understand Wittgenstein's relation to Hertz that we can appreciate the full importance of Weininger's work for his development. Intertextual evidence that the breakthrough of July 1916 was connected to reading Weininger can be found in the following passages: "What is it to be happy?" "What is it to live without fear and hope?" (14.VII.16); "How is the subject a limit of the world?" (2.VIII.16; 2.IX.16); "Man is the microcosm" (12.X.16); "The spirit of animals is your spirit" 14.X.16); "I have to judge the world" (2.IX.16). All of these matters were intimately linked to the problem of solipsism and Schopenhauer's philosophy in Wittgenstein's eyes.

David Pears has produced an insightful account of how the confrontation with solipsism as the limit of language forms an axis around which all of Wittgenstein's thinking revolves,[27] which is particularly relevant to grasping what he took over from Weininger. Beginning from his encounter with Russell's views about solipsism in 1913, where Russell observes that my experience of any given object is somehow more than that object because it is my object, Wittgenstein became increasingly fascinated by the way in which the self is a correlative of the world. However, in the course of the war there was a radical transformation in Wittgenstein's attitude to this problem, connected to the way the world and the self mutually limit one another, that is foreign to Russell but became increasingly important for Wittgenstein. Indeed, Russell's way of conceiving the problem of the relation between the self and the world could hardly inspire the sort of "obsession with limits"[28] that we find in Wittgenstein's *Notebooks* and that would characterize all of his future philosophizing. Neglecting Weininger, Pears ascribes that transition to the influence of Schopenhauer, who transformed not only Wittgenstein's thinking about the matter but also the intensity with which he pursued the issue. In this context Schopenhauer gave Wittgenstein a complex picture of the self according to which it was at once the seat of representation and thinking, but, at the same time, a nebulous set of prerational urges that I am, namely, the Will. This twofold notion of the self had profound implications inasmuch as it helped to establish a metaphysical significance for art as a release from willing and a way of contemplating the world as a whole.

His encounter with Weininger would intensify their significance for him. Both the testimony of his colleagues and intertextual evidence point to the centrality of Weininger at this crucial stage in his development. It seems that in his description of the "criminal" Weininger gave him something philosophically vivid that he could ruminate upon with his entire personal intensity. Of course the "influences" of Schopenhauer and Weininger would complement each other, with Schopenhauer having already contributed much to Wittgenstein's development ten years earlier (as well as having profoundly influenced Weininger).[29]

Finally, we come to the crucial point in our story. How, then, did Weininger further help Wittgenstein in his effort to let the problems of life dissolve of themselves? The answer is not that Weininger provided him with a solution to his problems, but that he gave him a striking Hertzian alternative to the conventional picture of the relationship between the self and the world, the will and the facts. Moreover, it was less the "truth" of Weininger's ideas than their power to grip him intellectually, that is, to help him restate his problem so that it "dissolved," that was crucial.[30] The technique bears a certain similarity to the practice of classical skepticism by Sextus Empiricus where one neutralizes metaphysical beliefs, thus ensuring mental health, by seeking alternatives that contradict them.[31] But that is another matter. How does the picture of the self that Weininger presented to Wittgenstein look? How did Wittgenstein use it? These are our next questions.

To begin with, we must grasp that Weininger is not concerned with making empirical generalizations about the mentality of actual people; rather, he is producing a thought experiment about the nature of immorality with a view to establishing by implication what genuine moral behavior is. The point of producing this quasi-phenomenological description is to move the reader to reflect upon what it really is to be happy and to lead a good life by giving us the negative example of their opposites. Weininger's criminal is that person who lives as though there were no limits upon him. In developing this picture Weininger in fact describes the polar opposite of Kant's autonomous human being – and the Christian notion of doing unto others as you would have them do unto you. Thus Weininger takes criminality to be a continuation of original sin. The criminal's sin, like original sin, is nothing other than selfishness, the will to self-assertion, the pursuit of happiness at any cost, the refusal to acknowledge any authority outside of one's self. Ultimately immorality, here termed criminality, is to be understood in terms of successfully living without limits, that is, possessing wonderful things without having worked for them. It is nothing other than the vulgar concept of "happiness." To this end the criminal will manipulate anything that he can get hold of. Indeed, he views everything as an extension of himself, subject to his Will and existing for his pleasure. On this view of human life there is no room for guilt whatsoever. Yet, unbeknown to himself, the criminal is in fact the "unhappiest man" because he has encapsulated himself solipsistically in his "earthly" existence by virtue of his very successes.

The criminal world is psychologically egoistic, morally nihilistic and ontologically accidental. It has no principle of inner unity. The reality of things is a function of the criminal's ego. It is only coherent as long as the criminal is successful; in failure everything falls nightmarishly to pieces. In all situations he is master or slave, possessor or possessed. The criminal wants to destroy everything that he cannot possess – or be destroyed by it. There is a certain flip-flop in his character, whereby greed and fatalism are two sides of a single coin, for he is a fatalist with respect to what he cannot have or has lost. Thus he goes to the gallows without feelings of guilt or remorse but, nevertheless, resigned that it is simply his lot. Being dominated is entirely consistent with the desire to possess; it is simply its obverse, namely, being possessed by Fate.

The criminal's world is the opposite of that of the Nietzschean *Übermensch,* who affirms the order in the world and its suffering as he finds it.[32] Since the principle of reality is the fulfillment of the criminal's wishes, the criminal's world is a curious kind of expressionistic dreamworld, in which fear and hope reign supreme (adding boredom to the constellation, you get a scenario not unlike Kierkegaard's analysis of Don Juan in *Either/Or* or his discussion of selfhood and possession in *The Sickness unto Death*). The past and the present are uninteresting to the criminal. Only the prospect of future self-aggrandizement interests him. He is essentially antisocial because he is incapable of recognizing the intrinsic worth of the Other, who is, as Other, a limit upon him. He can never be a comrade, for he enters relationships with a view to exploiting the Other. Thus the sexual exploitation that Don Juan embodies is a paradigm case of criminality inasmuch as the Don can never relate to the other as an "I" to a "Thou." Weininger goes so far as to insist that Don Juan's exploitation of women is morally equivalent to murder. Beyond that, it certainly would not have been lost on Wittgenstein that Weininger's criminal is compulsively talkative,[33] always chattering to somebody, even when he is alone. However, his words are never true, but only a function of his wishful thinking. Like the alcoholic who despises drunkards, he experiences anxiety and disgust when confronted with his own self-image. He cannot bear to be alone. Thus he has no real life of his own, which is reflected in his lack of respect for others. Being spiritually dead, he is capable of killing the Other without compunction. Finally, and perhaps most significantly in connection with Wittgenstein, his very attitude to knowledge is determined by wishful thinking:

> His drive to know is never pure, hopeful, needy, longing, never directed against insanity, never an inner need for self-preservation, rather he wants to force things and also to know. The idea that something should be impossible for him contradicts his absolute functionalist mentality that will join itself to everything and everything to itself. Therefore, he finds the idea of bounds or limits, even of knowledge, intolerable.[34]

It is precisely here that Wittgenstein found the common solution to both his existential and his intellectual problems. Henceforth they both must be solved in the only rigorous way: on the basis of drawing limits from within (*F*, 23, undated).

This is a completely different approach to the problem of solipsism from the one we find in Russell's reflections in "On the Nature of Acquaintance," which is purely epistemological. However, Wittgenstein seems to have sought and found a connection between them in the acknowledgment that the self is mysteriously linked to the limits of language: "It is true: Man is the microcosm. I am my world" (*N*, 12.X.16). Precisely this notion of man as microcosm seems to provide him with a key to both his philosophical and his existential problems.

The notion of the microcosm would seem to be exactly Wittgenstein's "mystical" point of departure in the discussion that appears so abruptly in the notebooks of 1916 about God and the meaning of life. His remarks proceed from the curious notion that despite its independence from the world my will penetrates the world, without being able to change any of the facts – a view that is clearly continuous with Weininger's concerns in "Animal Psychology." In fact, Wittgenstein's emphasis that my will is independent of the facts is the exact obverse of the Weiningerian criminal, who wallows in his own causality as it were. All of Wittgenstein's questions and remarks in the 1916 notebook can profitably be read against the background of Weininger's view of the "functionalist" criminal who refuses to recognize any ethical or logical limits to his action.

In this scenario logic and ethics are *both* "transcendental," that is, they are conditions of the world as I find it, precisely because the will or the self at once penetrates the world (as good or evil, happy or unhappy) and constitutes the facts that are its substance in the application of logic. Just as logic must take care of itself, the problems of life must be solved in the living and not in a set of beliefs about it or expectations from it. In both instances the problems must disappear (*N*, 6.VII.16). Happiness is a matter of learning that I can only master the world (the facts) by making myself independent of them. Wittgenstein claims in a Spinozistic turn – here again the project character of the enterprise is emphasized – that independence is a matter of taking a position with respect to the world ("*eine Stellungnahme zur Welt*"[35]). At this juncture (*N*, 2.IX.16) Wittgenstein insists with Weininger that "I must judge the world, measure things." This is neither Schopenhauer nor Russell nor even Tolstoy, but it is Weininger: "Judging is a phenomenon of the will;

the Criminal does not judge [things]."[36] To will is not merely to wish but to act, to live fully in the present without fear and hope. Fear and hope, it should be noted, presuppose that I identify myself with what I possess or what I want to possess – in the most extreme case with life itself considered as something I have, as opposed to something I *am*. Fear and hope presuppose loss and gain, as well as a past and a future in which said loss or gain can transpire. When I abandon the idea that life is a possession to be hoarded, the problem of life disappears. I have nothing more to fear. Thus it would seem that an evil life would be one in which I expected to be rewarded for my actions. In the end the happy life is a life in which our actions are by their nature rewarding because they are "harmonious." Thus the Spinozistic element is transformed into an Aristotelian point here as ethics and aesthetics become one in a profound sense. Such a happy life is an active one, dedicated to work in the form of the pursuit of knowledge, that is, exactly what those "Secret Diaries" show him striving for.

Yet, it is certainly not accidental that one of the only propositions from the logical part of *Tractatus* to be found in the "Secret Diaries" is proposition 6, which states that simultaneous negation is the general form of the proposition (*GT*, 21.VIII.14). Nor is it accidental that that proposition should also be reflected upon in the 1916 notebook (*N*, 13.VII.16) in the middle of his ruminations about God and the world. Logic exists only in its application, which determines a state of affairs in the world. Ethics too is a matter of recognizing in action that the self or the will and the world mutually limit one another. The "I" (the self or the will) is a limit of the world: the facts of themselves, neither happy nor unhappy, limit what I am. It seems as though through the application of the Sheffer stroke "p|q" (neither p nor q), simultaneous negation somehow provided Wittgenstein with the key to understanding both logic and ethics. On the one hand, when simultaneous negation is given truth and falsity and therefore the condition of the possibility, as it were, of all other truth functions is also given, that is, all possible propositions are given. On the other hand, the vain attempt to deny that the world is neither a happy nor unhappy world produces insight into the fact that the world is always *my* world. Its substance always has a "mood," as Heidegger puts it.[37] Simultaneous negation "shows" both the general form of the proposition, that is, as truth function, and also that inarticulable relationship between the self and the world that Heidegger attempts to capture with the phrase "*Jemeinigkeit der Welt.*"[38] Indeed, this seems to be the difference between the mere facts and "the world" for Wittgenstein. Everything that bears upon the world as my world and the form of the world as such must take care of itself. Problems with both logic and ethics must be solved in action, that is, in application. The application of logic shows us the nature of the world as it confers form upon it. Furthermore, the act of applying logic shows us an aspect of reality which we know with certainty without being able to describe in propositions, namely, the self that we are.

How is this reflected in the later Wittgenstein? To answer that question we should consider the fact that at roughly the same time that Wittgenstein came under the influence of Weininger he also realized that the problems of philosophy were rooted in a quasi-transcendental source, namely, our tendency to misunderstand the logic of language. This is one of the important features that unite the two Wittgensteins, early and late. Moreover, the idea that philosophical problems rest upon misunderstanding how language works, which he attributes to Paul Ernst,[39] is intimately related to the task of showing the limits of language from within. This is a point where we ought to feel Weininger's influence as well; for the whole point of Weininger's philosophizing, as we have seen in connection with his discussion of "Judaism," was to demonstrate that there is within human nature something like a transcendental source of self-deception (which his theory of bisexuality could *inter alia* explain).[40]

With that in mind let us look at Wittgenstein's mature view of philosophy. What is most striking at first glance is Wittgenstein's notion of philosophy as an activity directed against traditional philosophy in all its forms, not only its metaphysical (Scholastic or Cartesian) and transcendental (Hegelian or Kantian) forms, but also its traditional empiricist and conventional analytic forms.[41] In this respect his program resembles that of William James. Both of them ask traditional philosophers whether their theories really make any difference to the practice of science or for that matter to art or religion or anything whatever. Wittgenstein fully rejected the idea that philosophy could actually produce theories, not simply because he wanted to reform it, but on the grounds that all theories are as such on the same level: none is privileged in the sense of being any deeper than the others. Where there is theory, there is science, regardless of what it calls itself.

Try as we might, we can never succeed in producing a genuinely philosophical theory any more than we can succeed in producing a private language. However, in rejecting the idea that philosophy could be a science, Wittgenstein was not prepared to dismiss the problems that troubled philosophers as mere pseudo-problems. On the contrary, for him the roots of the confusing pseudo-problems of philosophy are "deep disquietudes" (*tiefe Beunruhigungen*) rooted in language itself inasmuch as we do not have a direct grasp of its workings (*PI*, 111). Thus they are a subject for profound reflection, but the results of that reflection will not be a theory. Wittgenstein was grateful to Paul Ernst for supplying him with an apt expression of the kind of difficulty we face here as we fail to understand the logic of language.[42]

Despite the huge literature on Wittgenstein, it has for the most part passed unobserved how radically his later conception of language as a plurality of game-like activities deviates from the standard views of philosophers and linguists.[43] For Wittgenstein, language is not a matter merely of words, signs, symbols, and sentences, but also of how they are interwoven in gestures to form meaning. One of several functions of the game analogy is to emphasize what a small role semiotic units and syntax play in it. Indeed, apart from instinctive behavior, such as that of the baby who pulls its hand immediately from the fire,[44] all human action is constituted through language inasmuch as nobody ever learns anything, including how to walk, without someone talking to them. However, what is said in the course of teaching a child to walk has more to do with encouragement than it does with information. For lacking the ability to speak and thus to understand, words can only function as cues in guiding the child to grasp what we want it to do. Thus the notion that play is the first vehicle through which we come to understand how experience hangs together is another important and often neglected aspect of the idea that language is constituted as we play with words. On Wittgenstein's view we all learn the most basic things we know through experience, but not our own experience. Be that as it may, the point is that if we only look at words, signs, symbols, and sentences, the pragmatics of meaning, the activities through which the significance of those units is constituted, will be wholly opaque to us. This is his point in wanting us to ponder the interactions of a group of builders who only use the words "block," "pillar," and "beam" as a complete primitive language (*PI*, 2); he wants to emphasize how much linguistic theorists from Plato to Chomsky have left out of their accounts of language. However, it is not a matter of mere ignorance: the very prominent role of referring expressions in language continually tempts us to reduce meaning to semantics and/or syntactics at the expense of pragmatics.

No small part of Wittgenstein's well-deserved status in the pantheon of twentieth-century philosophers attaches to the fact that, contrary to the positivists, he was convinced that it was not mere superstition or ignorance (that is, prejudice or empirical factors) that had prevented philosophers from seeing this. Rather, this tendency was transcendental inasmuch as it was rooted in a temptation presented by the way the very forms of words and sentences incline us to misconceive them. Put differently, those very linguistic structures that make knowing and acting possible tend to deceive us when they themselves become the objects of inquiry. When we try to fathom what meaning is without taking pragmatics into consideration, we find ourselves plagued by "deep disquietudes."

Given the predominant role of representational expressions (nouns and verbs) in language as it is normally understood, we are tempted to reify them, that is, to forget that the representational function is but one of many linguistic acts and a highly developed one that rests upon more primitive functions such as, say, ordering (as in the "builders"). It is not that the forms of language themselves are essentially deceptive, but that they tempt us to see language and ourselves wrongly. Here, as in the *Tractatus*, the point of philosophy is to help us see the world aright. Philosophical problems originate when words like "know," "judge," and "thought," as well as "language" itself, are confusedly taken to refer to things in the way that words like "cat," "fork," or "bicycle" do, that is, such that we are inclined to understand them in the same ways. Thus we tend to look for specific things corresponding to them, rather than for a number of loosely related activities linked to each other on the basis of various sorts of analogies. However, the danger of reification is only part of the problem for Wittgenstein, because what we must learn to see is that there is in fact something corresponding to such words, but not one thing. Instead, we must learn to see the plurality of loosely related referents as a family of more or less closely related members rather than members of a single species capable of being defined by genus and specific difference.

Let us consider how the word "know" epitomizes this point. Typically nurses, golfers, and opera singers have little facility in articulating what they know in their proper functions as nurses, golfers, and opera singers. However, Socrates was wrong to infer from that that they did not know anything at all. Rather, their kind of knowledge, unlike geometry and physics, does not lend itself directly to verbal expression. As Saint Augustine pointed out with respect to the concept of time, there are many things that I clearly grasp in practice so long as I am not asked to explain the matter (*PI*, 89).[45] Wittgenstein strove to develop a technique for coping with the problem by assembling reminders of the multiplicity and nuances of those particular activities and, above all, he strove to dissuade us from invidious comparisons; in this case from equating all knowledge with, say, physics. His task, in his own eyes, was a literary effort to remind us of striking facts that the very nature of language tends to tempt us to pass over – for example, the plurality of activities that correspond to the many modes of "thinking." This is why he insisted that philosophy must be analytic without its being what is conventionally understood under the rubric analytical philosophy.

Moreover it is precisely here that the idea of the limits of language – Otto Weininger's influence – enters into Wittgenstein's mature philosophy. The most important presupposition of Weininger's work is that we cannot trust conventional notions or values. Thus Weininger insists with critical theorists from Kant to Habermas that we must take an actively critical stance in relation to conventional ideas and beliefs – and in the end toward our very selves. Wittgenstein transforms this into skepticism of the idea that we in fact know what language is.

He would dismantle the Cartesian *Fragestellung* of classical modern philosophy on the basis of inventing and/or discovering new analogies and comparisons that show in an incontrovertible way that we were in fact confused when we sought to define "knowledge" and "certainty" once and for all. He would thus "dissolve" the problems of philosophy by showing us insight into the actual workings of language. In fact Descartes did not doubt systematically enough. He never questioned the meanings of the words he employed in doubting. Had he done so, it would have become clear that he must presuppose language to formulate his very doubts. A more radical systematic doubt would show that the foundations of knowledge lie elsewhere than in reason or sensation as conceived by classical modern philosophers.

Wittgenstein sought to develop a technique that would introduce such clarity into the question of, say, what it is to "know," that the question would simply cease to interest us as we gained insight into the natural history of an animal that speaks. However, it became increasingly clear to him that a single technique could never suffice to show us how language works; for it is as complex as the human organism itself. He would assemble reminders of the complexity and nuances of human knowing and acting in aid of disabusing us of the desire to ask oversimplified questions, employ misleading examples and form crude judgments on the basis of misconstruing the logic of language.

Thus philosophy ends up being a matter of coming to grips with our own animality. Wittgenstein's reaction to Weininger here was not simply to affirm his view but, as Rhees has suggested with respect to Judaism, he used the striking example that Weininger presented to him to understand just how the animal is "in" human nature.[46] In effect Weininger helped him to rehabilitate the old Aristotelian view of the human being as the ζωον λόγον εχον, which, after the later Wittgenstein, might be translated "rule following animal." Here we see the personal and the philosophical coming together in Wittgenstein's work across the decades.

In 1916 we find him making the following crucial observation about himself in battle, remarking almost despairingly, "From time to time I become an animal. Then I think of nothing other than eating, drinking, sleeping. Dreadful! And then I also suffer like an animal without the possibility of inner rescue" (*GT*, 29.VII.16). This thought is the remote ancestor to section 475 of *On Certainty*: "I want to regard man here as an animal; as a primitive being to which one grants instinct but not the power to reason. As a being in a primitive condition. Any logic good enough for a primitive means of communication needs no apology from us." Moreover, in *On Certainty* Wittgenstein finds himself all but compelled to assert that this "animal Logic," if you will, cannot be described (in the way that description is conventionally understood by analytical philosophers). Here we find ourselves running up against the limits of language. Wittgenstein would remind us that we never entirely cease to be an animal and that it is sometimes necessary for the philosopher to pay close attention to the beast in us.

The mature Wittgenstein, unlike Weininger, was convinced that philosophical problems about knowledge, thinking, certainty, mind and body, and the like could only be "solved" by being dissolved on the basis of an understanding of the natural history of the human species. For the mature Wittgenstein we see the world rightly when we consider philosophical problems against the background of those general, completely uncontroversial, facts of nature pertaining to how a language-using animal in fact functions. This is principally a matter of looking closely at how human beings learn to perform the most fundamental tasks in life, that is, those survival skills that are the indispensable prerequisites if thinking is to be at all possible. Thus, his reminders show us how traditional philosophical problems rest upon oversimplified questions, misleading examples, and misconceived comparisons that arise because we have not taken a hard look at human natural history. For Wittgenstein, unlike Weininger, it is not a matter of transcending nature but of acknowledging nature. Thus Wittgenstein recognizes, while Weininger fundamentally rejects, our animality. Hence, in his last work he insists upon considering man as an animal to the point of asserting that even logic had to be understood from this point of view: "Am I not getting ever closer to saying that in the end logic cannot be described? You have to look at the practice of language, then you see it" (*OC*, S. 501). From the point of view presented here this was already implicit in the idea, formulated as early as 1914, that logic must take care of itself. What Wittgenstein got clearer about is how difficult it is to develop the idea that logic must take care of itself.

Wittgenstein's great achievement turns on his showing us how the logic that confers systematicity (*OC*, S. 410) upon human activity and therefore underlies experience is not formal logic. Wittgenstein's position follows upon the central insight in his mature epistemology, namely, the idea of following a rule where no formal rule is present. The most primitive sort of human knowledge is constituted in practice alone, without recourse to explicit rules (*OC*, S. 95). Thus, Wittgenstein could refer to the picture of the world immanent in a particular mode of rule-following as a "kind of mythology" (*OC*, S. 475). It is fundamental to this mythology that our very participation in the myth hinders us from forming an accurate account of the practical basis of knowing. Formal (that is, propositional) knowledge is a matter of representation. Yet, in the very context of the everyday this is a considerably more complex procedure than we tend to believe. Further, the ability to form representations is learned only after we have mastered a number of other tasks, principally that of executing commands. Representation already assumes other practical abilities that have to be drilled into us (*abgerichtet*). Such dressage issues in what we might call "knowing in the body," rather than "knowing in the mind." Thus when required to explain certain things that we know perfectly well in practice, we find ourselves in the same position as Augustine confronted with the question, "What is time?" Again, think of nurses, golfers, or opera singers. The question perplexes us precisely because we are tempted into thinking that what we need is a theory to penetrate its depths when the solution in fact can be read on the very surface of our conduct. Thus Wittgenstein must remind us of any number of things that we normally accept without question concerning the world and ourselves.

Philosophers have a way of regularly overlooking precisely those aspects of practical knowledge and learning that are the key to understanding why the questions that they pose are misconceived. Their need for clarity concerning those misconceptions is linked to a fundamental misapprehension of the logic of language. Thus the clarity Wittgenstein strives for differs radically from that of the formal logician. It is a matter of seeing a certain subject rightly and realizing that there is really nothing more to question: the practice can take care of itself. Be that as it may, that difference dictates Wittgenstein's philosophical strategy. It accounts for the reason why aphorisms, questions (often unanswered), and thought experiments are so central to his way of doing philosophy. The task is, then, to dissolve philosophical problems by gesturing convincingly at practice, thereby showing us why there is no need for inquiry in the first place. It is not a matter of analysis, but of looking at the practice. Anthony Kenny has rightly argued that this notion of philosophizing bears principally upon the will rather than the intellect.[47] The notion is in fact Weiningerian.

Our inclination to be dazzled by the surface grammar of language has roots as deep as language itself. It can only be countered by *doing* something that traditional philosophical education excludes, namely, to take a look at those roots, at what we normally do and how we normally do it. The very familiarity of the practical foundations of knowing, we discover, explains why Wittgenstein's reminders have to be striking in character and also why they are often examples in the form of fictive natural histories. They should show us clearly and incontrovertibly how human experience hangs together and by demonstrating what would be the case, say, with respect to meaning, if we were differently endowed by nature concerning our fundamental modes of learning.

Thus we arrive at the point where Wittgenstein meets Weininger. For both of them, philosophical problems can only be eliminated on the basis of what Pascal calls a change of heart, that is, a change in our comportment: "Difficulty of philosophy, not the intellectual difficulty of science but the difficulty of a conversion. Resistance of the will has to be overcome."[48] The requisite transition from a theoretical to a practical point of view – for Weininger in ethics, for Wittgenstein in metaphysics and the theory of knowledge – is little less than a transformation. It is certainly not merely an intellectual matter. The source of temptation to confusion lies in a way of life. Weininger was the one who unambiguously and unequivocally presented a striking alternative to that lifestyle on the basis of the recognition of transcendental limits to thought and action. Yet, it would be wrong to think that Wittgenstein simply discovered profundities in Weininger and subsequently incorporated them into his thinking lock, stock and barrel. It was more that Weininger painted a radically different portrait of the self and the world from our conventional conceptions of them, which Wittgenstein ultimately used as a key for grasping what goes wrong in philosophy between Descartes and Russell. Thus the challenge to Wittgenstein was to dismantle the very *Problemstellung* of classical modern philosophy on the basis of insights into the nature of practice that showed the superfluity of those very questions. The power of the critique of language that constituted his response has been so immense that its full impact upon philosophy and culture has not yet been felt today, more than fifty years after his death. Weininger was indispensable to him in that Herculean enterprise.

Notes

Otto Weininger's works are referred to by title.

——— (1980). *Geschlecht und Charakter.* Munich: Matthes & Seitz.
——— (1980). *Über die letzten Dinge.* Munich: Matthes & Seitz.

Ludwig Wittgenstein's works are referred to using the following abbreviations.

CV (1980). *Culture and Value.* Edited by G. H. von Wright and Heikki Nyman. Translated by Peter Winch. Chicago: University of Chicago Press.

F (1969). *Briefe an Ludwig von Ficker.* Edited by G. H. von Wright. "Brenner Studien" vol. 1. Salzburg: Otto Müller. Letter numbers and dates given.

GT (1992). *Geheime Tagebücher.* Edited by W. Baum. Vienna: Turia & Kant. Dates are given, with month in Roman numerals.

N (1961). *Notebooks 1914–1916.* Edited by G. H. von Wright and G. E. M. Anscombe. Translated by G. E. M. Anscombe. Oxford: Basil Blackwell. Dates are given, with month in Roman numerals.

OC (1969). *On Certainty.* Translated by G. E. M. Anscombe & Denis Paul. (New York: Harper's). Section numbers are given.

PI (1958). *Philosophical Investigations.* Edited by G. E. M. Anscombe and Rush Rhees. Translated by G. E. M. Anscombe. Second Edition. Oxford: Basil Blackwell. Paragraph numbers are given.

RKM (1974). *Letters to Russell, Keynes and Moore.* Edited by G. H. von Wright. Second edition, revised. Ithaca, NY: Cornell University Press. Letter numbers are given.

TL-P (1961). *Tractatus Logico-Philosophicus.* Translated by D. F. Pears & B. F. McGuinness. London: Routledge & Kegan Paul. Proposition numbers are given.

1. See Allan Janik and Stephen Toulmin, *Wittgenstein's Vienna,* second edition, revised, Chicago: Ivan Dee, 1996, 32.
2. The term is a complete misnomer with little more than a polemic sense, as William Barrett pointed out in an (unpublished) address to the American Philosophical Association in the early 1980s. For example, what is normally understood as "Continental philosophy" has precious little to do with philosophy in such countries as Portugal, Poland, Holland, Belgium, Austria, Sweden, Norway, Finland, etc. "Analytic" philosophy is equally confusing for reasons partly explained in this essay.
3. "A son enterrement on vit Ludwig Wittgenstein, Karl Kraus, Stefan Zweig." Otto Weininger, *Sexe et charactère,* ed. Roland Jaccard, Lausanne: Editions l'Age d'Homme, 1975, dust jacket. The editor was not able to inform me of his source for this information beyond saying that he read it somewhere in Stefan Zweig. Personal communication from Roland Jaccard, Paris, 1977.
4. Personal communication from the late Dr. Thomas Stonborough.
5. Wittgenstein to Russell, 22 June 1912, *RKM,* R2.
6. Norman Malcolm, *Ludwig Wittgenstein: A Memoir,* Oxford University Press, 1962, 66–7.
7. On Weininger's "intentions" see my *Wittgenstein's Vienna Revisited,* New Brunswick and London: Transaction Publishers, 2001, 251, n. 3.

8. My citations from *Geschlecht und Charakter* are from the 1980 edition, which is the most convenient edition of Weininger's main work. However, it is not the definitive edition, as Waltraud Hirsch has shown in her "'26. unveränderte Auflage' – Bemerkungen zur Textgeschichte von Otto Weiningers *Geschlecht und Charakter*," *Mitteilungen aus dem Brenner Archiv* 13 (1994): 59–73. All translations from this and *Über die Letzten Dinge* are my own.
9. See, for example, George Mosse, *The Crisis of the German Ideology: Intellectual Origins of the Third Reich*, New York: Grosset & Dunlap, 1964.
10. Steven Beller, *Vienna and the Jews 1867–1938*, Cambridge: Cambridge University Press, 1989, 223, 226–9, 234–7.
11. Ray Monk, *The Duty of Genius*, London: Jonathan Cape, 1990, 313–18.
12. Rush Rhees, ed., *Ludwig Wittgenstein: Personal Recollections*, Oxford: Basil Blackwell, 1981), 195–6.
13. This should not be taken to indicate that I endorse the idea that there are two distinct Wittgensteins that have nothing to do with one another. My point is that it makes sense in certain contexts, such as with respect to the account of language, to speak of two Wittgensteins; whereas in others it makes less sense, as is the case with the concept of philosophy, as the substance of this contribution shows.
14. Conversations with Monika Seekircher have helped to clarify my thinking about the role of the technical in Wittgenstein's thought.
15. Brian McGuinness, "Wittgenstein & the Unsayable," typescript of an unpublished lecture at the University of Siena, 1999, 9–10. I am grateful to Brian McGuinness for putting his text at my disposal.
16. Ibid.
17. See my "On the Limits of Language and other Nonsense," in Rudolf Haller and Klaus Puhl, eds., *Proceedings of the 24th International Wittgenstein Symposium*. Vienna: OBV & HPT, forthcoming, 171–5.
18. On Engelmann, see my "Paul Engelmann's Role in Wittgenstein's Philosophical Development," in J. Bakacsy, A. V. Munch and A.-L. Sommer, eds., *Architecture, Language, Critique: Around Paul Engelmann*, "Studien zur österreichischen Philosophie" vol. XXXI; Amsterdam: Rodopi, 2000, 40–58.
19. See my *Wittgenstein's Vienna Revisited*, 147–70 for a full account of how Hertz influenced Wittgenstein's notion of philosophy as showing.
20. Otto Weininger, *Über die letzten Dinge*, Vienna and Leipzig: Braumüller, 1904, 115–21. This work in now available in English as *A Translation of Weininger's Über die letzten Dinge (1904/1907) On Last Things*, trans. Steven Burns, "Studies in German Language and Literature," vol. 28; Lewiston, NY: Edwin Mellen Press, 2001.
21. I have drawn the parallels between them in my "Schopenhauer and the Early Wittgenstein," *Philosophical Studies* XV, Maynooth, 1966: 76–95.

22. Russell was, of course, also preoccupied with other aspects of James's thought, namely, his so-called "neutral monism" as is clear from his article, "On the Nature of Acquaintance," in R. C. Marsh, ed., *Logic and Knowledge: Essays 1901–1950*, London: Allen & Unwin, 1984, 125–4.
23. *GT*, passim.
24. See his question about the kind of "philosophy" that would help his brother, Paul, after losing his profession due to the loss of his right arm: *GT*, 28 October 1914.
25. Hermine to Ludwig, in Brian McGuinness, Maria Concetta Ascher, and Otto Pfersmann, eds., *Wittgenstein Familienbriefe*, Vienna: Hölder-Pichler-Tempsky, 1996, 27.
26. Personal communication from G. H. von Wright in Philadelphia, 1966; See also his "Biographical Sketch," in Malcolm, *Ludwig Wittgenstein* 21, n. 7.
27. David Pears, *The False Prison*, 2 vols., Oxford: Clarendon Press, 1987 and 1988.
28. I owe this apposite phrase to Kjell S. Johannessen.
29. It should go without saying that the notion of "influence" is not unproblematic. On the problem of influence as it bears upon Wittgenstein see, my "Wie hat Schopenhauer Wittgenstein beeinflußt?" *Schopenhauer Jahrbuch* 73 (1992): 27–43.
30. This is why he could agree with Moore that Weininger was "fantastic" but nevertheless "great and fantastic," Wittgenstein to Moore, 23 August 1931, *RKM, M.* 17.
31. See Julia Annas and Jonathan Barnes, *The Modes of Scepticism: Ancient Texts and Modern Interpretations*, Cambridge: Cambridge University Press, 1985.
32. This is hardly accidental given Nietzsche's profound influence on Weininger. See my paper, "The Dionysian Element in Kant or How Friedrich Nietzsche Influenced Otto Weininger," delivered to the Nietzsche and Central Europe symposium held in Vienna, 2002. (Proceedings forthcoming, edited by Jacob Gomomb, Published by Wiener Universitaets Verlag.)
33. This text certainly bears examination in the light of Wittgenstein's injunction to silence at the end of the *Tractatus* and vice versa.
34. Weininger, *On Last Things*, 119.
35. At this point, as well as several others, Anscombe's translation is misleading: "*Stellungnahme*" refers to a position, taking a stand, making a commitment. "Attitude" only catches part of the word's sense. Similarly, "*das erlösende Wort*" is more than merely "the key word"; "the redeeming word" or the "saving word" would be closer.
36. Weininger, "Tierpsychologie," *Über die letzten Dinge*, 116.
37. Martin Heidegger, *Sein und Zeit*, Tübingen: Max Niemeyer Verlag, 1967, S. 29, 134–40 and passim. Wittgenstein's similarities with Heidegger and Nietzsche stem largely from Weininger and through him from the so-called South-West German School of Neo-Kantianism. On the South-West

German School in general, see Lucien Goldmann, *Lukács et Heidegger*, Paris: Denöel, 1973.

38. Heidegger, *Sein und Zeit*, S. 9, 42–3 passim.
39. "If my book is ever published the preface must contain a reference to the foreword to Paul Ernst's edition of Grimm's fairy tales which I should have mentioned in the *Logische-philosophische Abhandlung* as the source of the expression 'misunderstanding the logic of language,'" (*Wittgenstein, Philosophische Bemerkungen*, 184, Bergen Edition, my translation).
40. Janik, *Wittgenstein's Vienna Revisited*, 52–3.
41. Anthony Kenny, *Wittgenstein*, Harmondsworth: Penguin, 1982, 13.
42. "At a certain level of their development human beings get the idea that objects that appear to us to be dead have a soul like we do. Whether the idea originates from the interpretation of a misconstrued propensity of language or from the thought that the souls of dead people migrate into the objects is not taken into consideration here." (*Auf einer gewissen Entwicklungsstufe haben die Menschen die Vorstellung, dass auch uns heute tot erscheinenden Gegenstände eine Seele haben wie sie selber; ob die Vorstellung aus der Deutung einer missverstandenen Tendenz der Sprache entsteht, oder ob aus dem Gedanken, dass die Seelen der verstorbenen Menschen in die Gegenstände gezogen seien, kommt hier nicht in Betracht.*) Paul Ernst, *Kinder und Hausmärchen gesammelt durch die Brüder Grimm*, 3 Bde., Münich & Leipzig: Georg Müller, 1910, III, 273. The contrast between Ernst's formulation and what Wittgenstein makes out of it is noteworthy. It is a good indication that we cannot take Wittgenstein's remarks about being a merely "reproductive" thinker as seriously as he would have us take them. I am indebted to Dr. Josef Rothhaupt for providing me with a copy of this text, which is not easily accessible.
43. See my "Wittgensteins revolutionäre Auffassung der Sprache," *Wissenschaftliche Nachrichten* 80, Vienna, April 1989: 5–7.
44. Norman Malcolm, "Wittgenstein: The Relation of Language to Instinctive Behavior," *Philosophical Investigations* 5 (I), 1982: 3–22.
45. See St. Augustine, *Confessions*, trans. Rex Warner, New York, 1963, 14.
46. This is the explicit subject of Weininger's essay, "Über Henrik Ibsen und seine Dichtung *Peer Gynt*," in *Über die letzten Dinge*, to which the fragment on animal psychology is an appendage. See *On Last Things*, trans. Steven Burns, 1–40, and my *Wittgenstein's Vienna Revisited*, chs. 3 and 8.
47. Kenny, *Wittgenstein*, 26.
48. Wittgenstein, *Wittgenstein's Nachlass: The Bergen Electronic Edition*, Oxford: Oxford University Press, MS 213, Big Typescript, 406, my translation.

3

Sex and Solipsism

Weininger's On Last Things

Steven Burns

Introduction

This essay is a contribution to the study of the intellectual life of Vienna as it influenced the philosophy of Ludwig Wittgenstein. Everyone who explores this territory (first marked out in 1973 by Stephen Toulmin and Allan Janik in *Wittgenstein's Vienna*) is obliged to repeat that Wittgenstein acknowledged deep debts to Viennese mentors, Karl Kraus, Adolf Loos, and Otto Weininger, as well as to the obvious philosophers, Schopenhauer, Frege, and Russell,[1] They then have to say that Weininger published an enlarged version of his doctoral thesis, as *Sex and Character*, at the age of twenty-three (in 1903), and a few months later shot himself. *Sex and Character* soon became notorious, not for its author's dramatic demise or for what strikes us today as its antifeminism and anti-Semitism, but for its deep and systematic critique of Viennese modernism and for its embodiment of what struck fin-de-siècle Vienna as genius.

It was in Vienna, in 1977, that I discovered that Weininger had left behind essays and aphorisms and that these were posthumously published as a second book, titled *Über die letzten Dinge*. Unlike the first, which promptly appeared in English, the second volume, although it, too, sold well in German, was not translated into English. Over the years, mostly during subsequent sabbaticals, I would reread bits of that second book, and ponder what Wittgenstein had found so impressive in it. Finally, since no one else seemed to want to do so, I translated it.[2] What I propose to do here is first to describe briefly the contents of that book, highlighting some connections with Wittgenstein's work and philosophical methods. Then I shall discuss two particular points of influence that I think are of philosophical interest: the first concerns sex, and the second, solipsism.

Weininger in Translation

At the end of the nineteenth century, Henrik Ibsen was considered by many to be the greatest of the modern artists. In the first and longest of his essays,[3] Weininger takes up the challenge of explaining what *Peer Gynt* is really about, and what makes it Ibsen's greatest play. Weininger is a sort of pioneer "supertextualist" – someone who treats Ibsen not as primarily a poet, nor as a social realist with a political agenda, but as an artist expressing a *philosophy.* He argues that Ibsen, although not a learned philosopher or psychologist, nonetheless has an intuitive understanding of human psychology. The theory is that it is the *individual* that is the locus of moral value, and that each person has a vocation, a purpose, to seek the highest value possible for his life. Ibsen shows his intuitive understanding of this by portraying Peer Gynt as the exact opposite. He is an inconsistent, deceitful and self-deceitful character. Weininger has a clever footnote about his name: "Has it been observed what kind of name Ibsen has chosen for his hero? Peer Gynt – it has so little *gravity.* The name is like a rubber ball that keeps bouncing off the ground" (8, n. 14). Of course the name fits perfectly a character who has no gravity. Peer has no sense of guilt. He flits hopefully from adventure to adventure, always seeking a meaning for his life, but it is clear that he would not recognize such a thing if he found it. It is worth remarking that the feeling of guilt was one of the key examples of an experience of the ethical offered by Wittgenstein in his "Lecture on Ethics." This ethical dimension is exactly what Peer Gynt lacks.

In this Ibsen essay, Weininger will sometimes use "God," "Absolute," and "Higher Value" interchangeably. This has led one commentator to reconstruct Weininger's thought as a religious system, with a primal metaphysical unity as the transcendental condition of the dualities of experience.[4] I have argued that a secular reading will suffice, at least for present purposes, since Peer illustrates a Kantian moral thesis.[5] Peer is essentially heteronomous. He does not know himself, and is driven by wants and desires that are not his real needs. Only a person who strives for a higher, more valuable existence can attain autonomy, that is, in Kantian terms, be self-directed and responsible. Ibsen's intuitive grasp of this ethical truth is what first wins Weininger's praise. (This moral seriousness, in turn, is one of the things that earns Weininger Wittgenstein's respect.)

A remarkable feature of the Ibsen essay is its apparent digression – at its midpoint – into a typical Weininger distinction: "People can be divided into those who love themselves and those who hate themselves" (22). This is an exercise in what he calls characterology, the study of pure types, or characteristics, in terms of which individual human character is to be analyzed. He allows hybrid cases – people can exhibit a mixture of self-love and self-hatred. He even allows a case in which the division fails: Immanuel Kant, claims Weininger, is so lacking in subjectivity that he is neither able to be loved or hated, by others or by himself! But the basic division is between people who are pleased with themselves and those who are self-critical. "The former readily pardons himself . . . the other tears himself apart, silently, mercilessly" (23). The self-lover affirms, the self-hater denies.

Weininger then leads the reader to a further observation: "The self-loving person is strongly and constantly erotic. One must first love or hate oneself in order to love or to hate other people" (23). He quickly identifies this with a further distinction: "the self-loving man is also really, strictly speaking, a *father*" (24). He is the person who, loving himself, wishes to procreate and see himself in the other, in the *son*. On the other hand, "He who feels like a son can only hate himself" (25). And as if that were not stretching things too far already, Weininger then claims that the self-loving type is also the *teacher*, the person who likes to re-create himself intellectually. Thus, the connection of ideas runs from the self-lover through eroticism through fatherhood to the teacher.

How, one wants to ask, could a reader as astute as Wittgenstein think that passages like this were a product of genius? It is possible that at some level he thought that they applied to him: he was not a self-lover, but intensely self-critical; he was deeply troubled by all manifestations of the erotic, "even the slightest manifestation of sexual desire";[6] he was not inclined to fatherhood, and "had absolutely no intention of having children"[7] – which made it perfectly clear to Marguerite Respinger that despite Ludwig's intention of marrying her, she would find it impossible to be married to him; he resisted the conventional role of teacher and was horrified by the thought of re-creating himself intellectually in his students. Nonetheless, however much he may have seen himself in some of Weininger's categories, could he have taken such claims literally? Weininger certainly invites us to. "One sees how fatherhood, teacherhood, and self-love are always present or absent together" (25). It looks as though we should think that this proposition, that everyone is either a self-lover or a self-hater, is guaranteed by the law of excluded middle, and that the further extensions to fatherhood and teacherhood are *deducible* from the original insight. A skeptic, however, would immediately object that the law of excluded middle would only guarantee that everyone is either a self-lover or not a self-lover, which is not the same thing at all. Another objection might be that not every self-lover is a self-hater, but every father is a son – so the dualisms are not even of the same sort. Moreover, while claiming that the Christian Jesus is a quintessential "son," Weininger is driven to the expedient of calling him a prophet *and not a teacher*, in order to maintain the parallel dualisms. The critical reader, that is, would read Weininger's digression as a hodgepodge that only a gullible reader could take seriously.

I have caricatured the gullible and the skeptical readers. Wittgenstein clearly was neither, and the basis of his thinking that Weininger wrote with genius is not to be found in his taking derivations like these literally. We might say that there are at best family resemblances here, rather than essences that overlap. Weininger has shown us some ingenious ways in which we can see fatherhood and teacherhood as similar. What we are given is not a proof of congruence, but insight into a fresh way of associating some ideas. Wittgenstein's respect for Freud as "someone who had something to say"[8] is based on a similar kind of reading. Freud claims to be scientific, but what he offers are new ways of seeing: speculations which belong to the stage that *precedes* the formulation of hypotheses; not a scientific explanation but a "new myth."[9] If people are inclined to accept such a new way of seeing things, it "makes it easier for them to go certain ways. . . . They have given up one way of thinking and adopted another."[10] We should not, however, think (as Weininger seems to) that it could not be otherwise, that these ideas *must always* coincide.

Giving Weininger's digression on self-love and self-hatred a Wittgensteinian reading allows us to see and say some new things, without thinking that they are the only things that can be said here. To exploit a *Tractatus* metaphor, he has "expanded logical space," allowing more things to be and to be said.[11] It also illustrates one way in which we may think of Weininger as having a serious influence on Wittgenstein. We can see Wittgenstein putting a negation sign in front of the relentless essentializing and dichotomizing that characterizes Weininger's work, while recognizing the brilliance of his insights into the connectedness of concepts that might normally not seem to be related. As he said of his own work: "What I invent are new similes." "A good simile refreshes the intellect."[12] My suggestion is that he took Weininger's comparison of self-hatred and "sonhood" in the way one might take a surprising but fruitful figure of speech.

It is worth remarking that the concept of self-hatred may be best known to us in the expression "Jewish self-hatred," of which Weininger has been said to be a classic case (for example, by persons as different as Theodor Lessing, Adolf Hitler, and Sander Gilman). This account of Weininger has been disputed at systematic length by Waltraud Hirsch. She aims to revise his current status as just a foil for feminists and antiracists. "Anti-feminism and anti-Semitism in Weininger can only be understood within his system. In that system they lose their conventional meaning. That is to say, that almost all that has been written about Weininger's hatred of women and Jews indicates a misunderstanding of his fundamental idea."[13] This fundamental idea is the metaphysical one that a primal unity is presupposed by any drawing of distinctions. Judaism and Christianity are metaphors, respectively, for the original state of undifferentiated consciousness and the state of self-consciousness. (Christ is the Jew who distinguishes himself from that unity. He thus represents self-consciousness distinguishing itself from mere consciousness; he represents the higher potential of the transcendental ego.) So self-hatred in Weininger is directed at a person's tendency to subside into the empirical ego. This is only *Jewish* self-hatred in the sense of the very extended metaphor. I cannot pursue these topics here; suffice it to say that Weininger returns from his digression on self-love and self-hatred to claim: "A man who has written *Peer Gynt* can only be a self-hater" (29). I return to this theme in the section on sex.

The second chapter of *On Last Things* is a collection of "remarks that have remained in aphoristic form." Although it is rare for philosophers to write aphoristically, since it seems to omit the argumentative context of the thought, aphorisms can be strikingly powerful in the hands of a Pascal, a Nietzsche, or a Wittgenstein. The subtitle of this chapter ("the psychology of sadism and masochism, the psychology of murder, remarks about ethics, original sin, etc.") suggests that sadism and masochism are a major theme. They are discussed in a sustained essay fragment (56–9), as well as in individual aphorisms. The masochist sounds a good deal like the self-hater, but the contrast is a different one. Its origin, however, is in a similar metaphysical distinction between the one and the many. Human experience is always of pieces lifted from an infinite whole. Two types of character are then possible: there are people who seek reality in the whole, and for whom every individual thing is only a *part*; there are people who find each discrete thing fully real, a thing in itself, and only imagine the whole when it is symbolized by the completeness of a discrete thing. The former is the masochist, the latter the sadist. Immediately Weininger takes us a step sideways. The (male) masochist cannot love a woman, because she is not real for him, he seeks something other than the woman in her, and women therefore do not find him attractive. The sadist finds individual women to be very real, and they in turn find him attractive.

So far this masochist and sadist are not the familiar characters who take pleasure in their own pain, or in the pain of others. Weininger was quite familiar with de Sade and Sader-Masoch, and the uses they served for sexologists and psychologists like Havelock-Ellis and Freud. Nevertheless, in his own theory he puts the emphasis on the character's relation to the world: the masochist suffers because he is embarrassed in front of women, and passive toward sensations; the sadist rejoices in the confrontation with a woman, and can be absorbed in a sensation, but equally eagerly moves on to the next. Clearly, the potential for pain is evident in these examples, but the usual emphasis on finding enjoyment in it is absent. Instead, Weininger hurries on to align new associations with his original dualism. The sadist can tell stories and jokes, while the masochist cannot hold the little narratives together; for him the story spreads out into a part of the story of everything, and it loses its point. The masochist is dismayed by change, the sadist surprised by duration. In music, rhythm – "which attends precisely to every individual note" – is sadistic, while harmony and melody – "in which the individual notes do not emerge as such" (57) – are masochistic. The same holds for geometry and arithmetic, or as we might say, the analogical is masochistic, the digital is sadistic. What is holding these very diverse concepts together is their relation to the holism and atomism with which we started. We should then see, Weininger thinks, that the mystic "is identical with the masochist" (57).

The third chapter, "Characterology," discusses the character of two artists, after first developing another of Weininger's paradigmatic dualisms. This time he distinguishes seekers from priests:

> The seeker searches, the priest informs. The seeker searches above all *himself*, the priest reveals *himself* above all to others. The seeker searches his whole life long for himself, for his own soul; the priest's ego is given from the outset as a presupposition of everything else. The seeker is always accompanied by a feeling of imperfection; the priest is convinced of the existence of perfection (68).

Weininger then excoriates Friedrich Schiller, that icon of German literature, as a failed priest, as incapable of tragedy, or of recognizing the struggle between human grandeur and pettiness: "Schiller hardly seems to have known the enemy *in one's own breast*, loneliness and its terrors, human fate" (71). He is, in Weininger's most scathing epithet, really just a journalist. Wittgenstein seems to have shared Weininger's unusually critical view, not only of writers for journals but also of Schiller.[14]

Richard Wagner, on the other hand, though he ends as a great priest, starts out as a seeker. Weininger is interested, as he was with Ibsen, in the philosophical structure of his work, and contends that "The problems that he has chosen as his subject are the most enormous that any artist has chosen" (75). Like Ibsen he is concerned with human redemption, but in *Parsifal*, his last music drama, Wagner reaches a different final view of woman from that achieved by Ibsen. The latter believed in "the resurrection of the woman, in a higher life of man and woman together" (37). This might have been Wagner's view, too, at the time he conceived Siegfried and Brünnhilde, and Tristan and Isolde, but by the time he wrote *Parsifal* his main female character, Kundry, suggests that the woman's place in the universe is to be the *object* in which "only a *subject* will be able to attain consciousness of itself" (40). That is, the woman is the negative pole, the mirror of the man's striving for self-discovery. This thesis, too, I revisit in the section on sex.

The fourth chapter is titled "On the Unidirectionality of Time: and its ethical significance. . . . " Weininger singles out circles, epicycles and backwards motion as symbolically contrary to morality. That is why he thinks men are reluctant to return home by retracing their steps; going backwards indicates a lack of resolve or imagination. Going around in circles is also a failure of will, this time via frivolity or purposelessness. He offers the merry-go-round and the Viennese waltz as amusing instances. The point of this chapter, however, is to argue for a conception of the seriousness and directedness of moral behavior. It is to be understood in relation to the fact that time only flows in one direction, so to speak. The past grows and the future diminishes; it is never the other way around. To lie is to try to alter the past rather than to acknowledge the truth. Thus the greatest of moral questions, whether to be honest or deceitful, whether to be honest with yourself or self-deceitful, whether to live by the truth or the lie, is closely related to the nature of time.

This moral theme is echoed in the fifth chapter, the most bizarre of the essays. It is called "Metaphysics," but contains a section on animal psychology that Wittgenstein gave G. E. Moore to read. On the surface, this seems to be about why dogs symbolize criminality and horses symbolize madness. The eye of the dog "evokes the impression that the dog has *lost* something. . . . What he has lost is the ego, self-worth, freedom" (103). The horse's wild eyes and tossing of the head symbolize insanity. What lies behind this dichotomy is the claim that criminality and insanity are the two fates that threaten the genius. "Genius is either the *reverse* of perfect insanity, or the reverse of perfect criminality. Each genius lives in fear of one or the other" (106). In his self-doubt about his own originality, Wittgenstein sometimes insisted that he had only talent, not genius. If we do insist on his genius, however, it is clear that his was the type that lives in fear of insanity.[15]

This attempt to say something about how the world has meaning for human intelligence is the focus of David Stern's essay in this volume. He sees Weininger's interest in the psychology of animals reflected in Wittgenstein's frequent use of animal examples, especially in the *Philosophical Investigations.* As Stern explains, Wittgenstein is concerned to understand what it is to be in an intentional state: to wish, hope, fear, expect, and so on. The limits on what a dog can expect show us something about the complexities that underlie human expectation: a person, unlike a dog, can expect to go for a walk in Point Pleasant Park the day after tomorrow at noon. Seeing what sort of limits these are can help us to understand another intentional state: how it is that we can *mean.* Thus Stern links Weininger to the central problem in Wittgenstein's philosophy.

Quite aside from Wittgenstein's use of animal metaphors, I think that his conception of personal morality owes a good deal to Weininger's account of the criminal character that is symbolized by the dog. The criminal is the person who "lives his entire life without real 'unity of consciousness', without a continuous, unitary ego that is always aware of whatever it is doing, and holds itself responsible for it all" (98). The criminal has renounced autonomy, uses himself as a means to an end, or is a *function* of external forces; "his psychic life is discontinuous and broken to pieces" (101). This character cannot know his higher self, and lives a life that is a kind of deceit. Rush Rhees is surely right in claiming that "for Weininger the dread of such a *Lebenslüge* [lying life] was as terrible as it was for Wittgenstein."[16]

The last of Weininger's essays (Chapter 6) compares science and culture, proposing a critique of contemporary science that deserves comparison with Wittgenstein's actual preface and its early draft for *Philosophical Remarks.*[17] I shall return later to this essay (in the section on solipsism), and shall conclude the present sketch of *On Last Things* by saying that it ends with a set of aphorisms taken from those Weininger feverishly wrote down during his final few days in Vienna. A translator's appendix contains a few more remarks from letters that Weininger wrote to friends during his visit to Italy in the months just before his death. Weininger wrote: "Suicide is not a sign of courage, but of cowardice, even if it is the least of the cowardly acts" (157). Wittgenstein seems to have feared his own cowardice during much of his life. And while that thought did not save Weininger from his fate, it may well have helped Wittgenstein through some dark periods.

Given Wittgenstein's claim that reading Weininger had a great effect on him, I have proffered rather a thin list of effects to attribute to Weininger's *On Last Things.* Allan Janik has written extensively on this topic, and I recommend especially his recent "Weininger, Ibsen and the Origins of Viennese Critical Modernism."[18] I have already quoted from Rush Rhees's judicious essay concerning Wittgenstein's relation to Weininger. Rhees's essay is judged "somewhat too defensive" by Chandak Sengoopta.[19] I do not intend to survey the literature here. Suffice it to say that Rhees's "notes" are defensive in that he carefully distinguishes what Wittgenstein wrote and said about Jewishness from what Weininger wrote. In particular, claims Rhees, although he was acutely interested in what was Jewish in his thinking, Wittgenstein had no inclination to "overcome " this in himself. Nonetheless, Rhees puts the question of Weininger's influence in the context of Wittgenstein's passionate striving to be honest with himself. This is surely the right context. Wittgenstein thought a good deal about writing an autobiography as a means of being truthful about himself.[20] Weininger wrote: "A gifted human being," in contrast to the "criminal" already discussed, "does not recall the single incidents of his life as so many discrete images of situations which come to his mind. He *understands them together,* in some way."[21] This is undoubtedly one of the seeds of Wittgenstein's concern with self-knowledge and self-deceit. Rhees goes on to say: "in this case, as always, the seed which fell in Wittgenstein's soil grew into something quite unlike the plant it came from."[22] That judgment, too, seems to me to be right.

In general, one sees best how Wittgenstein learned from Weininger if one takes the moral and intellectual earnestness of Weininger's questioning, together with his ingenious and often insightful comparisons, and then inverts the main Weininger method. Instead of the Victorian dualisms, and the insistence that everything is either A or not-A, seeker or priest, male or female, sadist or masochist, criminal or madman – or some mixture of two polar opposites – Wittgenstein offers rich multiplicity and a new method of assembling reminders of differences.[23] I shall now return to the Weininger text, and discuss two examples of his striking way of thinking. They deal with topics that I have called "Sex" and "Solipsism," and which have a place among the "lines of thought" that Wittgenstein says he "seized on . . . with enthusiasm for my work of clarification."[24]

Sex

Weininger's most notorious dualism, of course, is that between Male and Female. His first book, *Sex and Character*, proposed to give a scientific and philosophical account of human (moral) character. He discusses this in terms of two extreme ideals, labeled "Man" and "Woman," which he treats as Platonic forms, as archetypes. All actual human beings, he claims, are to some extent bisexual, neither perfectly M nor perfectly W. Nonetheless, each person's character can be measured by his or her place on the continuum between the M and W "types." To be dominated by W-nature is to succumb to "passivity... to the flesh... to sleep of the spirit... to procreation,"[25] while to fulfill an M-destiny requires prodigious effort, creativity, genius. It will surprise no one that this book has a reputation for being the source of modern antifeminism. It is also interesting, however, because of the philosophical foundations of the characterology.

Ibsen was unacquainted with philosophical literature.[26] Otherwise, Weininger argues,

> he would have to have known that *his poetry is Kant's philosophy.* No one else, only Kant and Ibsen, took truth and the lie to be the deepest problem of ethics.... They were the only ones who recognized that truth can only flow from having an ego in the higher sense, having individuality. This, however, is the lesson of Ibsen's *Peer Gynt* no less than of the *Critique of Practical Reason.*
>
> ... the only thing that lends a person value is the possession of an ("intelligible") *ego*, of a *personality*, and ... when this is lacking in a person, he needs to assume value from somewhere else outside of himself. Nietzsche's great realization, that the will to power lies endlessly deep in all living things, has been long under-appreciated.... Particularly relevant for humans, however, and lying even deeper in them, is not the will to power but the *will to value*, which I believe is what finally distinguishes them from the animals. From the lack of value in itself comes the striving to gain value from elsewhere; that is the source of all fame-seeking, and all confidence trickery in the wider sense. All humans, man *and* woman, are constituted as such by the will to value. If someone cannot create value of and for himself – and this is *always* the case with women – then he tries to get it from someone else and for someone else; one always acts for the audience that makes the value judgement. In contrast to animals, which strive only for pleasure, for the satisfaction of natural drives, every human being constantly seeks, wherever and however, *to gain* the greatest possible *value for himself.*

We learn in Act 1 that Peer Gynt has no such value in himself, when we get to know him right away as a braggart and a showoff. (7–8)

It is a stroke of genius that leads Weininger from this analysis of the ethical basis of the play to a reevaluation of its most striking structural feature: that Peer is redeemed, in the end, by the love of Solveig. At the beginning of the essay, Weininger tells us that: "The central point of *Peer Gynt* concerns the role of the loved woman in man's life, and one cannot hope to understand man until one has got clear about woman" (5). After some twenty-two pages, in which he comments on the play and its major episodes, Weininger begins the digression on self-love and self-hate (discussed earlier). When he returns to his theme, he maintains that the author of *Peer Gynt* must be a self-hater. That puts him in the company of Goethe and Beethoven, among others, but Weininger does not explicitly say why he *must* hate himself. One of the reasons is that Ibsen is not complacent; on the contrary, he exposes to ridicule Peer's complacency about his empirical ego. (Of course, any reader who thinks the play is an affectionate, picaresque account of a simple everyman will have fundamentally missed the point.) Another proof of his being a self-hater is Ibsen's understanding that Peer is incapable of loving a woman. There is plenty of evidence of this: Peer's absconding with a bride on her wedding day (I:3), his dalliance with the dairymaids (II:3), his interest in the Troll King's daughter (II:6), and his temptation by the Bedouin Anitra (IV:6). Ibsen, the self-hater, is capable of seeing the moral shabbiness of these otherwise exuberant episodes; Peer, the self-lover, *affirms* the empirical world and its fleeting sensuality.

The main purpose of the digression, however, is not to categorize Ibsen, but to prepare us to understand the two most difficult themes in the play. First is the character of the great Boyg, who is "the most puzzling and at the same time most original figure in the work" (29), and who has been so much misunderstood. Weininger thinks that, armed with his account of morality and the self-love/self-hatred distinction, we can now understand him as "the whole force of the empirical ego. . . . It is the redemption-negating principle in general" (30). The Boyg raises itself again and again as an amorphous obstacle to the intelligible ego. Second, and the main purpose of the digression, is to prepare us to understand the theme of redemption through a woman's love.[27] Weininger explores the familiar parallels – in works by Goethe and Wagner, for instance. Although the theme may be a commonplace in literature, he thinks that as ordinarily conceived it is incoherent. It is unintelligible that a person's moral value should be determined by an external influence. No one can be redeemed by something external.[28] To understand such redemption through a woman's love we must think that the man "*projects onto the woman* his better self" (32). It thus cannot be Solveig, no matter how much she may love him, who causes Peer's redemption. It must be "the Solveig within him" who redeems him from hatred of his higher self, makes possible a higher sort of self-love, and thus leads him to the recognition of his higher moral potential.

It is an interesting consequence of this ingenious view that Peer in the final analysis must be using the *actual* Solveig as a *means.* This paradox leads Weininger to conclude his essay with a consideration of male/female relations in some of Ibsen's other plays, as well as in some of Wagner's works. It is here that he expresses the dismal view that the woman (at least as pure archetype) may have only negative potential, as "the mirror of the man's striving for self-discovery" (40). But now I am in danger of digressing.

My reader may be thinking that – apart from its being a plausible sketch of his own conception of the demands of morality – this has little to do with Wittgenstein. But look closely at this love. Peer has until the last moment "led a completely lying life; he never was himself, he has no *I,* and thus is third-person (a he, she or it)" (17). In the moment of redemption he recognizes love. However, he loves not the real Solveig, but a Solveig who is an aspect of his own inner potential. Sex, when it really is intercourse with another, is either the opposite of solipsism or is made bad by it; bad sex happens when the Male/Female relation is in practical terms one in which "there is no other mind there." Solipsistic sex, if I may put it this way, is conducted in a logically private language; there is no verifiable communication with another person in the sex act, no *intercourse.* Someone with a little imagination might see in the many sorts of failures to connect, to understand, to cooperate or coordinate with, to empathize with, and so on, that can infect our attempts at close relationships (or in our resorting to silence, to force, or to solitary pleasures), some variations on that theme. If indeed Weininger and Wittgenstein had much in common in their sexuality, then it is revealing that Weininger accepted the truth of solipsism, while Wittgenstein struggled against it throughout his life.

Solipsism

If skepticism about *other* minds normally assumes that at least one has a mind of one's own, and if solipsism is a sort of skepticism about the external world but not about one's self or its *internal* world, then I am inclined to say that Weininger thought that the most fundamental philosophical problem was the question whether *he* even had a self. The proof that he did was to be found in an ethical commitment that included a commitment to the principles of logic. As a result the question was for him neither an empirical one nor an a priori one, but a question of will. It was a sort of corollary that for many others this commitment, and thus a real self, would not be realized. It was to his discredit, and to some extent to our confusion, that he called these two extremes – the tendency to strive for a self, and the tendency not to want one – Male and Female. This is, of course, an indefensible sexism, but it can be separated from the moral metaphysics that Weininger was also concerned with.

Consider Weininger's own rhetorical question from *Sex and Character*: "Is the present generation with its electrical railways and empirical psychology so much higher than these earlier times? Is culture, if culture has any real value, to be compared with science, which is always social and never individual, and to be measured by the number of public libraries and laboratories? Is culture outside human beings and not always in human beings?"[29] The implied answer is that culture is not external, not a matter of museums and libraries, but is essentially a matter of the individual's consciousness. This is explicitly argued in the second longest of the essays in *On Last Things*, "Science and Culture." It is structured in three parts, the first is on the concept of science, the second is on the concept of culture, and the third gives a critical assessment of science from the point of view of culture.

Culture, he argues (in section 2), is essentially rooted in the individual and his sense for the problematic: "All culture is founded on *individuality*; because there are problems only for *individualities*" (130). Nonetheless, it is not confined to the individual, for the sense that there are deep problems forces the individual to transcend himself. The person of genius "stands in a conscious relation to the universe, so the pulse of the thing-in-itself, the breath of the world as a whole, will also have to be detectable" in his works (131). Weininger is convinced that, judged from the standpoint of this free commitment of the individual to transcendental problems and tasks, contemporary science is merely objective, merely a group activity conducted with merely mechanical methods: "To put briefly what today's science is and what it is not, we can say that this science enjoys results, and sets itself tasks, but has no more problems" (138).

What is of most interest to us here is the first section, on the essence of science, in which Weininger begins by distinguishing knowledge from hypothetical conjecture and from personal belief. Science tries to replace belief with knowledge (by way of hypotheses and evidence), only to find that "the belief which [it] aims to eliminate proves to be its very foundation" (121). The argument for this is especially interesting to anyone who recalls Russell's report that, on asking Wittgenstein whether he was struggling with logic or his sins, Wittgenstein replied: "Both."[30] Why it should *of course* be both is perhaps to be understood as one of Wittgenstein's debts to Weininger. For the latter develops here a view of the unity of logic and ethics. Ethics he treats in a Kantian fashion, as presuming a subject that *wills*. A *free* subject is self-legislating, *choosing* to accept moral maxims as rules for his own conduct. We are inclined, as Kant was, to think that this is a unique imperative, and to think that logic, on the other hand, is not something that is subject to the will. Weininger thinks that this is a mistake; the cases are in fact parallel. The principles of logic, too, "must be tied to the assent of the individual" (115). This is a "*second* categorical imperative which demands unconditional obedience, and whose source is just as much to be sought in our intelligible essence as is that of the other imperative, which Kant erroneously considered to be unique – doubtless because at bottom both are one" (116). Logic and ethics, that is, are at bottom one.[31]

That they *appear* not to be one Weininger readily admits. "Ethics says what ought to be, logic says what is. . . . Thus ethics gives to human birth a meaning relative to death; logic relieves human death of its meaninglessness in that from birth on it denies that *everything* will be forfeit to it" (116). The translation of this sentence is problematic.

The original edition reads: "logic relieves human striving [*Streben*] of its meaninglessness"; in the Matthes & Seitz edition of 1980 this is corrected to "human death [*Sterben*]." The transposition of two letters is a small matter, but standards of typesetting were high throughout the original edition of this book. Even if *Streben* is what Weininger wrote, however, the case for thinking that he *meant* to write *Sterben* is strong. It is "death" that contrasts properly to "birth," and gives the sentence its parallelism. Moreover, it does not make much sense to think that everything is forfeit to striving. The point is that everything that we strive for is made pointless by the fact that in the end we die. Weininger is challenging this common idea with the double claim: first, that ethics, if it does anything, makes claims on us that are temporally located – there are things that we ought to do *before* we die; while, second, logic makes claims that are timeless, and as true after our deaths as before, so that it is false that all meaning or value dies when we die.

That is intended to explain the appearance of difference. What is the ground of the more interesting claim that ethics and logic are at bottom one? The link is this: like the categorical imperative, which Weininger takes to have the status of moral law only because it is acknowledged by a free being, so too the law of identity ("that A = A," as he puts it) is only binding on a free being who posits it as an absolute standard. "The fact of the standard, i.e., that there *is* a standard, is *my free act*" (116). Were I to attempt to refute the law of identity (or its related formulations, the laws of non-contradiction and excluded middle), "in so doing I would have to make use of logic, i.e., of exactly this proposition. . . . [It is] the standard which I work from as soon as I begin to deduce" (116). Something like this move has been familiar since Aristotle's *Metaphysics*, but Weininger wants to draw from it the conclusion that the laws of logic remain theses *that can neither be proven nor disproven.* I cannot be forced *by logic* to embrace them. So logic and ethics are at least in the same position. It is worth adding that Weininger offers "this demonstration that logic is a spontaneous commitment of the intelligible subject . . . as a completion of the Kantian philosophy" (117).

If the ultimate laws of both ethics and logic are thus unprovable, but must be adopted by a free being, then "neither can be *known*, but only *believed*" (117). A good Kantian would be able to show that this is not *echt*

Kantian, but at best *neo*-Kantian. Moreover, it does not show that logic and ethics are *one*. It does, however, show why Weininger thought that they have the same status, and why one could not *selectively* make this act of faith; anyone committed to the categorical imperative must have accepted also that the true is to be preferred to the false, and anyone committed to the laws of rationality is thereby implicated in the moral life. "He who renounces logic, renounces thinking. He who renounces thinking, surrenders of his own free will to arbitrariness. . . . The logical standard is a 'law of freedom' no less than a moral duty" (117). Let us say, then, that Weininger defends the view that if logic and ethics are not identical, they are at least mutually implied, and that someone thinking of logic would of course also have been thinking of his sins. But, my patient reader will want to know, what has this to do with solipsism?

The link is provided by the idea that neither the laws of logic nor the moral law can be *proven*; they are presupposed by any act that might conceivably serve as a demonstration. Here is the paragraph to which I have been slowly making my way:

> [T]he idea of truth [cannot] be demonstrated; for if it were to be demonstrated, then I might have wanted the truth for the sake of something else. Likewise my own existence, the "I" or ego, if it is to have value, cannot be proven; and likewise the "you", when it is not the consequence of a reason and cannot be used as the means to an end, cannot be demonstrated. *The refutability of solipsism* is no more compatible with *ethics,* than is the possibility of *proving* the existence of one's own ego. It is therefore contained in the idea of the self that neither one's own self nor that of another can be demonstrated. If it were deducible, it would not be ultimate. Refutations of the thesis of solipsism are constantly being sought; not one year of the last twenty has passed without bringing at least one attempt at its refutation. Obviously people do not understand at all the pathos that underlies the sentence, "The world is *my* representation." It means, *"Something will be altered when I no longer exist."* I become *substance,* and "There are not two substance of the same nature". (Spinoza, *Ethics* II, 10n.) To recoil from solipsism is to be incapable of giving independent worth to existence, to be incapable of abundant solitude, it is to need to hide in the crowd, to *disappear* into a throng, to *perish.* It is craven. (118–19)

This is a remarkable paragraph. One way in which it is remarkable is that it immediately links solipsism to ethics. Note the formulation of the original argument: if something cannot be demonstrated, it cannot be used as the means to an end. It would violate the Kantian moral injunction to treat someone as the conclusion of an argument. Of course a person's *action* can be so treated, as if it were derived as a maxim from a universal law, and so on. But a person, considered as a free being and a moral agent, is not to be treated as something determined by reason, nor as a means to an end. That, Weininger seems to leap to thinking, implies an autonomous self, radically responsible for value and the world, and therefore condemned to embracing an unprovable solipsism. One cannot both embrace the ethical standpoint and reject the solipsism of accepting that I alone am responsible for my world. Anything else would be "craven." Cowardice is the basis of our tendency to seek a social concept of the self, as is our craving for the anonymity of the crowd.

A second way in which the paragraph is remarkable is the way that solipsism does not seem to be a form of skepticism. It is not necessary to disprove it in order for rationality and objectivity to be possible. Weininger clearly thought that his project of embracing himself as autonomous subject was the first step for a philosopher. That in turn makes logic and ethics possible. Only then does there arise the equally unprovable positing of the existence of other such selves. Coincidences between their worlds and mine are the territory of the objective sciences, and thus metaphysics is completed. Wittgenstein would of course find that in England this was unacceptable metaphysics, and he would have to rethink what he had accepted from Schopenhauer and Weininger.

A third way in which it is a remarkable paragraph is the sureness with which it links Schopenhauer (via Spinoza, indeed) to Wittgenstein. It is not just one thesis of Schopenhauer's, but the opening sentence and central theme of the whole of *The World as Will and Representation* that is invoked.[32] To understand that the world is my representation is to begin to understand why Wittgenstein claims that "what solipsism *means,* is quite correct, only it cannot be *said,* but it shows itself."[33] It is, Weininger claims, as unprovable a thesis as are the categorical imperative, the law of identity, and the presumption of self. But likewise it is not a *refutable* thesis. What it means is quite correct.

Solipsism is a key theme for Wittgenstein scholars. It links the *Tractatus* and the *Philosophical Investigations* in many interesting ways. The most superficial use of this obvious claim is to think that Wittgenstein offered two solutions to the problem, first in the *Tractatus* and then in the *Investigations.* Thus it may be claimed that in the *Tractatus* Wittgenstein solved the problem of solipsism by showing that it is coincident with pure "realism." That, of course, is the line uttered at 5.64: "Here we see that solipsism strictly carried out coincides with pure realism." This is the conclusion of an argument. The argument begins with the solipsist's claim that "I am my world" (5.63), then it is observed that if I wrote a book "The World as I found it," it would not be able to mention the metaphysical ego, because the "subject" is not an "object in the world." The argument then concludes that even on the assumption of solipsism the objective world remains the same: hence solipsism and pure realism coincide. I think that to take this argument as a refutation of solipsism is to miss something obvious enough in the *Tractatus,* but made even more obvious by its debt to Weininger's formulation. It *embraces* solipsism, but in a way that defuses its orneriness and its skepticism.

The early reception of the *Investigations* claimed again and again that the problem of Other Minds had been resolved by the later Wittgenstein; from Peter Strawson's critical notice through the book of essays edited by Harold Morick, to Peter Hacker's *Insight & Illusion.* Hacker admits that the early Wittgenstein accepted solipsism, but that the later work presents a radical change of view. He identifies the *Tractatus* doctrine as "transcendental solipsism," and Wittgenstein's view during the transitional period of the early 1930s as "methodological solipsism," a positivist view in which one assumes solipsism, and denies that problems with it can be meaningfully formulated. In the *Investigations,* however, solipsism is finally refuted. Hacker construes the anti–private language argument as the most important of the later Wittgenstein's arguments in final refutation of both solipsism in particular and idealism in general.[34] The very existence of a language in which to formulate the skepticism presupposes language users and their varying forms of life. Skepticism, of course (fomented not least by Saul Kripke's Humean interpretation of the anti–private language argument as the corollary of a skeptical solution to a newly invented skeptical doubt), has raised its head again, and those who are content with Wittgenstein's solution, or are content to read him as Hacker does, are for the moment condemned to be old-fashioned.

My suggestion is that it would be odd for Wittgenstein, not many years after reading Weininger's snide remark about a new refutation being published every year for the last twenty, to have produced another refutation. Other recent commentators can be called to my aid. I am sure that Hans Sluga is at least half right, when he subtly develops the thesis that Wittgenstein did not offer a new theory of the self. His conclusion, however, that this is "one more nail in the coffin of objectivism"[35] suggests that some form of subjectivism must be right. I think of Wittgenstein as working not on a refutation, but on a diversion. Something goes wrong when we embrace the objectivism/subjectivism dualism. Weininger's line, that only if dualism is inescapable can monism make any sense, has an air of self-refutation about it. Wittgenstein showed us how many other paths there are than just two. Naomi Scheman's proposal is that we approach the old question of whether one is in or out of a form of life not by arguing for one side or the other, but by adding others; in particular, she suggests adding the diasporic person, the refugee, and the immigrant, for whom the questions "are you at home here or not; here or elsewhere?" are not well-formed questions.[36] This can serve as a model of a philosophical method that seeks to construct a diversion from, rather than a refutation of, the problem of solipsism.

Conclusion

What I have tried to do in this paper is to give a sketch of the Weininger-Wittgenstein relationship with particular reference to essays of Weininger that were previously untranslated. I have stressed the way in which Weininger insisted that moral improvement must come from within, and cannot be thought to come from without (as the theme of redemption through the love of another person seems to imply). Then I have claimed that this inner/outer dichotomy is dramatically reconceived by Wittgenstein, in an attempt to take the threat of solipsism more seriously than Weininger did, but nonetheless to respect his claim that it is irrefutable.

Notes

This essay began as a paper presented at a symposium on Weininger's influence on Wittgenstein, at the annual meetings of the Canadian

Philosophical Association, at Université Laval, Québec, in May 2001. I am grateful to Béla Szabados for organizing that event, and am indebted to him and to the other participants, Daniel Steuer and David Stern, for their stimulating contributions both to that discussion and to this, much revised, essay.

1. See Wittgenstein, *Culture and Value,* 19. For more on Kraus's relevance to Wittgenstein, see Sawicky, *Wittgenstein's Art of Investigation,* especially ch. 1.
2. Weininger, *On Last Things.* Page numbers in my text refer to this work.
3. "*Peer Gynt* and Ibsen," Weininger, *On Last Things,* 1–40.
4. Hirsch, *Eine unbescheidene Charakterologie.*
5. Weininger, *On Last Things,* xxxi.
6. Monk, *The Duty of Genius,* 584.
7. Ibid., 318.
8. See "Conversations on Freud," in Wittgenstein, *Lectures and Conversations on Aesthetics, Psychology and Religious Belief.*
9. Ibid., 51. His remark about speculation is on 44.
10. Ibid., 44–5.
11. For a discussion and application of this idea of expanding logical space, see Rorty, "Feminism and Pragmatism."
12. Wittgenstein, *Culture and Value,* 19 and 1, respectively.
13. Hirsch, *Eine unbescheidene Charakterologie,* 17. On Jewishness and self-hatred in Weininger, see also 75–89 and 203–9.
14. See Wittgenstein, *Culture and Value,* 65–6. Weininger's critique of Schiller is discussed further in Daniel Steuer's contribution to this volume.
15. "I am often afraid of madness." Wittgenstein, *Culture and Value,* 53.
16. Rhees, *Ludwig Wittgenstein: Personal Recollections,* 207–8.
17. Compare the early draft for the preface, published in *Culture and Value,* pp. 6 ff.
18. Janik, *Wittgenstein's Vienna Revisited,* 59–84.
19. Chandak Sengoopta, *Otto Weininger,* 224 n. 80.
20. For a discussion that transcends the merely biographical, see Béla Szabados, "Autobiography after Wittgenstein."
21. Rhees, *Ludwig Wittgenstein,* 201. (Rhees's own translation of lines from *Sex and Character.*)
22. Ibid.
23. I propose this at greater length in the Preface to Weininger, *On Last Things,* xx–xxvi.
24. Wittgenstein, *Culture and Value,* 19.
25. The terms are taken from Le Rider, *Der Fall Otto Weininger,* 23.
26. This is Weininger's view. In his brief, early, critical writings Ibsen does offer some secondhand Hegelian ideas, which Brian Johnston makes the theme of his interpretation of Ibsen. See Johnston, *To the Third Empire,* Minneapolis: University of Minnesota Press, 1980.
27. This is evident, if from nothing else, from the fact that this discussion occupies the whole final quarter of the essay, 31–40.

28. Weininger considers this an unanswerable objection. Someone who wished to challenge him on this point might invoke Professor Dumbledore's words to Harry Potter: "[l]ove as powerful as your mother's for you leaves its own mark.[t]o have been loved so deeply, even though the person who loved us is gone, will give us some protection forever. It is in your very skin." J. K. Rowling, *Harry Potter and the Philosopher's Stone*, London: Bloomsbury, 1997, 216. The efficacy in this case, however, is admittedly magical.
29. *Sex and Character*, sixth edition, 276 [E. 211]
30. Russell, *The Autobiography of Bertrand Russell*, 132.
31. Rudolf Haller quotes Wittgenstein's *Notebooks 1914–1916* to this effect: "Ethics must be a condition of the world, like logic" (24 July 1916, 77e), and adds: "This is the view of the young Wittgenstein of 27 years, a view which, if I am right, he never changed": see Haller, "Wittgenstein and Austrian Philosophy," 110.
32. See also Weininger's aphorisms about Schopenhauer. Weininger, *On Last Things*, 47, 51.
33. *Tractatus Logico-Philosophicus*, 5.62.
34. Hacker, *Insight and Illusion*, 201.
35. Sluga, "'Whose house is that?' Wittgenstein on the Self," in Sluga and Stern, *The Cambridge Companion to Wittgenstein*, 320–53. Quote is from 350.
36. Naomi Scheman, "Forms of Life: mapping the rough ground," in Sluga and Stern, *The Cambridge Companion to Wittgenstein*, 383–410.

References

Burns, Steven (1981). "Was Wittgenstein a Genius?" In E. Morscher, R. Stranzinger, eds., *Ethics: Foundations, Problems, Applications*. Vienna: Hölder-Pichler-Tempsky, 315–18.

Hacker, P. M. S. (1972). *Insight and Illusion*. Oxford: Clarendon Press.

Haller, Rudolf (1981). "Wittgenstein and Austrian Philosophy." In J. C. Nyríri, ed., *Austrian Philosophy: studies and texts*. Munich: Philosophia Verlag.

Hirsch, Waltraud (1997). *Eine unbescheidene Charakterologie: Geistige Differenz von Judentum und Christentum; Otto Weiningers Lehre vom bestimmten Charakter*. Frankfurt am Main: Peter Lang.

Janik, Allan (2001). *Wittgenstein's Vienna Revisited*. New Brunswick and London: Transaction Publishers.

Klagge, James, ed. (2001). *Wittgenstein: Biography and Philosophy*. Cambridge: Cambridge University Press.

Le Rider, Jacques (1985). *Der Fall Otto Weininger: Wurzeln des Antifeminismus und Antisemitismus*. Translated by Dieter Hornig. Vienna and Munich: Löcker.

Monk, Ray (1990). *Ludwig Wittgenstein: The Duty of Genius*. New York: Free Press.

Morick, Harold, ed., (1967). *Wittgenstein on Other Minds*. New York: McGraw-Hill.

Rhees, Rush (1981). "Postscript." In Rhees, ed., *Ludwig Wittgenstein: Personal Recollections.* Oxford: Basil Blackwell, 190–219.

Rorty, Richard (1995). "Feminism and Pragmatism." In Russell B. Goodman, ed., *Pragmatism: a contemporary reader.* New York and London: Routledge, 125–48.

Russell, Bertrand (1969). *The Autobiography of Bertrand Russell: 1914–1944.* New York: Bantam Books. First published 1951.

Sawicky, Beth (1999). *Wittgenstein's Art of Investigation.* London: Routledge.

Sengoopta, Chandak (2000). *Otto Weininger: Sex, Science, and Self in Imperial Vienna.* Chicago: University of Chicago Press.

Sluga, Hans, and David Stern, eds. (1996). *The Cambridge Companion to Wittgenstein.* Cambridge: Cambridge University Press.

Szabados, Béla (1992). "Autobiography after Wittgenstein." *Journal of Aesthetics and Art Criticism* 50: 1–12.

Toulmin, Stephen, and Allan Janik (1973). *Wittgenstein's Vienna.* New York: Simon & Schuster.

Weininger, Otto (1975). *Sex and Character.* New York: G. P. Putnam's Sons. A reprint of the anonymous and incomplete 1906 translation of the second edition of *Geschlecht und Charakter,* first edition 1903, second edition with many corrections by the author, 1904.

——— (2001). *A Translation of Weininger's Über die letzten Dinge, 1904/1907/. On Last Things.* Translated by Steven Burns. Lewiston, NY: Edwin Mellen Press.

Wittgenstein, Ludwig (1922). *Tractatus Logico-Philosophicus.* Translated by C. K. Ogden. London: Routledge & Kegan Paul. Second edition, 1933.

——— (1953). *Philosophical Investigations.* Translated by G. E. M. Anscombe. Oxford: Basil Blackwell.

——— (1966). *Lectures and Conversations on Aesthetics, Psychology and Religious Belief.* Edited by Cyril Barrett. Oxford: Basil Blackwell.

——— (1969). *Notebooks 1914–1916.* Edited by G. H. von Wright and G. E. M. Anscombe. Translated by G. E. M. Anscombe. Oxford: Basil Blackwell 1961.

——— (1975). *Philosophical Remarks.* Edited by Rush Rhees. Translated by Raymond Hargreaves and Roger White. Oxford: Basil Blackwell.

——— (1980). *Culture and Value.* Edited by G. H. von Wright. Translated by Peter Winch. Oxford: Blackwell. Revised second edition, 1998.

——— (1993). "Lecture on Ethics." In *Philosophical Occasions, 1912–1951.* Edited by James Klagge and Alfred Nordmann. Indianapolis, IN: Hackett, 37–44.

Zwicky, Jan. "Review of Janik's *Essays on Wittgenstein and Weininger.*" *Canadian Philosophical Reviews* 6 (8), 1986: 386–8.

4

Wittgenstein and Weininger

Time, Life, World

Joachim Schulte

We know that Wittgenstein had a high opinion of Weininger. What we do not know is what his opinion rested on. It is extremely difficult to identify passages in his writings where a clearly Weiningerian thought is discussed; but that may be for the reason that there is no such thing as a clearly Weiningerian thought.[1] All attempts to clarify the relation between Weininger and Wittgenstein face a number of difficulties. Wittgenstein's philosophy is generally seen as firmly anchored in, or forming part of the foundations of, the analytic tradition, and the name of Weininger – a thinker who is evidently remote from this tradition – is unlikely to crop up in this context. If, on the other hand, a reader happens to come across Weininger in connection with other figures associated with fin-de-siècle Vienna,[2] he is unlikely to know enough about Wittgenstein's philosophy to make much of the fact that Wittgenstein thought highly of Weininger.

Weininger's world, the Vienna of his and the young Wittgenstein's day, is far removed from us and the styles of thinking we are familiar with. Of course, we are often told that many products of that time go to form essential parts of what we still tend to regard as *our* culture: there is the music of Gustav Mahler and the second Viennese school – Schönberg, Berg, Webern; there are the frequently exhibited and reproduced paintings of Klimt, Schiele, and Kokoschka, the admired architectural designs and buildings by Otto Wagner and Adolf Loos; there are highly recommended and much anthologized writings by

Hugo von Hofmannsthal, Arthur Schnitzler, and Stefan Zweig; there is Karl Kraus, who read and defended Weininger; and there is Freud, who felt compelled to distance himself from Weininger and his ideas. These are just a few of those names that are generally connected with Weininger's time and place, and for many of us they are household names. The people and works referred to by these names seem to belong to a kind of pantheon of modernity: they appear forever young, radical, virtually our contemporaries.

The same is true of Wittgenstein: he too appears forever young, radical, virtually our contemporary. But if you are told that Weininger, who was born in 1880 – that is, nine years before Wittgenstein – was one of the latter's heroes and for that reason open a musty copy of *Geschlecht und Charakter* or a tattered paperback called *Über die letzten Dinge*, you will all of a sudden notice how far away all this is and that the appearance of everlasting youth is largely imaginary. You will notice that the best you can do is *approach* these people and their works; they will never become our contemporaries. Our attempts to translate their thoughts into words familiar to us are bound to be tentative, and the correctness of such translations will to some extent remain undecidable.

Only if one develops some feeling for the remote culture and context out of which Wittgenstein's (Schönberg's, Freud's, etc.) personality and works grew will one have a chance of understanding what his apparent contemporaneousness may be due to. And to develop that sort of feeling one will have to be able to contemplate the products of those years with a certain degree of sympathetic understanding. This does not mean that one should completely identify with the life of that time and place, but one will constantly misunderstand Wittgenstein's (or his contemporaries') works unless one is seriously prepared to ask oneself what growing up in fin-de-siècle Vienna may have been like and to wonder what counted as a matter of course and what as an obvious absurdity in that context.

To be sure, even in the best of cases one will at most manage to come close to that kind of understanding. I think that when we are dealing with the times of Locke or Goethe, Giordano Bruno or Couperin, no one will need this sort of caution. But strangely enough, as soon as we come to those times and places which are still – after a hundred years of rapid developments – characterized as seedbeds of modernity, we tend to expect to be able to judge people and their works without allowing for the enormous distance that lies between them and us. This attitude appears all the stranger if one remembers that in at least two respects we have irremediably lost our innocence; we have lost an innocence that was theirs. The first respect in which that world was innocent is that it had not seen a world war. One of the lessons you learn from reading works by people who, as adults, lived through the days of, or fought in, what used to be called the Great War is that after 1918 nothing was the same as before. And the Second World War confirmed that no bridge led back to the age of innocence before 1914. The second respect in which this age was innocent was that it did not know, and probably did not guess at the possibility of, the Holocaust. This affects the very use of our words. Today expressions like "anti-Semitism" or even "Jew" lack many shades of meaning they used to have. These shades of meaning are irrevocably lost because the corresponding uses of these words are unimaginable. Here there were meanings, connotations and possible allusions that cannot be recovered. This is a fact, a fact that concerns not only what one may wish to call *Geistesgeschichte*, or a history of ideas, but also the possibility of gaining an understanding of that remote period in which Weininger wrote *Geschlecht und Charakter* and Wittgenstein grew up to become an icon of Cambridge philosophy.

To my mind, these remarks are truisms. But when, after rereading Weininger, I went through some of the literature on him and on Wittgenstein's attitude toward Weininger I became aware of the fact that not everybody seems to share my feeling that these remarks express truisms. On the contrary, there seem to be many people who believe that there are certain more or less clearly defined doctrines called "antifeminism" and "anti-Semitism," that these doctrines have advocates as well as adversaries today, and that these identical doctrines had advocates as well as adversaries in 1983, 1963, 1943, 1923 and so on back to Weininger and beyond. People who look at the matter this way cannot help seeing Weininger as a particularly ferocious campaigner for both causes; in their eyes he chiefly is a contributor to, or a cofounder of, two terrible ideologies. The attention his work was given by more noble characters such as Karl Kraus, Arnold Schönberg and other representatives of modern culture can then be cited as a cause of *their* moral defects. Thus Weininger is doubly culpable – first for disseminating those repulsive views and second for corrupting the minds of our cultural models. These cultural models, on the other hand, can then partly be whitewashed – it was not really their fault that they held odious views on women or expressed some of their ideas in racist terms. Weininger was the culprit. Similarly with Wittgenstein: it is held that his prejudices against women came from Weininger, who, according to this view, also is to blame for Wittgenstein's somewhat opaque but surely unpalatable remarks on Jews.[3]

It goes without saying that I am out of sympathy with this attitude and that I deplore this whole way of looking at Wittgenstein and his time or at developments in the history of ideas in general. I think the notion that the people living in those days were *ipso facto* much stupider and probably morally more deficient than ourselves is benighted and should never be allowed to tinge our descriptions of the past or our judgments about it. The tendency I object to finds expression in the account that Ray Monk, who has written a biography of Wittgenstein, gives of Weininger and his influence on Wittgenstein. Monk asks himself and his readers:

> But why did Wittgenstein admire the book so much? What did he learn from it? Indeed, given that its claims to scientific biology are transparently spurious, its epistemology obvious nonsense, its psychology primitive, and its ethical prescriptions odious, what could he *possibly* have learnt from it?[4]

Monk does give an answer to this last question, and this answer is based on his decision to turn away from Weininger's psychology of Woman and to focus instead on the psychology of Man, where he is able to unearth a few notions (especially those connected with Weininger's idea of genius) that seem to chime with Wittgenstein's outlook on life. The unwary reader, however, will find these notions cranky at best. In Monk's summary, Weininger comes across as a swaggering fool and a wicked fraud, who (as Monk nearly suggests) committed suicide to promote the sales of his book. Accordingly, Wittgenstein himself looks a bit like a fool and a bit like a fraud for having found something positive to say about Weininger. Of course, a glance at his own summary should have told Monk that this cannot have been the whole story: either there was something wrong with this way of summarizing Weininger's book or the mere possibility of giving this kind of summary should serve to indicate that there may be other, and very different, ways of reading the book.

I shall come back to this point. But first I want to look at some of the evidence for saying that Wittgenstein "admired" *Geschlecht und Charakter.* In the literature, all the relevant passages have been discussed at length. But I feel that my way of reading, or contextualizing, these passages is sufficiently different from other interpretations to justify my quoting and examining some of them afresh. Probably the best known of these passages is a remark from a notebook written in 1931. Here Wittgenstein lists ten people who in his view have influenced him. These ten people are Boltzmann, Hertz, Schopenhauer, Frege, Russell, Kraus, Loos, Weininger, Spengler, and Sraffa. Originally the list had been much shorter and only comprised the names of Frege, Russell, Spengler, and Sraffa. The other six names were added above the line, and it is clear that Wittgenstein tried to put down these names in chronological order, that is, the first influence comes first, the second influence second, and so on. Obviously, Spengler's influence comes after 1918,[5] and Sraffa belongs to the time after Wittgenstein's return to Cambridge early in 1929. The influence exercised by Frege and Russell dates from 1911 and the years immediately following that. Boltzmann, Hertz, and Schopenhauer can safely be assigned places in the intellectual life of Wittgenstein the schoolboy and, perhaps, the young university student, while the influence of Kraus, Loos, and Weininger seems to be ascribed to the years after the first impact of Frege and Russell. At the same time we may assume that the names – and probably more than just the names – of Kraus, Loos, and Weininger had been well known to Wittgenstein before he met Frege and Russell.[6]

Clearly, the concept "influence" was a problematic one for Wittgenstein. In a remark jotted down in 1929 he claims that it is a good thing that he does not let himself be influenced (*Culture and Value,* 3). In another notebook from the early thirties he talks about the way artists can be influenced by others and says that this sort of influence will often not be more than eggshells, which "will not give us spiritual nourishment" (*Culture and Value,* 27). In a very late remark (30 March, 1950) he mentions Weininger and talks about the way a person's character may be influenced by his environment (*Culture and Value,* 95).

But obviously the passage mentioning the ten influential authors from Boltzmann to Sraffa is the most interesting one. It was written down in a spirit of self-reflection and self-criticism and is the second of an entire series of observations. The first of these observations uses concepts reminiscent of Weininger. The word "genius" (in the phrase "Jewish 'genius' ") is put in quotation marks – and of course the idea of a genius is one of the central notions discussed by Weininger. Wittgenstein proceeds to say that even the greatest Jewish thinker is no more than talented. And "talent" too is one of those Weiningerian concepts. In *Geschlecht und Charakter* it is contrasted with "gift" (*Begabung*) and said to be one of those Female/Jewish accomplishments, which count incomparably much less than the Male/non-Jewish (Aryan)[7] achievement of *Begabung*.

After this introduction Wittgenstein says that there is "some truth" in his idea that he is really only reproductive in his thinking. He says that he has "never *invented* a line of thinking" (*Gedankenbewegung* – perhaps, a "thought-move" or "thought-gesture"). He supposes that all he has done is assimilate such thought-moves and "passionately"[8] take them up for his "work of clarification." The ten authors mentioned are examples of people who have given Wittgenstein the opportunity to take up such *Gedankenbewegungen* and bring his work of clarification to bear on them. (Here it is worth remembering that some of the influences mentioned by Wittgenstein, and notably Weininger, were Jewish.) Still, he does attribute to himself the power to invent something, namely the power to invent similes (or comparisons – *Gleichnisse*). The remarks following this one are also interesting but a discussion of the whole sequence (*Culture and Value*, 16–17) would distract from the main point. What should be taken into account, however, is that the last of these remarks seems to contain (a partial) disclaimer of what was said before. Here Wittgenstein says: "when I was in Norway during the year 1913–14 I had some thoughts of my own, or so at least it seems to me now. I mean that I have the impression of having given birth to new lines of thinking at that time." And then he goes on (partially) to withdraw *this* remark by adding in brackets the words "But perhaps I am mistaken." For the time being I want to content myself with mentioning this succession of (partial) disclaimers.

In a sense the ten authors[9] listed are examples supporting the general self-criticism of being a merely reproductive thinker. In another sense, however, the aim of listing these names seems to go beyond that, for the remark looks as if it were part of one of Wittgenstein's attempts at settling accounts with himself. He wants to get things exactly right and is extremely scrupulous when it comes to mentioning names and putting them in a certain order. We can be sure that the influences mentioned are neither "merely theoretical" ones nor general *Bildungseinflüsse.* He names neither Goethe nor Gottfried Keller, neither Dostoevsky nor Tolstoy, neither Nestroy nor Kürnberger. It is intelligible yet worthy of note that no composer is listed: neither the "actual sons of god," Mozart and Beethoven,[10] nor his hero Brahms are mentioned. So it is reasonable to suppose that with every single one of these ten references he wants to mark a relatively *specific* trait[11] of his own personality or his work (if such a distinction can be made in Wittgenstein's case). In some of these ten cases it is not particularly difficult to think of specific features Wittgenstein may have had in mind when writing down his list. Two or three cases may prove harder. In a way Weininger may be the most puzzling case of all. At any rate, the attempt to find out why his name is on the list is a very interesting exercise. Let's see what we can do.

In the year 1931 (when the list was written) we find two further prominent references to Weininger: one comes from a letter to G. E. Moore, the other from a conversation with Wittgenstein's then student and later friend Drury. Both passages are worth quoting. Drury reports as follows:

> [Wittgenstein] did advise me to read Weininger's *Sex and Character,* saying it was the work of a remarkable genius. He pointed out that Weininger at the age of twenty-one had recognized, before any one else had taken much notice, the future importance of the ideas which Freud was putting forward in his first book, the one in which he had collaborated with Breuer, *Studies on Hysteria.* When I had read *Sex and Character* I spoke to Wittgenstein.
>
> DRURY: Weininger seems to me to be full of prejudices, for instance his extreme adulation of Wagner.
> WITTGENSTEIN: Yes, he is full of prejudices, only a young man would be so prejudiced.
>
> And then with regard to Weininger's theme that women and the female element in men was the source of all evil he exclaimed: "How wrong he was, my God he was wrong."[12]

Naturally the reader must allow for the fact that these are notes taken from memory – notes written down by a young man who probably was "full of prejudices" of his own. The real exchange between those two men must have been much fuller than the brief account quoted. Still, the passage contains several elements worth bearing in mind.

First, there is the fact that Wittgenstein explicitly recommended reading Weininger's book, accompanying his advice with words to the effect that in his opinion it was the "work of a remarkable genius." It is clear from Drury's report as well as from correspondence and the accounts given by other students and friends that, for Wittgenstein, recommending books was a token of goodwill and a way of disclosing features of his own personality. Advising another person to read a certain book was, roughly speaking, tantamount to saying: "If you read this, it may do you good and you will gain a better understanding of myself." Thus it is likely that by advising people to read Weininger, Wittgenstein wished to lay bare what he himself perceived as an important part of his own character. Recommending not *Über die letzten Dinge* but *Geschlecht und Charakter* need not mean much, as only the latter book was available in English translation. Yet it is likely that Wittgenstein would not have suggested reading the book if he had thought much less highly of it than of the other work. The connection with Freud and Breuer, however, must be taken with a pinch of salt. In 1931 the relative value of their contributions to *Studies on Hysteria* was on Wittgenstein's mind anyway.[13] But from the way Drury reports what Wittgenstein told him one might get the impression that Wittgenstein wanted to praise the depth of Weininger's psychological insight. That impression, however, would be misleading. Psychological insight of the Freud/Breuer kind would not have impressed him sufficiently to speak of an "influence." After all, Freud (whose work Wittgenstein was familiar with) is not on the list.

Second, to Drury's complaint about Weininger's prejudices Wittgenstein reacts by agreeing that, indeed, Weininger *was* prejudiced and adding that his way of being prejudiced was the way typical of a young man. Presumably in this attitude of Weininger's Wittgenstein recognized something he had discovered about his own younger self and diagnosed as the fault of "dogmatism."[14] That does not mean that Weininger's dogmatism was of the same kind as Wittgenstein's. What it means is that a certain manner of clinging to one's principles is characteristic of young men – at least of young men attempting to produce ambitious works. What may also be implied is the view that such works can be successful only if they are produced from a prejudiced or dogmatic perspective (but that would be a secondary consideration).

Third, it is worth noting that, as far as we know, Wittgenstein does not respond to Drury's specific complaint regarding Weininger's adulation of Wagner. Probably he does not respond because he does not agree with Drury's criticism. Weininger's expressed attitude towards Wagner is part and parcel of the book: *Geschlecht und Charakter* would not be the kind of book it is unless it were a kind of Wagnerian rhapsody. I shall come back to this in a moment.

Fourth, even though Wittgenstein agrees that Weininger's claim about the generally baleful influence of the female element is wrong, he apparently does not regard this as a reason for having a low opinion of Weininger's work. It is obvious that Wittgenstein did not need Drury's comment to become aware of the "wrongness" of that claim. He recommended the book notwithstanding his judgment that what appeared to be one of the main theses of the work was wrong. He would not have done so if he had thought getting things right was the chief objective, or one of the chief objectives, of that kind of book.

The third and fourth points especially raise the question of what kind of work Weininger's book was in Wittgenstein's opinion. Clearly he did not think of it as a scientific treatise in psychology, characterology, racial or feminist studies or what have you. Had he seen it as a treatise of that sort, getting things right would have mattered to him.

Usually, the title of a book is the place where one expects to find some information about the type of work one is confronted with. The main title of Weininger's work – *Geschlecht und Charakter* – sounds instructive enough. It indicates that sex, masculinity, and femininity, as well as certain aspects of the relation between the sexes are being dealt with; and it also suggests that the character of people, in particular their character *as* men or *as* women, is another main subject. So far, so good. But what about the subtitle of the work – *Eine prinzipielle Untersuchung*? What kind of (sub)title is that supposed to be? "A philosophical investigation" or "A psychological examination" – these would have been subtitles of the usual, more or less informative kind, telling prospective readers (or librarians) what kind of interest the author hopes to cater to. It is difficult to render the particular flavor of "*Eine prinzipielle Untersuchung*" in English. I am fairly sure that "A principled investigation" is useless. One might try "A matter of principle" or "A question of principle," but these proposals are misleading insofar as they lack the peculiar aroma of willful noninformativeness distinguishing the German title. In a sense, the German subtitle amounts to saying "This is a general book" or "A book." In another sense, it manages splendidly to give an idea of the characteristic *tone* of the book. The most instructive parallel may be with half-programmatic musical titles describing the mood supposedly expressed or captured by a piece, such as "*Lyrische Suite*," "Rhapsody in Blue," or "Mood Indigo." But what this parallel fails to highlight is the peculiarly teasing quality of Weininger's subtitle: it provokes certain expectations, it frustrates these expectations, but at the same time manages to get across something unexpected. Exaggerating slightly, one might claim that the subtitle says "This is a prejudiced, a dogmatic, book," and simultaneously conveys that the book is going to play with prejudices and dogmas.

What is a real achievement is Weininger's way of topping the conceit inherent in the subtitle of his book by slyly concealing his ironical intentions through the following ostensible explanation of that subtitle:

> This investigation is not a specialized but a general [*prinzipielle*] one. It does not despise experimental work, even though the means afforded by laboratories seem to be restricted [*or.* narrow-minded – *beschränkt*] if compared with the accomplishments of analysis by self-observation. Even an artist describing a female may be able to render something typical without having legitimized himself before a guild of experimental Beckmessers [*vor einer experimentellen Merkergilde*] by citing numbers and frequencies.[15]

This passage not only contains the first link in a long chain of allusions to Wagner's works – the expression "*Merkergilde*," here translated as "guild of Beckmessers," clearly refers to *Meistersinger*, where the figure of Beckmesser plays the role of *Merker*, the narrow-minded stickler for traditional principles; it also manages to "explain" the subtitle's use of "*prinzipiell*" by setting the book's alleged principles in *opposition* to the quintessential defender of principle – Beckmesser, a comical and at the same time slightly tragic figure. And, of course, there is no author of a theoretical work whose character is completely free of all Beckmesserian traits.

There are several reasons why I have dwelled on Weininger's ironical play with the word "*prinzipiell.*" First of all it is a fine example of a general feature: Weininger likes to tease his readers and to convey a concealed message by a subtle strategy of saying and apparently unsaying things at the same time. Second, it is worth reminding readers of the existence of this relatively obvious irony, which is staring people in the face from the book's very title page, and makes it hard to understand why Weininger is generally taken to be nothing but a solemn, zealous and bigoted stickler for nasty and stupid principles. Third, the teasing quality of Weininger's writing is one among several characteristics of Weininger's work that may serve to explain Wittgenstein's liking for it. In my view, it is not far-fetched to suppose that the author of such a deeply ironical and often paradoxical work as the *Logisch-philosophische Abhandlung* (another teasing title, if you are looking for more examples) might like the works of another writer reveling in (mostly unobvious) irony and paradox.

The host of Wagnerian allusions to be found in Weininger's book may serve to highlight another aspect of the question "What kind of book are we dealing with when reading *Geschlecht und Charakter*?" If you look at the appendix with its more than 130 pages of "*Zusätze und Nachweise*" (Notes and Appendices) you may well be surprised by the medley of authors referred to. There are the names of classical and modern philosophers, such as Plato and Aristotle, Spinoza and Hume, Kant and Schelling, Mill and Dilthey, Pascal and Schopenhauer, of well-known scientists or philosopher-scientists, such as Mach and Boltzmann, Darwin and Krafft-Ebing, Johannes Müller and Claude Bernard, Wilhelm Wundt and Richard Avenarius, Lombroso and Havelock Ellis, a vast number of physiologists, psychologists, phrenologists, biologists and so forth of Weininger's day,[16] and next to, or interspersed among, these more conventional albeit fairly mixed authorities you will spot the names of writers, poets and musicians such as Goethe and Hebbel, Ibsen and Zola, Schiller and – of course – Wagner. The tone of Weininger's notes varies a great deal. Some of them are simple references; others contain short essays on characterology or morphology, on hero-worship or the psychology of criminals;

a third kind are mock-serious disquisitions on an apparently empirical subject culminating in a quotation from Ibsen or Wagner that is ostensibly meant to decide the matter once and for all. No summary can suffice to give an idea of the flavor of that sort of thing. But the main text abounds with similar passages, the occasional profusion of which may in some readers cause a feeling of giddiness and the desire for more of the same. The following passage is a brief example:

> Thus there really is such a thing as "Platonic" love, even if our professors of psychiatry do not think highly of that notion. I should like to go so far as to say: as regards *love,* there is none but the Platonic kind. For the other things called love belong in the realm of swine. There is only one kind of love, and that is love for Beatrice, the adoration of the Madonna. For one's coital needs one may turn to the Babylonian harlot.
>
> Should this remain tenable, Kant's list of transcendental ideas would need to be extended. Pure and high love free of lust – love in the sense of Plato and Bruno – would also count as a *transcendental idea* whose significance as an *idea* would not be affected by the fact that no experience would ever reveal it to be realized.
>
> That is the problem of *Tannhäuser.* On the one hand there is Tannhäuser, on the other Wolfram; on the one hand there is Venus, on the other Maria. The fact that two loving people who have really found each other for eternity – Tristan and Isolde – prefer death to their bridal bed is a proof of something higher, of something metaphysical if you wish, whose absoluteness equals that of the martyrdom suffered by Giordano Bruno.[17]

No doubt this is heady stuff, but often this sort of passage has an amazing internal logic; the narrative smoothly leads from one monument of Western culture to the next and frequently manages to surprise readers through the unexpectedness of its juxtapositions and comparisons. What is absolutely stunning is Weininger's daring use of all kinds of commonplaces and clichés. But as these commonplaces and clichés tend to be presented as the best products of the greatest (scientific and philosophic as well as artistic) minds the reader is constantly torn between his wish to despise or condemn the ideas and his desire to cling to his admiration for the great minds: it seems impossible to criticize the clichés without besmirching their authors. In sum, Weininger's tour de force is, among other things, an efficient exercise in cultural criticism. To what extent this criticism was planned, what this criticism was meant to teach us, or what feelings it was intended to provoke – these are entirely different questions that cannot be discussed here.

Another context in which Weininger proves himself to be a master of the use of clichés is the apparent main subject of the book – the relation between Man and Woman (unfortunately, it does not seem possible to find an adequate English rendering of Weininger's slightly archaic, slightly pseudo- or mock-scientific as well as slightly vulgar use of the German word "*Weib*"). Here I wish to cite only one example. In one of his two chapters on logic (or "logic") Weininger goes on and on about what he (I suspect) is not the only one to call "female logic," which is a euphemism for the inability to think straight. Thus he regards the tendency to commit the fallacy of *quaternio terminorum* and the complete lack of any understanding of the principle of identity as essentially female characteristics (*Geschlecht und Charakter* II, vi, e.g. 192). At the same time he never tires of reminding us that the male/female distinction is not a distinction between empirical men and women but a scientific and philosophical distinction between elements present in everyone's character, no matter if empirically male or female. But his accounts of fallacies and the inability to construct anything resembling a cogent argument seem to be taken from the cartoon pages of the daily press or cliché-ridden comedies, where those mistakes are (were?) – of course – typically committed by women. So on the one hand his graphic descriptions are suggestive of stock situations and stock characters normally showing women to be the intellectually inferior sex while on the other hand his interventions in his role as a conscientious scientist keep informing us that the "women" he is describing are not really, or not necessarily, female – they are 80 or 90 percent W but not women. On these pages, however, Weininger gets carried away by his own narrative: some of his descriptions are so hilarious and some of the quasi scientific babble is so mock-solemn that laughter seems the only fitting reaction. This is high comedy. And I am sure that Wittgenstein chuckled more than once when looking at this material. It must have been disappointing for him that the Cambridge friends to whom he recommended reading Weininger got so little amusement out of it.

G. E. Moore was another Cambridge friend whom Wittgenstein advised to read Weininger's *Sex and Character.* From a letter Wittgenstein wrote in August 1931 it becomes obvious that Moore was not very happy about Wittgenstein's recommendation. To Moore's complaint Wittgenstein replied as follows:

> I can quite imagine that you don't admire Weininger very much what with that beastly translation and the fact that W. must feel very foreign to you. It is true that he is fantastic but he is *great* and fantastic. It isn't necessary or rather not possible to agree with him but the greatness lies in that with which we disagree. It is his enormous mistake which is great. I.e. roughly speaking if you just add a "∼" to the whole book it says an important truth.[18]

Wittgenstein's words are puzzling. He *seems* to be saying that the book's content is great but mistaken and that, if the content of *Sex and Character* were represented by "p & q & r," then affirming "$\sim(p$ & q & $r)$" would express a true and a great statement. I do not think that this is what Wittgenstein has in mind. There are various reasons why, and an important reason follows from what I have already said: A book that keeps taking back things apparently said before, a book brazenly employing vast dualisms, which it then proceeds to dismantle, is not the sort of text that gains much by straightforward denial. I think what Wittgenstein is doing here is this: he is telling Moore how he should read the book to get something out of it. The crucial phrase is that a tilde is to be added to *the whole book* in order to yield an important truth. The tilde does not signify the negation of standard propositional logic; it signifies disagreement, and this is not disagreement with a complex statement about matters of empirical fact, but disagreement with an entire way of looking at the world.[19] A book consisting of a conjunction of statements that in your opinion are false is not the sort of thing you would greatly admire. But a book that expresses a view with which you happen to disagree or cannot help disagreeing may well be an object of admiration.

A corollary of this way of reading Weininger (and Wittgenstein's comment on it) is that, from a point of view from which the vision expressed by the book is one with which you disagree, this vision as well as the book itself is beyond repair however much you may admire it (and hence it would not help to affirm the opposite, whatever that might be). This consequence flows from perceiving the book as a whole, something complete in itself. In short, Wittgenstein is telling Moore to read the book as he would read an outstanding novel or poem or a great work of philosophy. You may admire Shakespeare but still disagree with his outlook (this was the case with Wittgenstein).[20] You may admire *Obermann Once More* and yet disagree with the vision behind it. You may admire the *Critique of Judgement* but disagree with the world view conveyed by it. What you would not do is revise Shakespeare's plays, Arnold's poem or Kant's philosophy and proceed to present the result as a better version of the original. If you attempted that, it would prove that you simply had not understood what a (great) drama, poem, or philosophical work is. These things are complete in themselves, and they are beyond repair. You may take them or leave them, you may love or hate, admire or despise them; but you cannot meddle with them.

Certainly, this is a speculative reading but my impression is that, in writing to Moore about Weininger, Wittgenstein is at the same time writing about his own early work. (Remember, we are in 1931 – the *Tractatus* was still casting a large shadow while Wittgenstein was busy defining his new project.) By now he has come to see – but did he ever think otherwise? – that tampering with the early book would be a mistake. *That* work was complete in itself, it was beyond repair, you had to take it or leave it.

So far I have spelled out two or three reasons why Wittgenstein may have appreciated Weininger and his work. I have done so by pointing out that appreciation by someone like Wittgenstein was possible only if Weininger's work was not read as a straightforward treatise on characterology, psychology, and so on. Only a reader who notices the irony, the teasing, the conceits, the criticism that colours the apparent adulation and many other tongue-in-cheek maneuvers will find something to admire in Weininger's writings. The presence of these features makes Weininger *palatable.* But that does not mean that these writings ought to be seen as nothing but irony and sleight of hand, nor that Wittgenstein respected only this aspect of Weininger's work. Another aspect he surely admired was Weininger's consistently moral way of looking at things: he just could not help writing from an ethical standpoint. And yet another aspect is Weininger's great admiration for works of art: for him it is a matter of course that Dante and Goethe, Beethoven and Wagner should have the last word. Wittgenstein would not have found it difficult to subscribe to the basic judgment implicit in Weininger's claim that "a great artist, just as a great philosopher, carries *the whole world in himself*." Every great artist is "a self-aware microcosm" while the microcosm present in an ordinary human being or in someone whose sole occupation is science is not consciously felt.[21] This attitude – Weininger's nearly instinctive admiration for great philosophy and great art – was naturally congenial to Wittgenstein, who wrote: "Scientific questions may interest me, but they never really grip me. Only *conceptual and aesthetic* questions have that effect on me. At bottom it leaves me cold whether scientific problems are solved; but not those other questions."[22]

While these considerations may go some way toward explaining why Wittgenstein liked or admired Weininger, we have not yet succeeded in describing a specific feature of Weininger's work that might suggest why Wittgenstein spoke of him as an *influence*. To be sure, we have mentioned the idea of man as a microcosm, whose only occurrence in Wittgenstein's *Notebooks* (12 October 1916) survived into the *Tractatus* (5.63). And the idea of man as a microcosm plays a great role both in *Geschlecht und Charakter* and in *Über die letzten Dinge*. But without further specification it may be advisable to see this idea as belonging to the general Schopenhauerian heritage and not as a specific trait due to Weininger in particular. Another point of contact is Wittgenstein's criticism of the conception of the soul current in the superficial psychology of the present day: "Indeed a composite soul would no longer be a soul."[23] This is the sort of thing Weininger says in various places when criticizing modern psychology, in particular the views of Mach and Avenarius: "I wish to point out how wrong the doctrine of present-day psychology is (according to which a human individual is nothing but an advanced recording instrument)."[24] But again I do not think that this is the kind of idea Wittgenstein saw as a specific influence.

People who are not used to reading lots of books from this period may be surprised by a number of parallels between Weininger's and Wittgenstein's writings which on closer inspection should be regarded as purely coincidental and simply due to the fact that we are studying authors from the same time and the same culture: these things were in the air. So one may be surprised at finding Weininger say that "every nincompoop from Bacon to Fritz Mauthner has practiced criticism of language"[25] and compare this harsh judgment with *Tractatus*

4.0031: "*Alle Philosophie ist 'Sprachkritik'. (Allerdings nicht im Sinne Mauthners)*" "all philosophy is a 'critique of language' (though not in Mauthner's sense)." But it is clear that this sort of coincidence does not add up to anything like influence.

What seems quite clear from reading our two authors side by side is that if any passages indicative of Weininger's influence can be found at all, they should be located in the 5.6's or the 6.4's of the *Tractatus* or in corresponding passages from the *Notebooks* (where many relevant entries can be found which did not survive into the published work). And certainly some of the things Weininger says about solipsism seem to fit Wittgenstein's ruminations on this topic. This is particularly true of Weininger's way of connecting the idea of solipsism with the notion of a world-soul.[26] But in this case too we are probably dealing with a vaguely Schopenhauerian idea, which he may have been familiar with anyway or which, alternatively, may have been transmitted to Wittgenstein via Weininger without his having felt that the latter was the real source of this idea. Wittgenstein's specific use of the idea may be unclear and all likely interpretations of it controversial, but what seems clear is that in Wittgenstein's thought it plays a role that is too remote from its possible roots in Schopenhauer or Weininger to receive much light from these possible ancestors.

At any rate, we have moved from *Geschlecht und Charakter* to *Über die letzten Dinge*, and Wittgenstein's correspondence with his sister Hermine suggests that it was *this* book that his relatives associated with Ludwig. In one letter Hermine writes: "I've brought your Weininger and I'm very happy about this book, which to a small extent serves as a substitute for your own presence."[27] And in another letter she makes an elaborate joke referring to an aphorism where Weininger concludes that milk is the only food really fit for human consumption: "Perhaps the reason why milk is the most wholesome kind of food is the fact that it is the most virtuous kind."[28] This book describes a certain *Gedankenbewegung* which may be the most likely candidate for a move or gesture that Wittgenstein could have seen as an influence on his own way of thinking.

The move I mean is complicated and, in Weininger's presentation, very difficult to comprehend. I do not think that all its aspects are relevant to what Wittgenstein may have derived from it. The basic idea is that of the unidirectionality of time. Weininger says that this, "together with the riddle of the world (the riddle of *dualism*), constitutes the deepest problem in the universe."[29] According to Weininger, the unidirectionality of time is more or less the same thing as the impossibility of a return of past events. The interesting fact about it is that it is the basis of all aversion to retrogressive or rotating movements. This sort of movement, Weininger claims, has been shown to be unethical. The unidirectionality of time and that aversion have a common ground in the ethical realm, and that connects the whole issue with the human will. To quote Weininger: "*Thus the unidirectionality of time is identical with the fact that in its essence a human being is a willing being. The ego as will is time.*"[30] So there are two important aspects of Weininger's notion that stand out: on the one hand, unidirectionality involves a boundary that cannot be crossed – you cannot return to the past; on the other, unidirectionality is connected with man's capacity for ethical conduct. Both aspects play a role in the following passage where, however, they are given a new twist:

> Thus the unidirectionality of time is identical with the fact of the irreversibility of *life*, and the riddle of time is identical with the riddle of *life* (though not with the riddle of the world). *Life is not reversible*; there is no way leading back from death to birth. *The problem of the unidirectionality of time is the question of the meaning of life.*[31]

I should be hard put to explain the full sense of Weininger's fragmentary thoughts on these matters. But I do not think that we have to understand them fully. What is interesting is that in Wittgenstein's notebooks we find a series of entries (12 October 1916) dealing with the question of unidirectionality. Some formulations seem to go back directly to Weininger's book – it is very likely that he was reading it in Olmütz when writing these entries. The idea as such, however, does not appear to impress Wittgenstein very much. He deals with it as one should expect: it is a formal property, belonging to the framework, and hence "time is unidirectional" must be nonsense. The entries of that day terminate in an early formulation of *Tractatus* 5.63: "It is true: Man is the microcosm: I am my world." Of course, these words *need not* be directly related to the remarks on unidirectionality but I think they *may* be connected with them: in a way they articulate what remains of the Weiningerian thought after the unidirectionality as a formal property has been disposed of.

In Weininger's account, the connection with boundaries and ethics culminated in the question of the meaning of life. And a partial answer to this question is indicated by Weininger when he says that willing to live in the present and thus deliberately respecting the boundaries that separate the present from the past and the future should be our aim in life: Man as a self-conscious microcosm may find himself in accord with the meaning (= *Sinn* = direction) of life if he strives to honor the boundaries of the present, which have their raison d'être in his own ethical character. In order to reach full agreement with the meaning/direction of life, Man as microcosm must try to *absorb* past and future in his omnipresence.[32] From this notion it is only a short step to the idea that "If by eternity is understood not infinite temporal duration but non-temporality, then it can be said that a man lives eternally if he lives in the present. In order to live happily I must be in agreement with the world. And that is what 'being happy' *means.*"[33] It may well be that the short remark on Man as microcosm was also meant to allude to this idea of the absorption of past and future resulting in omnipresence and happy agreement with the world.

This move of bringing oneself in accord with the direction of life and world involves respect for the boundaries of the present. In other words, it involves acceptance of what is given. For man to succeed in finding the meaning/direction of life he will have to say "yes" to the world as he finds it: this is an "enormous yes" of the kind Philip Larkin heard in Sidney Bechet's music. And it is also part of Job's praising the Lord who has deprived him of everything – an attitude Wittgenstein found expressed by Gottfried Keller, one of his favorite authors.[34] Weininger connects the idea with the genius in ourselves whose potential we are called upon to develop as fully as we can: "Man will become a genius through performing the highest act of will by affirming – accepting – the whole universe within himself."[35] I think this is the "fatalistic" attitude that, according to McGuinness, Wittgenstein got from Weininger.

But I think there is more to this story. According to Weininger, the only people who fully succeed in living entirely in the present are great men of action, emperors and leading statesmen. That may come as a surprise – after all, Weininger does not think very highly of these people. They are part of history but they do not create history. *That* is achieved by men of real genius who are capable of grasping the essence of the universe and expressing it in their works. By doing so they generate time and history; they transform what is essentially timeless into something that can be perceived within time but simultaneously as something standing outside time.[36] The trick is to preserve one's individuality while absorbing as much world as possible.

The perspective from which this can be achieved – the perspective from which works of real genius can be produced – is not that of perfect accord with the world and uninterrupted immersion in the present. It is a perspective that can be attained, *if* it can be attained, by succeeding in the attempt to move beyond the ordinary human station – ultimately by defeating time itself. Through obtaining the highest possible degree of individuality while gaining utter timelessness in the production of great works of art or philosophy, some people manage to indicate ideas and ideals that cannot be perceived from within the boundaries of time, life, and world. "As individuals, philosophers and artists are timeless; from within their time they can never be grasped and they can never be excused by blaming their time. In philosophers and artists there lies eternity."[37] Presumably by way of considerations of this kind Weininger is led to formulate his "ethical precept":

> Every action ought to reveal man's *entire* individuality; every action ought to be a consummate defeat [*Überwindung*] of time, of the unconscious, the narrowness of consciousness. . . . The present and eternity are kindred. . . . *And hence every present moment ought to enshrine the whole of eternity.*[38]

As this suggests, there is a dual thought-move to be found in Weininger, which, I submit, may have inspired Wittgenstein. The first part of this move involves acceptance of the boundaries and the meaning/direction of life and world. We have seen that echoes of this sentiment can be traced in the *Tractatus* and, in particular, in Wittgenstein's early notebooks. But reflections of the second part, too – of the precept to defeat time, to reach timelessness or eternity, a perspective from outside the given world – can be found in Wittgenstein's early writings. Five days before writing down his remarks on the unidirectionality of time he continued his earlier observations on works of art by saying (and here I quote only a selection from the relevant remarks):

> The work of art is the object seen *sub specie aeternitatis*; and the good life is the world seen *sub specie aeternitatis*. This is the connection between art and ethics.

The usual way of looking at things sees objects as it were from the midst of them, the view *sub specie aeternitatis* from outside.

In such a way that they have the whole world as background.

Is this it perhaps – in this view the object is seen *together with* space and time instead of *in* space and time?[39]

As we know, very little of this survived into the *Tractatus*.[40] To evaluate its relevance to Wittgenstein's early work, and especially to sections 6.4 and 6.5 in the *Tractatus*, would require a long and complicated discussion. But I am sure that looking at the earlier material and, perhaps, at its possible source in Weininger's writings may help us to understand what Wittgenstein is driving at. Perhaps his speaking of various riddles in 6.4312 and his claim that "*The riddle* does not exist" (6.5) are allusions to certain passages in Weininger's posthumous book, some of which I have already cited.

In this essay I have suggested a *Gedankenbewegung* in Weininger that may have influenced Wittgenstein, and I have also tried to indicate a few aspects of Weininger's work that might help explain why Wittgenstein found his books congenial. What I have not attempted to do is to summarize all the good stuff that can be found in Weininger's writings, which by itself would justify – if any justification were needed – why so many brilliant minds admired them in that remote age of innocence. True, in reading Weininger and Wittgenstein side by side one sometimes feels like a person trying to accommodate one of those sleek, and apparently timeless, objects designed by Loos and kindred spirits (like Engelmann and Wittgenstein) in the same room as some hefty pieces of obviously dated *Gründerzeit* furniture. But if you find it hard to combine them, you should remember that without those time-bound objects we should never have had these no doubt more gratifying works, which, after all, responded to earlier developments and may, in some barely visible crannies, show traces if not influences of what they responded to.

Notes

1. This is not meant as a criticism. What Weininger mostly did was take up other people's thoughts and process them – often until they were recognizable for what they really were (what Karl Kraus called "*zur Kenntlichkeit entstellt*").

2. This label has gained currency since the appearance of Carl E. Schorske's book, *Fin-de-Siècle Vienna: Politics and Culture*, London: Weidenfeld & Nicolson, 1980. If the index of Schorske's book can be relied on, Weininger is not mentioned at all. This fact is astonishing, especially if one remembers that some of the figures discussed at length (e.g. Schönberg and Kokoschka) were great and explicit admirers of Weininger.
3. Wittgenstein, *Culture and Value* (revised edition), edited by G. H. von Wright in collaboration with Heikki Nyman, with revisions by Alois Pichler, and translated by P. Winch. Oxford: Blackwell, 1998, 14–19 (remarks from 1931).
4. Ray Monk, *Ludwig Wittgenstein: The Duty of Genius*, London: Jonathan Cape, 1990, 23.
5. The first volume of Spengler's *Untergang des Abendlands* appeared in 1918, the second volume in 1922.
6. According to Roland Jaccard, editor of the French translation of *Geschlecht und Charakter*, there is "evidence that Wittgenstein attended Weininger's funeral in 1903." See Allan Janik, "Wittgenstein and Weininger," in Janik, *Essays on Wittgenstein and Weininger*, Amsterdam: Rodopi, 1985, p. 65. I am not sure if going to the funeral was in any way compatible with Wittgenstein's attendance at the *Realschule* in Linz. The story is repeated by Le Rider, in his *Der Fall Otto Weininger: Wurzeln des Antifeminismus und Antisemitismus*. Translated by Dieter Hornig, Vienna and Munich: Löcker, 1985, 46 (a revised and enlarged version of Le Rider's *Le Cas Otto Weininger*, Paris: Presses Universitaires de France), and, prefaced with a cautionary "allegedly," by Allan Janik and Hans Veigl, *Wittgenstein in Wien*, Vienna and New York: Springer, 1998, 213. I am sure that further repetition will one day turn the story into a fact.
7. Weininger's way of using the terms "Jew" and "Aryan" corresponds to his way of using the words "male" and "female": in Weininger's terminology, to characterize a person as "Jewish" does not mean that he or she is a Jew. It means, for instance, a lack of *verecundia* (truthfulness). See further, *Geschlecht und Charakter*, third edition, Vienna and Leipzig: Wilhelm Braumüller, 1904, note to chapter XIII, 427, quoting Schopenhauer's *Parerga und Paralipomena*, vol. II, S.132, and note to 445. In the latter, very important, note, Weininger writes that "'*Jewishness*' is a *category*, and hence cannot be reduced or specified any further; metaphysically, one may regard it as a *state prior to being*; introspectively, one does not get any further than to a point of inner ambiguity, lack of any kind of conviction, inability to love . . . and to make sacrifices." It is likely that this introspective report is meant to describe Weininger's own feelings about himself. In the main text (414) he says that the "anti-Semitism of a *Jew* demonstrates that no one who knows him – not even the Jew himself – will feel that there is something attractive about him; the anti-Semitism of an *Aryan* yields an insight which is no less significant, namely, that one must not confuse Jewish-*ness* and *Jews*. There are Aryans who are more Jewish than many a Jew, and there really are Jews who are more Aryan than certain Aryans . . . even *Richard Wagner*,

the *profoundest* anti-Semite, cannot be exonerated from being endowed with a pinch of Jewishness, which surfaces even in his art."

8. For Wittgenstein's use of the word "passionately," see my paper, "On a remark by Jukundus," to appear in a collection edited by Enzo De Pellegrin.
9. Of course, it is an open question whether Loos is mentioned in his capacity as a writer or as architect and designer or both. In the case of Sraffa we may presume that Wittgenstein refers to things said in conversation or, perhaps, to a *way* of saying things in conversation. Also in the case of some of the other authors (e.g. Frege and Russell) it may be that the influence intended by Wittgenstein is not only what was conveyed by their writings but perhaps comprises certain aspects of their personalities or their attitudes.
10. Letter to Russell, 16 August 1912, in Wittgenstein, *Ludwig Wittgenstein, Cambridge Letters: Correspondence with Russell, Keynes, Moore, Ramsey and Sraffa,* edited by Brian McGuinness and G. H. von Wright, Oxford: Blackwell, 1995, no. 5, 19.
11. A succinct and by and large convincing characterization is given by Brian McGuinness in his paper on the unsayable (here Spengler and Sraffa are, because of their chronological positions, left out of account). As McGuinness says, "there are traces of all the others in the *Tractatus* – Hertz for the whole picture theory, Schopenhauer for the attitude towards the world (where Wittgenstein attempts to accommodate both Schopenhauer's pessimism and Tolstoy's optimism), Frege and Russell for the treatment of logic and mathematics, Kraus for the refutation of positions from within the very language they are expressed in, Loos for a clear distinction between ornament and practical use (and hence for the idea that unnecessary units in a sign-language mean nothing), Weininger (in his 'Aphorismen') for a generally fatalistic attitude": see "The Unsayable: A Genetic Account," in McGuinness, *Approaches to Wittgenstein: Collected Papers,* London: Routledge, 2002, 162–3. McGuinness then proceeds to show that Wittgenstein was indebted to Boltzmann for his "paradoxically systematic rejection of theory" (166). To Spengler Wittgenstein claimed to owe the idea of family resemblance, and as far as Sraffa's influence is concerned, we can only speculate (see, again, McGuinness, 231–3, and also Wolfgang Kienzler, *Wittgensteins Wende zu seiner Spätphilosophie: 1930–1932,* Frankfurt am Main: Suhrkamp, 1997, 51–5; Kienzler also comments on Wittgenstein's relation to Weininger (40ff.). The extent to which I agree with McGuinness's description of Weininger's influence will become clear in the course of this paper.
12. Rush Rhees, ed., *Recollections of Wittgenstein,* Oxford: Oxford University Press, 1984, 91.
13. The passage containing the list of influences continues as follows: "Can one take Breuer and Freud as an example of Jewish reproductive thinking?"
14. See Friedrich Waismann, *Ludwig Wittgenstein and the Vienna Circle,* ed. Brian McGuinness, trans. Joachim Schulte and Brian McGuinness,

Oxford: Blackwell, 1979, 182ff. (9 December, 1931). According to Wittgenstein's own characterization the dogmatism of the *Tractatus* did not involve specific prejudices but the attitude expressing itself in the confident claim "that we can *discover* something wholly new" (183).

15. Weininger, *Geschlecht und Charakter*, "Vorwort zur ersten Auflage," v–vi. The editors of the present volume have called my attention to the important fact that many of the features I mean to emphasize in this paper can hardly be appreciated by readers of the hitherto sole available English translation of *Geschlecht und Charakter*. In this translation, I am told, Weininger's notes are simply left out, as are many of the less "scientific" passages in the body of the text. Even the subtitle, which I have discussed, is left untranslated. Relevant details are impossible to notice if one does not consult the German original. This can be seen from comparing my rendering of this quoted passage (a rendering which can no doubt be improved upon) with the text given in *Sex and Character*. "This investigation is not of details, but of principles. It does not despise the laboratory, although the help of the laboratories with regard to the deeper problems, is limited as compared to introspective analysis. An artist who wishes to represent the female form can construct a type without actually giving formal proof by a series of measurements" (New York: Heinemann, 1906, ix).
16. Allan Janik reports that he has counted "two hundred and thirty scientific works referred to by one hundred and sixty different authors as notes to the first part of *Sex and Character* (the first 89 pages)": Janik, *Essays on Wittgenstein and Weininger*, 68, n. 23. Janik continues by saying that there "can be little doubt that Weininger was aware of the most advanced researches in the biology and psychology of sex in his day." Le Rider, on the other hand, belongs to those who claim that Weininger "rests his claims on incomplete and in many cases obsolete evidence": Le Rider, *Der Fall Otto Weininger*, 69. I have no idea who is right, and I am not sure that it matters greatly.
17. Weininger, *Geschlecht und Charakter*, II, xi, 319–20.
18. Wittgenstein, *Ludwig Wittgenstein, Cambridge Letters*, 250.
19. Thus the truth yielded by disagreeing with the book does not follow automatically; only by way of seriously engaging with its reflections from a standpoint incompatible with that occupied by the book itself can one arrive at that truth.
20. See Wittgenstein, *Culture and Value*, especially 55–6 and 95–6 (remarks from 1946 and 1950, respectively).
21. Weininger, *Über die letzten Dinge*, fourth edition, Vienna and Leipzig: Wilhelm Braumüller, 1918, "Wissenschaft und Kultur," 169.
22. Wittgenstein, *Culture and Value*, 91, 19 January 1949.
23. Wittgenstein, *Tractatus Logico-Philosophicus*, trans. D. F. Pears and B. F. McGuinness, London: Routledge & Kegan Paul, 1971 (first edition 1961), 5.5421.

24. Weininger, *Geschlecht und Charakter,* II, v, p. 164–5. Starting from this criticism Weininger develops his program of "theoretical biography." Wittgenstein must have loved this notion; but I cannot see that it is connected with any special feature of his work. Rhees has a stimulating discussion of some related notions in his "Postscript," *Recollections of Wittgenstein,* 180–6.
25. Weininger, *Geschlecht und Charakter,* II, v, 176. Weininger compounds his derogatory judgment of Mauthner by adding a footnote to the effect that he wishes to apologize to Bacon's *manes* for mentioning his name in the same breath as that of Mauthner.
26. See Weininger, *Über die letzten Dinge,* "Wissenschaft und Kultur," 138–9. See also Wittgenstein, *Notebooks 1914–1916,* second edition, ed. G. H. von Wright and G. E. M. Anscombe, trans. G. E. M. Anscombe, Oxford: Blackwell, 1979, 23 May 1915: "There really is only one world soul, which I for preference call *my* soul and as which alone I conceive what I call the souls of others."
27. Brian McGuinness, Maria Concetta Ascher, and Otto Pfersmann, eds., *Wittgenstein Familienbriefe,* Vienna: Hölder-Pichler-Tempsky, 1996, 30, 18 November 1916.
28. Weininger, "Aphoristisches," in *Über die letzten Dinge,* 63; *Familienbriefe,* 83, probably 16 March 1921. Translations from *Über die letzten Dinge* are my own. The reason for this is that at the time of writing this paper it was impossible for me to lay my hands on a copy of Steven Burns's excellent translation. In the meantime, the editors of the present volume have kindly sent me copies of the relevant passages from the Burns translation. In essence, most of these renderings seem to agree with the results of my own efforts; and since I feel that it would be a shame to waste these results by simply replacing them with the Burns translations easily accessible to likely readers of this essay, I have decided to retain my renderings while adding page references to the Burns translation. For my readers this may have the beneficial effect of giving them an opportunity of comparing two translations, which may help them in figuring out Weininger's probable meaning. (In one or two places I have changed the wording of my original renderings in the light of Steven Burns's translations.)
29. Weininger "Das Zeitproblem," in *Über die letzten Dinge,* 101. What Weininger means by "dualism" is not obvious. Perhaps the following two passages help to see what he is driving at: "What cannot be grasped is the dualism in this world: *the motive of the Fall is the riddle,* the *ground* and *sense* and *end* of the fall from timeless being, from eternal life, into non-being, into sensual life, into mundane temporality." And: "Dualism lies in this: that we do not *create* the sensations we reflect on" from "Aphoristisches," in *Über die letzten Dinge,* 60 and 61.
30. Weininger, "Das Zeitproblem," 103.
31. Ibid., 104. The last sentence contains an untranslatable pun: "*Das Problem der Einsinnigkeit der Zeit ist die Frage nach dem Sinn des Lebens.*" The German word "*Sinn*" can mean both "direction" and "sense." The same ambiguity

is used by Wittgenstein when he says that "*Namen gleichen Punkten, Sätze Pfeilen, sie haben Sinn* – Names are like points; propositions like arrows – they have sense/direction" (*Tractatus*, 3.144).

32. Weininger, *Über die letzten Dinge*, 64: "The present is just as spaceless as it is timeless; and the object of man may be specified as the nothing-but-present [*Nurgegenwart*], as omnipresence. (By omnipresence one for the most part means only freedom from space instead of including in its meaning absorption of past and future, too, as well as of everything unconscious into the conscious present.) Our bounded consciousness ought to comprise the universe: only then will man be 'eternally young' and perfect."
33. Wittgenstein, *Notebooks 1914–1916*, 75, 8 July 1916; see also Wittgenstein, *Tractatus*, 6.4311.
34. See my paper "On a remark by Jukundus."
35. Weininger, *Geschlecht und Charakter*, II, viii, 236: "*Zum Genie wird der Mensch durch einen höchsten Willensakt, indem er das ganze Weltall in sich bejaht.*" It must be remembered that, according to Weininger, every man contains the seeds of genius in himself; he does not use the word with exclusive reference to the small group of people exemplified by Goethe, Beethoven, etc., even if these geniuses are the models that make us understand our own potential genius.
36. Weininger, *Geschlecht und Charakter*, II, iv, 177–8.
37. Weininger, "Wissenschaft und Kultur," in *Über die letzten Dinge*, 169.
38. Weininger, "Aphoristisches," in *Über die letzten Dinge*, 52–3.
39. Wittgenstein, *Notebooks 1914–1916*, 83, 7 December 1916.
40. See 6.45: "To view the world sub specie aeterni is to view it as a whole – a limited whole. Feeling the world as a limited whole – it is this that is mystical." Weininger has a number of interesting remarks on mysticism. The question of whether there are substantial parallels between his view of mysticism and Wittgenstein's would be an interesting one to discuss.

5

Uncanny Differences

Wittgenstein and Weininger as Doppelgänger

Daniel Steuer

In memory of my father
Herbert Steuer
Engineer and Inventor
1918–2001

Introduction: The Autobiographical Project and the *Doppelgänger*

The Weininger/Wittgenstein riddle is encapsulated in the concise, if enigmatic, formulation from Wittgenstein's letter to Moore where he claims that it is not necessary, or rather not possible to agree with Weininger, yet that "the greatness lies in that with which we disagree. It is his enormous mistake which is great. I.e. roughly speaking if you just add a '∼' to the whole book it says an important truth."[1] The nature of that negation, further qualified by "roughly speaking," is the object of much speculation. Yet it shouldn't be that way according to a passage from the *Big Typescript* section on "Philosophy": "Since everything lies open to view there is nothing to explain either. For what might not lie open to view is of no interest to us . . . The answer to the request for an explanation of negation is really: don't you understand it? Well, if you understand it, what is there left to explain, what business is there left for an explanation?"[2]

As the texts of both Weininger and Wittgenstein lie open to our view, does it follow that there is nothing to explain? Or rather is the feeling that there is a need for explanation due to our own system of categories and images which places too much intellectual space between Weininger and Wittgenstein? Is it troubling that one of the central figures in recent philosophy should admit to having been influenced by a second-, some would say third-class, thinker? Someone, to make matters worse, who seems to score extremely poorly with respect to late capitalist liberal values?

I shall try to understand the nature of Wittgenstein's truth-yielding negation – his metaphorical use of a logical sign – by looking for particular points of contact between Weininger and Wittgenstein: points which, roughly speaking, may serve as a hinge for the movement of the negation. For this is the way Wittgenstein describes, again metaphorically, the transition from his earlier to his later work: the prejudice concerning the formal unity of language, and of logic, as crystal clear is to be replaced by the network of language games, which bear more or less (or even, in some cases, no) family resemblance with each other. "One could say: The perspective of our investigation [*Betrachtung*] must be turned around, but with our actual need [*Bedürfnis*] providing the axis."[3] Note that the need remains the same, and that the change in perspective is not portrayed as something already accomplished. Rather, the turning around of the perspective is a continuous, or repetitive, task. Before this turn, words and their associated images may hold us captive because we perceive them as inevitable necessities. After this turn, they present no more than possibilities, which may also lead to new possibilities being perceived. This turn is the reason why, according to the later Wittgenstein, the problem of philosophy is to overcome a resistance of the will (or of feeling) rather than the intellect.

In what follows I shall assume that there is a psychological as well as a philosophical dimension to the role Weininger played for Wittgenstein. Especially after his so-called return to philosophy, Weininger served as a *Doppelgänger*, a double, that allowed him to turn around his philosophical perspective as well as to confront a part of himself with which he needed to come to terms. The term *Doppelgänger* is meant to emphasize that, uncannily, there must be something about Weininger that remained perfectly valid for Wittgenstein, while he must have rejected something else completely (something that was only too familiar to him). Weininger could only fulfill this role of the uncanny double because he shared Wittgenstein's "essential interest": to achieve clarity and peace of mind, to be awake and to be true to himself. But whereas this interest led to a fatal end in the case of Weininger (one he shared, we should remember, with three of Wittgenstein's brothers), Wittgenstein survived it.

One central point of contact between the two was the project of biography that Weininger alludes to at the end of his draft of "Zur Theorie des Lebens" (1902): "As a name for the one science which biology and psychology ultimately are, I suggest biography, because on the one hand it contains 'bios', and on the other it has a specific psychological sense today."[4] And in his chapter on "*Begabung und Gedächtnis*" (Endowment and Memory) in *Geschlecht und Charakter* he talks about an "*ontogenetic psychology* or *theoretical biography* which is destined sooner or later to displace today's science of the human mind."[5] Wittgenstein's idea that it should be possible to find reflected in the history of his spirit and of its moral concepts, together with an understanding of his personal situation, the specific movement of his philosophical thought is not identical with Weininger's "theoretical biography" but shares important features with it.[6] Both statements take biography as an enterprise that allows one to capture what must necessarily escape a reductive science of psychology or biology, and what lies beyond purely abstract philosophy. However, the task of Weininger's biography would be "to explore the unchanging laws of the *mental* development of the *individual*," and "to develop general points of view, to establish types" (*GuC*, 165). He entertained the idea that true genius – as the true *Gestalt* of an individual's *bios* – may eventually appear (albeit at the moment of death, see *GuC*, 164), whereas Wittgenstein was thinking about individual autobiography, and saw the life of the individual as incomplete, and sometimes ragged; he came to acknowledge that the autobiographical project, insofar as it aims to establish the complete truth about one's self, and to write objectively about oneself, was doomed to failure. There can be no complete recollection, no complete record of a life, no complete memory, and there is no uniform sense underlying a life.[7] And these insights are, of course, related to the turn in philosophical perspective already mentioned. This abolition of the idea of the ideal was not so much a failure but a liberation for Wittgenstein.

The seeming contradiction between Wittgenstein's philosophical anti-essentialism and his personal prejudices may disappear once we see that, in some sense, he held on to Weininger's theory of "double life" (*Theorie des zweifachen Lebens*), but transformed it into a double perspective on the self: a philosophical perspective *sub specie aeternitatis*, and an empirical perspective. The former excuses the deficiencies of the latter, so that the double perspective allowed Wittgenstein to alleviate, at least temporarily, his moral self-doubts.

Weininger's "Theory of Double Life": Genius or Criminal?

The essays collected in *On Last Things* are largely consistent with important parts of Weininger's philosophical argument in *Sex and Character*, and I shall base my exposition of his theory of double life on both publications. Five themes are of particular interest:

1. Weininger's theory of judgment;
2. his definitions of the criminal and of genius;
3. his notion of tragedy;
4. the quest for the self;
5. the place of logic and ethics

I shall then go on to discuss Wittgenstein's reevaluation of the arguments related to these five points.

Central to Weininger's thought is the absolute opposition between heteronomy (causality) and autonomy (freedom). In *Sex and Character* he juxtaposes "individuation" with "individuality," "recognition" with "memory," "lust" with "value," "sexual drive" with "love," "narrowness of consciousness" with "attention," and "instinct" with "will" (see *GuC*, 378, Table), finally asking: "What is the cause of this strange correspondence in spite of such a profound difference?" His answer is that one side is governed by causality from without, whereas the other binds itself to normative imperatives from within (*GuC*, 379). The resulting system of a metaphysical dualism suggests a discussion of my five themes, not one by one, but in pairs: first the theory of judgment and logic and ethics, then the quest for the self and the various definitions of the criminal and the genius and so on. Finally, "tragedy" will be the pinnacle, which we know that Wittgenstein (at least one side of him) came to reject: "In this world (my world) there is no tragedy & therefore nothing of all these infinities which produce, as their result, tragedy. Everything, so to speak, can be dissolved into the ether (of the world); there is no hardness. This means that hardness & conflict do not become something splendid but a *defect*" (*Culture and Value*, 12e, 1931; trans. mod.).

Theory of Judgment: Logic and Ethics

For Weininger, both logic and ethics were metaphysical as well as normative. The principle of identity, as the standard for all truth, cannot itself be a specific empirical truth: "The idea of a *standard* for experience, the *idea of truth*, cannot be situated in *experience* itself" (*GuC*, 247), just as "*The norm of thought cannot be situated in thought itself.* The principle of identity adds nothing to our knowledge. Rather than increasing a fortune, it provides the complete *foundation* for that fortune in the first place" (*GuC*, 200). The intelligible and autonomous self, in judging, has access to the principle of identity as logically, not just temporally, prior to any specific judgment, and this is the reason why it may give the dignity of identity to the empirical object thus judged, if and only if the judgment is guided by the idea of truth (the principle of identity) alone. Prior to any such empirical judgment, the principle of identity is applied to concepts and thus it secures their meaning: "*This* is the true function of the principle of contradiction and the principle of identity. *They constitute conceptuality*" (*GuC*, 201).

It is, thus, the use of concepts in empirical judgments that allows one to establish a stable reality. Concepts introduce form into the otherwise formless flow of perceptions.[8] They have thus the role of mediators between pure logic and the empirical world. The individual empirical subject is the arena in which this mediation takes place, the individual metaphysical subject is responsible for this process of mediation.[9] Only the metaphysical self can transform the indefinite object into a definite object, one that is no longer in danger of falling prey to accidental circumstances of perception and arbitrary judgment in the stream of life. The metaphysical self thereby gives, in one step, both itself and the object an absolute identity and value; or rather, this would be its proper task.

Two limitations are important in this context. First, as there is no purely logical thought free of psychological components, the ideal identity cannot be achieved in the empirical world (that would be "*the miracle*"; *GuC*, 201). Second, the system of metaphysical oppositions is beyond proof. In his essay on science and culture Weininger says: "Nothing is further from it than to raise even the slightest doubt about the absolute logicality of the universe. It is just as much permeated by its logicality as it is by its absolute ethicality. What I want to stress is that neither can be *known*, but only *believed*."[10]

Definitions (Criminal, Genius, Science, Culture, Religion, Philosophy): The Quest for the Self

In believing in a judgment, the believer commits himself to the objectivity of the judgment. He "vouch[es] for a problematic judgment" ("Science and Culture," 115): "Belief involves a gift on my part; I give the judgment in which I believe something of me. I give myself to it. . . . The believer, at bottom, can only believe in himself" ("Science and Culture," 122). But this belief in himself, in turn, rests on belief in the principle of identity. The metaphysical self, in an act beyond proof or demonstration, decides between lawfulness or chaos by applying the principle of identity with more or less discipline and rigor both to himself and to objects.

To make a judgment is to affirm a state of affairs as objective truth. To make a judgment is to commit oneself to a version of reality. Such affirmation and commitment distinguish what Weininger calls "problems" from "tasks." The scientist of his day he saw as merely attacking and solving tasks, never problems. A scientist "does not like questions, is not acquainted with them; at most for him the question is a means of forcing an answer, and he does not give answers, because inner clarification is not a moral need for him. Rather, the fundamental form of his answer is triumphant irony about the question" ("Science and Culture," 140). In other words, the scientist suffers from a loss of personal involvement with the truth; he has no metaphysical urge. He aims to establish universal causality, functionalism, un-freedom, and does not know that "Problems without tasks are pointless; tasks without problems are groundless" ("Science and Culture," 134). As opposed to a science that has cut itself off from final questions, culture and philosophy not only remain in touch with them, they are defined by this orientation.

Yet Weininger does more than just criticize science. At the very end of his essay, he correlates science, philosophy, and culture in a way that blurs the borders between science and philosophy. Philosophy is defined by:

1. the element of mysticism (the urge towards the absolute);
2. the systematic or theoretical element (the urge towards architectonics);
3. the element of knowledge (the postulate of, or demand for, deducibility and demonstration).

Philosophy is of cultural value because it is science, and because science is transcendental. Science itself, however, is only culturally valuable insofar as it is philosophical, i.e. does not set out from the start to prove theorems of a distinct philosophical system, but rather, in the spirit of the researcher himself, intentionally stands in a continuous and inextricable, devoted relation to the riddle of the world ("Science and Culture," 146).

I conclude from this rather tangled knot that philosophy without science becomes mysticism, that is, a form of religion, and ceases to be social and public. Science without philosophy becomes dogmatic empiricism, and as such is detached from human life. The term "culture" stands for the necessary translation between the individual and private struggle with problems and the empirical and public creation and fulfillment of tasks. Behind Weininger's idea of culture lies again his theory of judgment; not to be conscious of the judgments that are necessary for a particular state of affairs to exist is immoral. The purely empirical facts on which a form of life is based amount to no more than a machinery, a form maybe, but not a life.

Weininger's conception of the criminal and of the genius follow from that: "The criminal does not evaluate. He does not even evaluate himself, for he does not try to affirm an ego which would stand above his mental events; he is not self-observing, and lives unconsciously. Because he evaluates nothing, judges nothing, so too he does not evaluate himself; he has given up the freedom of judgment."[11] Dryly defined, crime is "the impulse towards functionalism;" expressed more vividly, "it is the need to kill God; it is supreme, universal negation" ("Metaphysics," 102). The intention to put the blame on others (God) is criminal (murder).[12]

The genius, on the other hand, "*lives in a conscious connection with the whole universe. Thus genius alone is the really divine element in humans*" (*GuC*, 222). There are two necessary conditions for genius, and only humans possess them: memory and apperception (see *GuC*, 147f.). Through apperception humans can incorporate what they experience, their perceptions, into personal memory. The genius remembers what is significant to his life and establishes an integrated version of it. This differs from a pure memorizing of facts (the methodological error of experimental psychology). The memory of a perfect genius would enable him to write the perfect autobiography.

From the advent of the self – the moment when a person first recognizes himself as an undivided consciousness – derives the core of a *Weltanschauung*, that is, a form of thought which perceives the world as a whole, even if some of the details remain to be filled in (see *GuC*, 216f.). The person now lives with a soul as a "hyper-empirical reality" (*GuC*, 218).

The possibility of becoming a genius is ever-present in every human being. It is not a matter of acquiring a new quality, but of "a supreme act of the will," the decision to affirm "the whole universe in himself" (*GuC*, 236), and thus to reach a stage of universal apperception.[13] The last obstacle the genius has to overcome on the way towards salvation is vanity, a theme that greatly occupies Wittgenstein. And the form of vanity typical for the genius is self-directed. However, it usually leads to vanity toward others as well, so that the wish to impress oneself and the wish to impress others fight against each other in a genius (see *GuC*, 226).

The weak point in Weininger's argument is that both the genius and the criminal are the product of "an incomprehensible, spontaneous renunciation [or affirmation] of individual value" ("Metaphysics," 98f.). Although these spontaneous acts of the will are, in the last instance, beyond comprehension, it is the battle surrounding this decision that constitutes the tragic structure of human life.[14]

Tragedy

Weininger's idea of the tragic can be elaborated from his criticism of Friedrich Schiller. Schiller's dramatic characters, he claims, have no inner personal past, and his plays portray the question of guilt not as something inherent in the individual, but as dependent on the constellation of the stars and their chance relation to human affairs; and "chance is absolutely *un-tragic.*"[15] According to Weininger, Schiller has no inkling of "the destiny within us" ("Characterology," 72), "the enemy *in one's own breast,*" he only knows the "meanness of the *external world*" and "the nasty neighbour" ("Characterology," 71). In Schiller's *Weltanschauung* there is no real conflict between the empirical and the hyper-empirical self: "his worldview is as little tragic as his tragedies" because he turns the resignation to which the critique of reason leads into a superficial and smug acceptance of the immanent as sufficient ("Characterology," 73). In short: "The limited and the unlimited in humans are not divided here; there is, here, no battle between the world of the mind and the world of the senses" ("Characterology," 71).

This battle is the ultimate meaning of tragedy for Weininger; it is the unresolvable conflict between the empirical and the metaphysical, as it appears in the irreducible form it takes in the life of an individual.

Even if Weininger's final verdict – "In hating Schiller, journalistic modernism only hates itself" ("Characterology," 73) – seems harsh, it does put a finger on an aspect of Schiller's intellectual style. While the *Letters on the Aesthetic Education of Man,* for instance, set out a utopian scheme for the reconciliation of the intellect and the senses, they have, however, no real sense of urgency about them. The balance between all human faculties, to be achieved through nurturing what Schiller calls "*Spieltrieb*" (the urge to play), and the freedom from one-sided determination, are presented effortlessly and without any sense of tension; as if the battle was already won, the utopia fulfilled.

Contrary to this, the acceptance of the "colossal tragedy of knowing" ("Science and Culture," 140 – "*die kolossale Tragödie des Erkennens*") and of judgment, the acceptance of guilt, and the striving for culture ("Science and Culture," 133f.), and the will to become a genius, despite the universal responsibility and the pain it entails (*GuC,* 236f.), are the ethical tasks of humankind for Weininger. The attempt to fulfill these tasks takes courage. "Courage is the self-confidence of the higher life." And "whoever is fully courageous, . . . is pure and guiltless" ("Science and Culture," 126).

Courage, as the opposite of vanity, will play a role for Wittgenstein as well. He pondered how the soul can be moved by vain thoughts (*Culture and Value*, 41; 1939–40), and his answer to the question of how one pays for valuable thoughts was: "I believe: with courage" (*Culture and Value*, 60e; 1946). In 1940 he defines genius thus: "One might say: 'Genius is *courage in one's talent*'" (*Culture and Value*, 44e). But there is an important twist in Wittgenstein's appropriation of this moral terminology. Whereas for Weininger it takes courage to strive towards becoming a genius, for Wittgenstein it takes courage to be a criminal; that is, to be someone who is honest enough to accept his own distance from genius, and who follows his intuition rather than a preconceived ideal of man or of himself. In February 1937 he writes that he believes the highest form of life must be the one guided by intuition alone, but that he lacks the courage to lead it, and hence he "must hope that this will not kill, *that is*, will not make me unhappy for eternity" (*DB*, 87f.).

The Form of Weininger's Thought
"+" Hyper-empirical ideal/... Empirical Continuum... /Hyper-empirical ideal "-"
The difficulty with Weininger's many dualisms, such as genius/criminal and man/woman, is that he provides no way of imagining, let alone explaining, transitions from the oppositional extremes to the continuum of mixtures that lie in between. The result, in each case, is a hyper-empirical opposition between a positive and a negative pole (or hyper-empirical idea), and, entirely separated from it, the empirical continuum they organize. The separation means that this structure is immune to criticism, and it is this structure that Wittgenstein, as I shall argue, negates. The immunity of the structure also protects those factual parts of Weininger's argument, which he can only postulate, but not explain further: the renunciation or not of the will, the fact that natural skill and sex are not inherited, and seem to "come into being, as it were, spontaneously" (*GuC*, 144), that "true love," always a sign of genius, is "entirely a matter of chance" (*GuC*, 154). In other words, the immunity of the structure also allows for the prejudice of the content, including the arbitrary evaluation of masculinity and femininity. Hence, Weininger's thought rests on fatalism, not on tragedy, insofar

as the incomprehensible renunciation (or affirmation) of the will can only be accepted as a fact.

> Wittgenstein's Negation: "I Cannot and Should Not Judge"
> ...x...x... Empirical Continuum...x...x...
> (containing relative a prioris established by ways of comparing and acting)

What Wittgenstein negated was not any of the content of Weininger's book, but the form of Weininger's thought. Within that form, the negation of any of his claims obviously would not yield a result that is more reasonable than the original proposition. What, then, could it mean to negate this form of thought? In the recently published notebooks, *Denkbewegungen*, there is a passage in which Wittgenstein talks about a cultural sea change:

> It was characteristic of the theoreticians of the past cultural period to want to look for the *a priori* where it wasn't to be found. Or should I say, it was characteristic for the past cultural period that it created the concept of the *a priori*.
>
> For it would never have created this concept, if it had seen the situation [*die Sachlage*] the way that we see it. (And in that case, a great – that is, an important – error would have been lost to the world.) But in truth it is impossible to think about it in this way, because this concept was rooted in the culture as a whole. (DB, p. 45; between 6.5.–12.10.1931)

"A great... error would have been lost to the world" echoes the enormous mistake that is great from the letter to Moore (written around the same time; 23 August 1931), and the term 'a priori' in this passage can clearly be related to the Weiningerian dichotomy of hyperempirical ideal and empirical continuum. Wittgenstein is not quite clear whether this is just another perspective or a false perspective, but he is unequivocal about two things: first, that we don't choose the perspective (it is rooted in the culture), and second, that his own perspective excludes the concept of the a priori in the old sense. However, the beginning of the quotation suggests that there is still something similar; a kind of a priori may be found, but somewhere else. Let us call the Weininger a priori absolute, and ascribe the concept of a relative a priori to Wittgenstein.

Immediately before these two paragraphs Wittgenstein discusses the concepts of comedy and tragedy as two ideal types. This passage can be read as a commentary on Weininger's criticism of Schiller:

The opposition between comedy and tragedy has, in the past, always been worked out as something which divides the concept of dramatic space *a priori*. And thus astonishing remarks were made, e.g. that comedy deals with types whereas tragedy deals with individualities. In reality, comedy and tragedy are not in that kind of opposition where the one fills that part of dramatic space which is left out by the other.... Rather, they are two of many possible types of drama, and they just seemed to be the only possible ones for a particular – and past – culture (*DB*, 45).

In other words, Weininger's empirical continuum becomes Wittgenstein's empirical space, and the hyper-empirical, absolute a priori becomes a relative a priori established through the choice of a standard of comparison from within the empirical. Thus, in some sense an a priori can still be found, but not where Weininger had been looking for it.

The biographical context of these remarks is Wittgenstein's relationship with Marguerite Respinger, of which he notes he can foresee a tragedy (*DB*, 42). Two years earlier, in 1929, Wittgenstein apparently had felt quite immune to the perils of love: "Tragically holding on, defiantly holding on to a tragic situation in love always seems to me quite alien to my ideal. Does that mean my ideal is feeble? I cannot *& should not judge*" (*Culture and Value*, 3f.). The 1931–32 and 1936–37 notebooks amply illustrate the transformation of personal reflections into philosophical statements, and the following quotation at the same time indicates that the relation between life and philosophy was not a one-way street for Wittgenstein:

As in philosophy, so in life we are tempted by false analogies between ourselves and what others do, or should be allowed to do. And in life, too, there is only one remedy [*Mittel*] against this temptation: to listen to the quiet voices which tell us that the situation here, after all, is not the situation there [*daß es sich hier doch nicht so verhält wie dort*] (*DB*, 48, between 6 May and October 1931).

The life of the individual is not excluded from the empirical play of relative a prioris, precisely because it is unique. The logical and ethical problem of the individual is not, as in Weininger, the tragical structure created between hyper-empirical and empirical self, but the uniqueness of the situation for each individual.

When Wittgenstein observes, "The ultimate ground (I mean the last depth) of my vanity I will, anyway, not uncover here" (*DB*, 48), he is still thinking within the framework of Weininger's project of the (auto)biography of the genius. But vanity, now, is no longer a deficiency that stands in the way toward the absolute; it is the tendency to cling on to something of limited value as if it possessed absolute value, and, as a result of this tendency, not to follow one's intuitions (I will return to this in the epilogue). Wittgenstein, personally, thought one should have an ideal, and remain aware of the fact that one falls short of it (*DB*, 73, 28 January 1937). To insist on the personal ideal was for him a medicine against vanity, and his insistence on the incomparable uniqueness of each life, at the same time, meant the dissolution of tragedy. The impossibility of writing one's own life thus results from the fact that there is no objective method by which to measure the tension between the reality of someone's life and his or her ideal. All the ideal does is indicate to the individual his or her level of vanity. Through this double perspective – essentialist on the personal level, anti-essentialist on the public, or social, level – Wittgenstein tried to measure his distance from himself. It did not alleviate all moral self-doubt, but it provided a necessary balance to the ongoing temptations of Weiningerian absolutism. Before I return to this theme of an ongoing struggle, I take a look at Wittgenstein's aesthetic theory of judgment, and his ideas on the foundations of logic and mathematics.

An Aesthetic Theory of Judgment

In "On the Scientific Justification of a Conceptual Notation" (1882), Frege compared two different states of perception and the subsequent processes of sensation formation: one in the absence of signs, the other in the presence of signs. In the absence of signs perceptions stir further sensations from memory (*Erinnerungsbilder*) without limitation. Thought has no control over the free play of association. Once a sensual sign is attached to a sensation, this sensation becomes a fixed center to which thought can hold on. With the help of signs we can then actualize what is not present, what is invisible, even what is purely abstract:

> Thus we penetrate step by step into the inner world of our sensations [*Vorstellungen*], and we move about there at will by using the sensual itself in order to free ourselves of its compulsion. Signs have the same importance for thought which the invention to use the wind to sail against the wind possessed in seafaring. Thus, let no one despise signs! A lot depends on the appropriate choice of signs.[16]

This image of sensual signs necessary for intellectual orientation within the empirical flow of sensations can easily be seen to resemble Weininger's theory of the "henids" (*Heniden*), those initial, vague and hazy mental entities in which feeling and thought are still undifferentiated, and which have to be developed into clear and distinct ideas and thoughts.[17] In both cases the ideal is one of exactness within the transcendental Kantian project. The border between thought and experience, between the logical form of thought and the empirical flow of impressions, between mind and world, is to be determined exactly. It is this ideal of exactness, still accepted in Wittgenstein's early work, that he attacks, and undermines, in his later work.

One expression of this criticism is the variation of the Fregean imagery in the remarks on certainty. Using examples from Moore's article "A Defence of Common Sense" – "These are my two hands," "I was never far from the surface of the earth," and so on – as his starting point, Wittgenstein circles the question of how we can be certain of those judgments of which we are, as a matter of fact, absolutely certain. The examples are slowly reinterpreted by Wittgenstein until, finally, they appear as sentences that "play a peculiar logical role" within the system of empirical sentences.[18] They are sentences that not only Moore can be sure about. We all can, but – without knowing how (*On Certainty*, s. 84). The important point here is that Wittgenstein again and again realizes that he has no method to categorically distinguish between such sentences and others where a doubt about their status is perfectly possible. There is no sharp border between those empirical sentences that can be looked at as hypothetical and those that can't (*On Certainty*, s. 52).

Wittgenstein also rejects the recurrent temptation to see certain sentences, for whatever reason, as absolutely foundational for his system of beliefs, his "*Weltbild*."[19] There are no sentences that reflect natural laws or the nature of all human judgment so as to be unconditionally excluded from doubt. The picture his convictions and beliefs paint of the world remains in motion: "Not as if I could describe the system of these convictions. But my convictions form a system, a building" (*On Certainty*, s.102).

There is also no hierarchical relation between certain sentences and the conclusions drawn with their help: "The system is not so much the point of departure [*Ausgangspunkt*] for the arguments, but the medium in which they live [*Lebenselement*]" (*On Certainty*, s. 105). And: "It is not that individual axioms seem plausible to me, but a system within which conclusions and premises mutually support *each other*" (*On Certainty*, s. 142).

We learn to make judgments against the background of such systems, and we "do not learn the praxis of empirical judgments by learning rules; we are taught certain *judgments* and their connection with other judgments. *A totality* [*Ein Ganzes*] of judgments is made plausible to us" (*On Certainty*, s. 140). "When we begin to believe certain things, we do not start by believing individual sentences, but a whole system of sentences. (The light, by and by, dawns over the whole.)" (*On Certainty*, s. 141)

The picture of the landscape of concepts and of the judgments made with their help that emerges from Wittgenstein's later writings amounts to an aesthetic theory of judgment. The basis of the order we introduce into our experience is the act of making a comparison, and whether this is an intellectual comparison or based on perception, it involves the capacity to "see" similarities. This is still, just like the judgment in Weininger, at the same time an ethical and a logical act insofar as our decision to accept certain comparisons decides what we consider to be the nature of certain phenomena, and hence it decides how we treat them. But with the nature of things thus established, the order introduced into experience remains flexible.[20] The hyper-empirical ideals as endpoints have disappeared: ideals are standards of comparison taken from within the empirical space.

Logic and Ethics: The Philosopher as Criminal

In his transitional phase Wittgenstein also gave up the picture of an absolute and abstract foundation for logic and mathematics: "Logic and mathematics do not *rest* on axioms; just as a group does not rest on the elements and operations which define it. It is therefore a mistake to consider the self-evidence of the basic laws as a criterion of correctness in logic. A foundation which rests on nothing is a bad foundation."[21] The imagery here is that of an organic self-referentiality (as in a mathematical group, where all parts mutually support each other and hence the whole), and, in principle, it is the same imagery that we find in the remarks on certainty some twenty years later. Within a system or calculus, there is no hierarchical dependency between sentences. Axioms and first principles take on the role of representatives of a system, rather than its foundation. And, most importantly, the elements of a system have their meaning only within that system. There is no meta-system that would integrate all systems of logic or mathematics (or any other kind of systems). Wittgenstein's finitism, his antiformalism, his views on the nature of a mathematical proof, and his talk of the mathematicians' superstition concerning contradictions all follow from or are at least closely related to this change of imagery.[22] It is no longer isolated axioms or propositions that carry the weight of evidence for truthfulness; the systems must display their meaning as a totality.

Independent of a specific system (or specific language), basic principles, such as the principle of identity, are simply meaningless. Whereas Weininger used the principle of identity and of the excluded middle as a foundation for his argument, Wittgenstein negates these principles and their role as foundational: "The law of identity, for example, seemed to be of fundamental importance. But now the proposition that this 'law' is nonsense has taken over this importance" ("Philosophy," 169).

The philosopher should behave like one of Weininger's criminals: he should adapt to any environment, to any system. Because he is, in this sense, an intellectual opportunist he can avoid the mistake of expecting something from one system that only holds true in another, or of looking for a truth that would be independent of any system.

What becomes foundational, the basis of the order we introduce into our experience by creating systems, is the faculty to form concepts by way of comparison: "The limits of the empirical are not unconfirmed assumptions, or assumptions intuitively known to be correct; rather, they are [established by certain ways] of comparing and acting" (*BGM,* 387, my translation; *RFM,* 387). "The limit of the empirical is the *formation of concepts*" (*BGM,* 237, my translation; *RFM,* 237).

The Dissolution of Tragedy

Wittgenstein was looking for a way to sail with what he considered to be our reasonably reliable language against the essentialism of language, and against essentialist views of knowledge and certainty. His negation of Frege and Weininger allowed him to challenge philosophical essentialism while maintaining a kind of absoluteness, or nonrelativism, on the personal level.[23] "Think of the words lovers use," Wittgenstein says: they certainly cannot be exchanged for any other words. They are irreplaceable gestures. As such they are learned, they take their importance not from corresponding to natural facts or from being part of our nature. The gesture "is the result of education, but it is *assimilated*," and this is not pure mythology because, at the end of the day, the "characteristics of assimilation are that I want to use this word, and that I would rather use no word at all than one forced upon me, and similar reactions."[24] The personal choice of words, the individual style, has nothing arbitrary about it; still, it may change. The tendency in the later Wittgenstein to emphasize that we make up and change the rules as we go along also puts his earlier fixation of character into perspective. A born aristocrat may sink, a street bum may rise.[25] What is and what is not a lie about oneself depends on the present state of character, and thus he can finally write in 1950: "It is not unheard of that someone's character may be influenced by the external world (Weininger). For that only means that, as we know from experience, people change with circumstances" (*Culture and Value,* 95e). And in his diary of 1937 we find the following remark relating to the preface of the *Philosophical Investigations*: "It is possible after all that, following several coherent chapters of my work, I am only capable of writing, *and should* only be writing, scattered remarks. I am, after all, a human being & dependent on how things go. But it is difficult for me to really accept that" (*DB*; 208).

The ethical rigorism of Weininger's quest for genius is thus replaced by simple acceptance of the self for what it is at present, good or bad, low or high. Self-deception, or vanity, remains the only danger, and the only obstacle on the path toward clarity and peace. And into his battle against vanity, Wittgenstein at times reintroduced all his capacity for self-torture and self-doubt. But in principle he now had a double perspective, which was useful against this tendency. In his philosophical perspective every life and every possibility has to be accepted (a nonjudgmental perspective), and from this perspective the prejudice and imbalance of individual existence (which constitutes the second perspective) is no longer tragic, it is just an empirical fact: life is judgmental. It seems to me that this form of detachment was necessary for Wittgenstein's psychological survival. Still, the a priori that enabled him to carry out his negation of Weininger is perhaps just as uncanny as the double himself.

Conclusion: Wittgenstein's Double Perspective: General Relativism versus Personal Fundamentalism

It is most likely that the tension between Wittgenstein's perspective in philosophy and his attitude toward his own life was never fully resolved. And there is no inconsistency in this. It is one thing to say there are many possible lives – and I should not judge. There is not one ideal way to live one's life, no ideal that would be binding for everyone, including the ideal of "having an ideal." And it is another thing to say it is therefore perfectly acceptable for someone to feel that he should have an ideal, and then not to follow it at all. What emerges from the tension in Wittgenstein is a relativist ethics as far as the differences between individuals are concerned, and a fundamentalist ethics as far as one's allegiance, or commitment, to an ideal is concerned, including the ideal of "not having an ideal." But there can be no universal ethics: "All that philosophy can do is to destroy idols. And that means not creating a new one – for instance as in 'absence of an idol'" ("Philosophy," 171).

What Wittgenstein, however, did not consider was the possibility that inconsistency may be fundamental to human nature, despite his willingness to see all thought to be, ultimately, based on a fixed image that can neither be justified nor refuted (this is transcendental resignation, in Weininger's words). The impartial philosopher, the one who does not reject any possible image out of hand, must, of course, take into consideration that some people's perspective on the world is entirely different from his own: "how can I know, what I would imagine as the only acceptable image of the structure of the world [*Weltordnung*], if I lived differently, totally different. I cannot judge this. A different life moves different images into the foreground, makes completely different images necessary" (*DB*, 75). The one last difference that remains, then, may be the one between the impartial (I am tempted to say "hyper-impartial," in order to express the negation of Weininger's hyper-empirical ideal) philosopher, who accepts all options as possible solutions to the problem of life,[26] and the cynical philosopher, who also pretends to practice unlimited tolerance, but without any feeling that there might be a problem of life other than how to gain his own advantage. There is an excruciatingly thin line between the two. Wittgenstein's Norwegian diaries make it clear that he belonged to the first category; in them, among other things, he is testing the possibility of the religious solution to the problem of life – as if his soul were a laboratory for metaphysical experiments: "Think, e.g., more of (your own) death, – & it would be strange, if that way you wouldn't get to know new ideas, new areas of language" (*DB*, 76). Five days later, Wittgenstein has followed his own advice, and notes (in coded script): "I often think of death now, & how I will master the distressing moment of death [*Todesnot*]" (*DB*, 77).

Thinking of the moment of death, Wittgenstein relapses into a Weiningerian mode of absolute possibilities. You may either tell yourself: "Now it is too late." Or you may say: "Now it is done." These two extreme possibilities are related to one of the mightiest tools of organized religion: the promise of heaven and the fear of hell. And Wittgenstein, straightaway, corrects himself: "I think that different grades must exist in this case as well" (*DB*, 81). This takes the urgency out of the image; it is now no longer a question of complete failure or success. The structure is no longer tragic, the tension is released. Almost. In the next sentence Wittgenstein switches to coded script: "But I myself, where am I? How far from what is good & how close to the low end!" (*DB*, 81) At least, this is how he feels in this particular moment in 1937.

Wittgenstein's later philosophy was a permanent battle against moral self-destruction. The remedy for Weiningerian introspective rigorism was the public and aesthetic nature of meaning and of all forms of judgment. It kept him alive, and it led to a new philosophical method. Therefore it is justified to say that philosophy and biography in Wittgenstein were indeed inseparable. His ultimate criterion for the value of a thought was whether it came from the heart. And this was not a criterion beyond logic. The solution he suggests for the paradox of the liar is: "Maybe we would say of someone like him, that he does not mean the same thing by 'true' and 'lying' as we do. Maybe he means something like: what he says flickers; or nothing really comes straight from the heart" (*BGM*, 255, my translation: *RFM*, 255). And what comes straight from the heart, and what doesn't, we can only decide "in the flow of life."

In his Norwegian notebook, his laboratory for metaphysical experiments, Wittgenstein wrote that he cannot accept that someone who does not believe in Jesus cannot be saved. This was the limit of his Christian faith – on that particular day. As he adds, he may be able to believe it at some point in the future. He compares this situation to the belief in the existence of witches: some ages believed in them, others didn't. We, at present don't, but the belief may return. Did Wittgenstein become a Christian? Maybe, and maybe he lost that faith again. In Wittgenstein, all that is left is the empirical continuum within the experience of the individual. Not only did he not want to spare his readers the effort to think (as he says in his preface to the *Philosophical Investigations*), he also left them to find their own certainties.

In order to do so, we have to listen to the quiet voices coming straight from the heart – an antimodern as much as an antipostmodern exercise. What hovers over Wittgenstein's philosophical work is a commitment to authenticity – but unlike Weininger's duty to oneself, this commitment, in his later work, is no longer based on abstract principles. It is based on our aesthetic faculty of judgment and of perception, both of the world and of ourselves.

Epilogue: Spirit and *Doppelgänger*

It is a great temptation to try and express spirit (*Culture and Value*, 11e, 1930; trans. mod.).

The task of philosophy is to reassure spirit concerning meaningless questions. Whoever has no inclination towards such questions does not need philosophy (*DB*, 65).

Spirit

When looked at in isolation, Wittgenstein's remark on the movement of his thought and the history of his spirit does not allow us to decide whether he thought of a parallelism, of influence (mutual or of one on the other), between his life and his philosophy or of a common source for both.[27] But in any case, his model of spirit is not necessarily associated with religion; it fits in well with Hamilton's interpretation of the *Bild*-theory, based on the principles of projective geometry. Given the projective rules one "can visualize relations that cannot be verbalized."[28] This turns the mysticism of the saying/showing dichotomy into problems of technical and artistic design. I would like to suggest that Wittgenstein's talk of spirit ("*Geist*") implies this model: we construct our own as well as other people's selves from expressive behavior – not once and for all, but in a continuous process of communication with ourselves and others, a kind of mutual, and often self-reflective, reading.[29] Sleepiness and wakefulness of spirit seem to indicate the degree of willingness to engage in this authentically, that is, with the highest possible attentiveness and accuracy. Failure to do so results in a kind of living death, characterized by a loss of radiance (*DB*, 199),[30] and by superstition (*DB*, 194); the latter understood as the magical employment of words (also in the process of reading) whereby reason becomes impure. With respect to eternal bliss, he notes: "if I have a right to think about it, then what I think must stand in an exact relation to my life; otherwise, what I think is either nonsense, or my life is in danger" (*DB*, 203f.).[31]

In accordance with the "moral imperative" of attentiveness and authenticity – speak and think always in accordance with the reality of your own being – Wittgenstein reproaches himself for his sleepiness.[32] If a sleepy person wakes up for a moment he is at once under the delusion of grandeur and genius. Here being awake seems to mean being in touch with the reality of our being without the veil of psychological and logical obstructions that usually dull our sense of it, in short: it means self-knowledge (*DB*, 91). The genius of this mode of being is not so much Weininger's idea of perfect recollection, but Wittgenstein's ideal of perfect presence of mind as a prerequisite for the purity of thought.

Yet spirit, the way Wittgenstein employs the term, has similarities with both Weininger's hyper-empirical soul and Kierkegaard's notion of the self. When Wittgenstein prays that spirit won't leave him, this can be interpreted as "may I not lose myself in despair, in theatricality."[33] Theatricality includes using expressions that belong to another, possibly higher, form of life than one's own. Honest self-observation (the self accepting itself for what it is, without vanity interfering) implies the permanent testing of the language used by the empirical self against his own spirit, as well as the individual publicly staking himself in making a claim for community. In both cases the ultimate standard of comparison is the "straight from the heart," or, in other words, whether or not the use of words is a true reflection of the speaker's spirit at the time. This is why Wittgenstein's highest ideal is to live by inspiration ("*Eingebung*") alone (*DB*, 194). When Wittgenstein tells himself that he is alone, that "there is no one here," this does not necessarily give expression to a paradoxical encounter with the higher,[34] it might simply be seen as an attempt to polish any traces of vanity (before a possible God as well as an inner spectator) off his inner vision, and this inner vision – devoid of distortions – could be understood as the absolute endpoint of any analysis, and at the same time as the basis for a positivism without any materialist or physicalist prejudice.

What is finally left of the notion of duty to oneself in the later Wittgenstein is total honesty in the face of whatever the inner vision may reveal. This ideal is threatened by any form of pretense, and by any desire to give permanence to what is only transitory ("*eitel*"), and by what he calls "ethical artistry."[35] Wittgenstein believed that it is important to live the right (authentic) life in order to have a good death, and, vice versa, the certainty of empirical death should compel you to lead your life in an authentic fashion. His concern is "to see reality as it is," including, of course, in the first place the reality of one's self (*DB*, 176). The thought of giving away even what is most treasured, be it a sweater or one's philosophical writings, must be acted upon if it occurs.[36]

Doppelgänger

There are two remarks by Wittgenstein on the theme of *Doppelgänger*; both relate to Adelbert Chamisso's *Peter Schlemihls wundersame Geschichte*: "Again and again I think that I am, or should be, a kind of Peter Schlemihl & if this name means as much as unlucky devil, this means that he is meant to become happy through external misfortune" (*DB*, 45, 1930).[37] In *Culture and Value*, he qualifies the kind of "external misfortune" he has in mind: "The story of Peter Schlemihl should, it seems to me, go like this: He makes over his soul to the Devil for money. Then he repents it & now the Devil demands his shadow as ransom. But Peter Schlemihl still has a choice between giving the Devil his soul or sacrificing along with his shadow life in community with human beings" (*Culture and Value*, 21e, 1931). Rank's interpretation also stresses the opposition between a common and vain social existence and a self-sufficient existence for one's higher self (Rank, 58), but Wittgenstein refuses to see the dilemma between soul and social life as tragic. As he finds himself losing his self whenever he seeks happiness in company (and he stresses his dependence on being liked by others more than once), he is forced to withdraw from seeking happiness externally, and instead to pursue happiness internally by seeking total honesty with himself; hence his concentration on decency as absence of vanity, of any form of theatricality, toward himself, which, if achieved, would mean salvation of his metaphysical self, and allow him a "good death."[38] The clarity Wittgenstein wanted to achieve would have coincided with him living by intuition alone, yet this clarity became impossible for him once he engaged in too much social and empirical life. In this form, Weininger's dichotomy between heteronomy and autonomy continued to haunt him; it was the conceptual framework within which he interpreted his social performance. In the empirical muddle of everyday relationships he couldn't keep up the close scrutiny of what these relationships really claimed from him, how far his authentic commitment to them really reached, and thus whether or not he behaved authentically or immorally.

In the classical psychoanalytic interpretation the shadow or double stands for death and fear of death, as well as representing a regression to the state of primary narcissism, total love of oneself. Weininger mentions the phenomenon of the *Doppelgänger*, and of anxiety in the face of the *Doppelgänger*, in a number of places. In his 1902 sketch "Zur Theorie des Lebens," the *Doppelgänger* heads a list of empirical evidence for the self:

> Empirical examples for the self: Fear of the double (model [*Urbild*] of all fear. First impression of oneself in front of a mirror; experiments with

animals!) . . . The fact of style! The primordial fact [*Urthatsache*] of shame! Immutability of character! Physical individuality! Naegeli, idioplasm! . . . Finally: Ethics! Unfaithfulness towards oneself! Desire for immortality! Superficial explanations for the latter! The satisfaction of belief in a soul, the truth that is felt in it! (*EP*, 200)

The same complex of phenomena is taken up again in *Sex and Character*:

Or how would Mach and Hume explain the simple fact of *style*, if not by individuality? Further: animals are never startled when they see themselves in a mirror, but no human being would be able to spend all his life in a room of mirrors. Or can this fear, the fear of the *Doppelgänger* (of which, characteristically, woman is free), also be explained in "biological" or "Darwinist" terms? One only needs to pronounce the word *doppelgänger* in order to make most men's hearts beat faster. Here any purely empirical psychology necessarily reaches its end, and *profoundness* is required (*GuC*, 274).

This passage appears within Weininger's discussion of the, prima facie, impossible scientific psychology of M, or the self. Whoever believes in free will must deny the possibility of a scientific psychology; whoever believes in the possibility of a scientific psychology must deny the free will (of the subject): "This dilemma explains the sad plight of today's psychology with regard to all questions of principle" (*GuC*, 271). At this point, a tension arises between Weininger's idea of a theoretical biography, which is, at the same time, an "*ontogenetic psychology* or *theoretical biography* which is destined sooner or later to displace today's science of the human mind" (discussed in the first section of this essay). For Weininger, the *Doppelgänger*, as empirical double, signifies nonbeing: "Fear, however, is always fear of losing one's individuality, of losing the connection with the absolute that is guaranteed only through the logical and ethical in his personality. With a little effort, one can derive from this general schema of fear, the fear of death, fear of the doppelgänger, . . . and fear of sin and insanity" ("Science and Culture," 123). The *Doppelgänger* thus symbolizes the worst fear of all: "fear of oneself," which is "fear of the empirical ego. Fear that the timeless personality will be reduced to an elementary point in time arises at every instant at which one becomes conscious of the present merely as a moment in time, instead of being somehow fulfilled by thinking of the future or the past, i.e. by behaving as a willing or thinking being" ("Science and Culture," 123). Weininger here describes, in Kierkegaardian terms, precisely the state of despair that results from losing one's grounding in the absolute; from a reduction to a discontinuous string of empirical moments that end with physical death. The opposite, and synonymous with the good death Wittgenstein had in mind, is expressed by Wilhelm Anz: "As existing individuals, we live our death before we die it. The manner in which we 'live' or experience our death is precisely the anxious looking forward which individualizes us in our lives and thereby places us in a necessary relationship to ourselves."[39] The "mental doppelgänger [*Doppelgänger im Geistigen*]" is uncanny because he takes away the uniqueness of this necessary relationship with myself, just as someone totally disagreeing with my world view produces an eerie feeling: "The former negates me, the latter negates the world" ("Science and Culture," 124, n. 14).

In short, the *Doppelgänger* violates the principle of identity, and transforms unique individuality into repetitive objectivity.[40] Thus he questions one part of the self when free of despair, in the definition given by Kierkegaard: the part that relates itself to the absolute. What is left is a self that relates itself to itself, but such individuality is just one breath short of true individuality even if the combinations of elements that make it up are almost certainly unique. We find it insulting to be subsumed under a class, and this is not only, as Weininger poignantly puts it, a case of "hurt calculus" ("*beleidigte Wahrscheinlichkeitsrechnung,*" *GuC,* 275). What we wish to insist on is that "*something will be altered when I do not exist*" ("Science and Culture," 118), and this, as Burns discusses in his contribution to this volume, is linked in Weininger to the question of solipsism as irrefutable because of the impossibility of proving empirically "the existence of one's own ego" ("Science and Culture," 118). This problematic status of the ego is shared by Wittgenstein's notion of spirit, and it points to Weininger's project (incomplete by the usual standards of philosophical argument, according to Burns) of reading ethics as the categorical imperative insofar as it affects us as temporal beings, and logic as the categorical imperative insofar as it affects us as timeless beings: "Ethics says what ought to be, logic says what is, *that something is,* that certain propositions have validity. Thus ethics gives to human birth a meaning relative to death; logic relieves human death of its meaninglessness in that from birth on it denies that *everything* will be forfeit to it" ("Science and Culture," 116).

If the reflections of this epilogue have some plausibility then Wittgenstein's philosophy was ultimately not a philosophy of language, or of mind, but a philosophy of spirit. However, he did not see himself as a religious person, but rather as someone who could not help seeing things from a religious perspective.[41] This perspective acknowledges the existence of spirit as the uncanny implicit double of the totality of what can be made explicit, and it insists on authenticity, even though the difference between authenticity and inauthenticity is yet another example of the uncanny. We feel this difference in our relation with others and with ourselves, but it is not possible to prove it by applying objective and general criteria.

Notes

The short titles and abbreviations refer to the following references.

BGM	Wittgenstein, Ludwig, *Bemerkungen über die Grundlagen der Mathematik*, Suhrkamp Werkausgabe.
"Characterology"	Weininger, Otto (2001). "Characterology" ("On Friedrich Schiller"). In *On Last Things*, 68–80.
Culture and Value	Wittgenstein, Ludwig (1998). *Culture and Value*. Revised second edition. Edited by Georg Henrik von Wright in collaboration with Heikke Nyman, with revisions by Alois Pichler, translated by Peter Winch. Oxford: Basil Blackwell.
DB	Wittgenstein, Ludwig (1997). *Denkbewegungen: Tagebücher 1930–1932, 1936–1937* (MS 183). Edited by Ilse Somavilla. Innsbruck, Austria: Haymon Verlag.
EP	Weininger, Otto (1990). "Zur Theorie des Lebens" (On a theory of life). In *Eros und Psyche*. Edited by Hannelore Rodlauer. Vienna: Verlag der Österreichischen Akademie der Wissenschaften.
GuC	Weininger Otto (1997). *Geschlecht und Charakter: Eine prinzipielle Untersuchung*. Munich: Matthes & Seitz. Quotations in English are taken from the new unabridged translation, *Sex and Character*, translated by Ladislaus Löb, edited by Daniel Steuer and Laura Marcus, with an introduction by Daniel Steuer, Bloomington: Indiana University

Press, 2004. Page references are to the German edition.

"Metaphysics" — Weininger, Otto (2001). "Metaphysics" ("Animal Psychology"). In *On Last Things*, 96–111.

On Certainty — Wittgenstein, Ludwig (1984). *Über Gewißheit* (*On Certainty*). Frankfurt/M.: Suhrkamp Werkausgabe 8.

"Philosophie" — Wittgenstein, Ludwig (1993). "Philosophie." Translated by C. G. Luckhardt and M. A. E. Aue. In *Philosophical Occasions 1912–1951*. Edited by James Klagge and Alfred Nordmann. Indianapolis, IN: Hackett, 160–99.

Rank — Rank, Otto (1993). *Der Doppelgänger. Eine psychoanalytische Studie.* Reprint of the 1925 edition. Vienna: Turia & Kant. First published as "Der Doppelgänger," in *Imago*, 1914. English edition, "The Double as Immortal Self," in Otto Rank, *Beyond Psychology*, Camden, NJ: Haddon Craftsmen, 1941.

RFM — Wittgenstein, Ludwig (1978). *Remarks on the Foundations of Mathematics.* Edited by G. H. von Wright, R. Rhees, and G. E. M. Anscombe. Oxford: Basil Blackwell.

"Science and Culture" — Weininger, Otto (2001). "Science and Culture." In *On Last Things.* Translated and with an introduction by Steven Burns. Lewiston, NY: Edwin Mellen Press, 114–46.

1. Ludwig Wittgenstein, *Ludwig Wittgenstein Cambridge Letters: Correspondence with Russell, Keynes, Moore, Ramsey and Saffra*, ed. Brian McGuiness and Georg Henrik von Wright, Oxford: Basil Blackwell, 1995, 250, 23.8.1931.
2. Ludwig Wittgenstein, "Philosophie." 177.
3. Ludwig Wittgenstein, *Philosophische Untersuchungen*, Frankfurt/M. Suhrkamp Werkausgabe 1, Suhrkamp, 1984, s. 108; my translation.
4. Otto Weininger, "Zur Theorie des Lebens" (On a theory of life), in *Eros und Psyche*, 208; my translation.
5. Otto Weininger, *Geschlecht und Charakter. Eine prinzipielle Untersuchung*, 165.
6. Ludwig Wittgenstein, *Denkbewegungen. Tagebücher 1930–1932/1936–1937*, "Normalisierte Fassung," 62. ("*Die Denkbewegung in meinem Philosophieren müßte sich in der Geschichte meines Geistes, seiner Moralbegriffe & dem Verständnis meiner Lage wiederfinden lassen*"; between 24 October and 15 December 1931). English translation in James Klagge and Alfred Nordmann, eds., *Public and Private Occasions*, Lanham: Rowman & Littlefield, 2003.
7. See, for instance, Wittgenstein, *Culture and Value*, 53e (ca. 1945). See also Béla Szabados, "Autobiography after Wittgenstein," *Journal of Aesthetics and*

Art Criticism 50(1): 1–12, and O. K. Bouwsma, *Wittgenstein Conversations, 1949–1951*, edited and with an introduction by J. L. Craft and Ronald E. Hustwit, Indianapolis: Hackett, 1986, 71.

8. "I can never say about a raw complex of sensations that it is equal to itself: the moment I apply to it the judgment of identity, it has already become a concept. Thus it is the concept that bestows *dignity* and *rigour* on any perceptual construct and any tissue of thoughts: *the concept liberates any content by binding it*" (*Geschlecht und Charakter*, 246). Compare this to Frege's argument on the importance of sign systems (discussed in this chapter).
9. Weininger's criticism of empiricist psychology, the link between logic and ethics, and the microcosm-macrocosm theory meet in the question of truthful judgments: "Therefore the ability to judge . . . is only the dry *logical expression of the theory of the human soul as the microcosm*" (*Geschlecht und Charakter*, 248).
10. Otto Weininger, "Science and Culture," in *On Last Things*, 117. This constitutes another parallel to Wittgenstein's suggestion that we must accept certain images and language games as "*Urphänomene*," i.e. as foundational for our thought and behavior: See *Philosophical Investigations*, s. 654, and *Culture and Value*, 95. The important difference is that in the later Wittgenstein there is a diversity of such images and games.
11. Otto Weininger, "Metaphysics" ("Animal Psychology"), in *On Last Things*, 99.
12. See Otto Weininger, "Final Aphorisms," in *On Last Things*, 148–51, here.
13. While for both Weininger and Wittgenstein the central problem of philosophy was one of the will, not of the intellect, in the case of Weininger it ultimately took the form of the question "whether *he* even had a self" (see Steven Burns's contribution, "Sex and Solipsism: Weininger and Wittgenstein," in this volume), whereas Wittgenstein tones this down to a necessary process of correcting self-delusion, and in particular delusions about one's self.
14. However, this incomprehensibility is not different, in principle, to that of Kant's spontaneous, synthetic apperception as the basis of human understanding ("*Verstand*"). See Immanuel Kant, *Kritik der reinen Vernunft*, Suhrkamp Werkausgabe III, ed. Wilhelm Weischedel, Frankfurt/M.: Suhrkamp, 1992, ss. 15–17, 134–40 (B, 129–39). Weininger's amalgamation of logic and ethics on a Kantian basis deserves separate attention.
15. Otto Weininger, "Characterology" ("On Friedrich Schiller"), in *On Last Things*, 71.
16. Gottlob Frege, "Über die wissenschaftliche Berechtigung einer Begriffsschrift," in *Begriffsschrift und andere Aufsätze*, ed. Ignacio Angelelli and Georg Olms, Hildesheim, 1964, 106–14, here 107; my translation. English edition: Gottlob Frege, "On the Scientific Justification of a Conceptual Notation," in *Conceptual Notation and related articles*, trans. and ed., with a biography and introduction, by Terrell Ward Bynum, Oxford: Clarendon Press, 1972, 83–9, here, 84.

17. On this term, coined by Weininger, see Chandak Sengoopta, *Otto Weininger: Sex, Science and Self in Imperial Vienna,* Chicago: University of Chicago Press, 2000, 52 and 180 n. 22.
18. Ludwig Wittgenstein, *Über Gewißheit* (*On Certainty*), s. 136; my translation.
19. Wittgenstein compares the sentences describing this "*Weltbild*" to a flowing river whose bedrock is given by momentarily hardened propositions: *On Certainty,* ss. 94ff. This use of the image differs significantly from earlier, Heraclitean or phenomenological, uses of it: "Unlike Wittgenstein's earlier river image, his later image accommodates both change and persistence, for he now holds that change is possible only against a background: in talking of change, one must hold some things constant, at least for the present": David G. Stern, *Wittgenstein on Mind and Language,* Oxford: Oxford University Press, 1995, 190. Wittgenstein's use of this imagery neither implies that the bedrock is, or reflects, the conditions of the possibility of our judgments, nor that it is possible to make it fully explicit.
20. And the relation between formal logic and the aesthetic logic of our language is changed: formal calculi are a special case of language games; they may serve as standards of comparison, but they are not the foundation of our language. This is argued in detail by Hans Julius Schneider, *Phantasie und Kalkül. Über die Polarität von Handlung und Struktur in der Sprache,* Frankfurt/M.: Suhrkamp, 1992.
21. Ludwig Wittgenstein, *Wiener Ausgabe* 2, ed. Michael Nedo, Vienna and New York: Springer, 1995, 260 (18 May 1930); my translation (MS 108, 166).
22. See, on contradiction as an object of superstition, and as a ghost, Ludwig Wittgenstein, *Bemerkungen über die Grundlagen der Mathematik,* 122 and 254. English edition: *Remarks on the Foundations of Mathematics,* 122 and 254.
23. Wolfgang Kienzler, *Wittgensteins Wende zu seiner Spätphilosophie 1930–1932,* Frankfurt/M.: Suhrkamp, 1997, points out that, in many respects, Wittgenstein's remark about the truth-yielding negation applies more to Frege than to Weininger. Wittgenstein, he writes, "put Frege from the head of pure thought onto the feet of human behavior" (200; my translation. See also 309, n. 82).
24. Ludwig Wittgenstein, *Letzte Schriften über die Philosophie der Psychologie (1949–1951). Das Innere und das Äußere I* (MS 169), ed. G. H. von Wright and Heikki Nyman, Frankfurt/M.: Suhrkamp, 1993, 30; my translation. English edition: *Last Writings on the Philosophy of Psychology (Vol. II). The Inner and the Outer 1949–1951,* ed. Georg Henrik von Wright and Heikki Nyman, Oxford: Basil Blackwell, 1992, 17e.
25. Wittgenstein, in 1931, uses the example of a "street bum" ("*Straßenköter*") pretending to be naturally noble when discussing the possible ways in which his autobiography may become untruthful. See *Wiener Ausgabe 3,* 305 (MS 110, 252–3).
26. Wittgenstein describes himself as "an amoral nucleus" to which the moral concepts of others become easily attached: *Denkbewegungen,* 109.

27. On the historical development he comments: "My main movement of thought is entirely different today compared to 15 or 20 years ago." *Denkbewegungen*, 141.
28. Kelly Hamilton, "Wittgenstein and the Mind's eye," in James Klagge, ed., *Wittgenstein: Biography and Philosophy*, Cambridge: Cambridge University Press, 2001, 53–97, 85.
29. See Cavell: "The inflection of the idea of the reader as fantastic . . . is thus an idea of the reader's willingness to subject himself or herself to taking the eyes of the writer, which is in effect yielding his or her own, an exchange interpretable as a sacrifice of one another, of what we think we know of one another": "The Fantastic of Philosophy," in *In Quest of the Ordinary*, Chicago: University of Chicago Press, 1988, 181–8, 187.
30. For Wittgenstein, our lives are illuminated by a light of which we are not normally aware. If it is missing we "suddenly realize that life is robbed of all value, meaning (or whatever expression one may choose)," and that "mere existence, as one is inclined to say, by itself is utterly empty and barren" (*Denkbewegungen*, 198f.).
31. The exact relation between language and life replaces Weininger's definition of the lie and immorality as the criterion for authenticity: "The definition of the lie itself is the best description of immorality: to postulate as real what is unreal, and also: incorporation into the self where such incorporation must not occur [*Einreihung ins Ich, wo Einreihung nicht erfolgen darf*]." (See *Taschenbuch und Briefe an einen Freund*, Leipzig: E. P. Tal, 1999, 662. For Weininger, such incorporation of empirical elements that do not genuinely belong to the self are theft, and characterize the criminal without a self. Wittgenstein's continuous attempts, in his notebooks, to measure the exactness of the relation between his words and his life give rise to what Sass calls his hyper-reflexivity, and, indeed, much of his later writing is devoted to securing an end to "endless critique": Louis Sass, "Deep Disquietudes: Reflections on Wittgenstein as Antiphilosopher," in Klagge, *Wittgenstein: Biography and Philosophy*, 98–155, 123. Against this tendency towards hyper-reflexivity his method aimed at a form of hyper-awareness where thoughts are "at peace" (*Culture and Value*, 50e), and where the method is not itself being called into question again (see also *Philosophical Investigations*, s. 133).
32. Wittgenstein uses the image of sleep in the same sense as early as 1917 in a letter to Engelmann (Paul Engelmann, *Letters from Ludwig Wittgenstein. With a Memoir*, Oxford: Basil Blackwell, 1967, 6; 9 April 1917). On sleepiness as a condition for philosophizing see Alfred Nordmann, "The Sleepy Philosopher. How to Read Wittgenstein's Diaries," in Klagge, *Wittgenstein: Biography and Philosophy*, 156–75.
33. See Søren Kierkegaard, *The Sickness unto Death*, Princeton: Princeton University Press, 1980, 14: "The formula that describes the state of self when despair is completely rooted out is this: in relating itself to itself and in willing to be itself, the self rests transparently in the power that established it." Kierkegaard, in a lengthy footnote, aligns the two possibilities of

despair resulting from this structure of the self to the sexes, pronouncing "in despair to will to be oneself" as the predominantly male form, and "in despair not to will to be oneself" as the predominantly female form.

34. Nordmann makes the case for this interpretation of the remark: "The Sleepy Philosopher," 169.
35. "(Ethical artistry is something I perform for others, or even only for myself, in order to demonstrate of what I am capable.)" *Denkbewegungen*, 125.
36. See *Denkbewegungen*, 153f., where Wittgenstein considers himself a slave rather than a free man because he is afraid of ridicule, and 177ff., where he discusses his inability to follow his intuition and give away his new sweater, and the possibility that he may feel that he has to burn his writings.
37. Chamisso's text is discussed at some length by Otto Rank in his classical psychoanalytic study of 1914, *Der Doppelgänger. Eine psychoanalytische Studie.* Freud's article "The Uncanny" (see *Standard Edition*, vol. 17, 219–52) first appeared in 1919, and was republished in 1924. Wittgenstein's reference to the etymology of the name, the details of which form a long footnote in Rank (58), as well as his interpretation, suggest – though obviously cannot prove – that he knew the text(s).
38. Whether or not he becomes entangled in the type of meta-moves that Sass mentions when trying to distinguish between "ethical artistry" and "authentic decency" is difficult to decide. On the whole, the diaries seem to display hyper-alertness to states of consciousness – an intense focusing on his own mental states – rather than hyper-reflexivity and cascades of meta-reflections.
39. Wilhelm Anz, "Kierkegaard on Death and Dying," in Jonathan Rée and Jane Chamberlain, eds., *Kierkegaard: A Critical Reader*, Oxford: Blackwell, 1998, 39–52, p. 49.
40. This is one reason why the *Doppelgänger* causes fear. Weininger suggests another in his *Taschenbuch*, the *Doppelgänger* as a collection of all evil properties: "The *Doppelgänger* is the ensemble of all evil properties of the self. Any specific fear is only part of this fear, the fear of the *Doppelgänger*." Likewise, the criminal must murder all witnesses of his crimes: "They all are his *Doppelgänger*." *Geschlecht und Charakter*, 611 and 625.
41. See Norman Malcolm: *Wittgenstein: A Religious Point of View*, London: Routledge, 1993. See also Philip R. Shields, *Logic and Sin in the Writings of Ludwig Wittgenstein*, Chicago: University of Chicago Press, 1993 (esp. "Writing to the Glory of God," 87–114). Wittgenstein, according to Shields, may have been looking "for a resting place, for thoughts that are at peace," but "remained troubled by the effects of our alienation, by the discrepancy between his religious vision and our own restless lives" (106).

6

Weininger and Wittgenstein on "Animal Psychology"

David G. Stern

Introduction

In November 1916, when Wittgenstein was serving in the Austro-Hungarian army, his oldest sister, Hermine, wrote to him that "I have taken your Weininger with me and am very happy with this book; it replaces you for me, a little."[1] It is not clear which Weininger book Hermine was referring to, but in another letter to her brother, written in 1931, she playfully refers to *On Last Things*: "I believe Weininger maintained that milk is the only innocent food, because it destroys no seed... "[2] The passage in question is part of the collection of aphorisms that makes up the second chapter of that book:

> The vegetarians are just as wrong as their opponents. Anyone who does not wish to contribute to the killing of living things may only drink milk, for anyone who eats fruit or eggs still kills embryos. That is perhaps why milk is the healthiest food, because it is the most ethical.[3]

At first sight, one might take the point of Weininger's aphorism to be to make fun of those whose logical consistency drives them to take up positions that cannot, in practice, be maintained. However, his rejection of both sides in this dispute closely parallels his own substantive ethical outlook, which also sets an impossibly high standard by which to judge human action. For Weininger maintains that to live a virtuous life one must not only reject immorality but also conventional mores, devoting oneself wholeheartedly to a life of celibacy and extreme self-denial.

Furthermore, as in the case of Weininger's discussion of vegetarians and meat-eaters, the depiction of a higher ideal turns, to a remarkable extent, on a morbid fascination with the failings of the positions he opposes.

Weininger was certainly on Wittgenstein's mind in 1916 and 1931; Weininger's influence on the composition of the *Tractatus* can be dated to the second half of 1916, and it was in 1931 that Wittgenstein included Weininger on a short list of writers who had influenced him.[4] In 1966, in his first conversation with Allan Janik, Georg Henrik von Wright drew Janik's attention to Wittgenstein's very serious interest in Weininger's *On Last Things*, and said that Wittgenstein spoke highly of the section entitled "Animal Psychology" late in his life.[5] In that text, Weininger maintains that "each species of animal has a *single* character common to all its members, but which among humans is possessed only by a certain few."[6] In other words, he maintains that a given species, or breed of dog, has certain essential traits, constituting a character that corresponds to a distinctive personality type among humans. Most of the discussion is devoted to the case for seeing dogs as exemplifying a set of character traits common to human criminals, with particular breeds of dog corresponding to different types of criminal. Toward the end, Weininger begins to sketch a typology of animal characteristics, maintaining that people with an inclination to immorality take on these animal physiognomies more and more as they get older:

> The dog, as criminal, is related to the wolf (the wolf is a symbol of *greed*, but perhaps also of something else), and the wolf is surely criminal. The horse is a symbol of insanity, the donkey of stupidity. (The donkey is above all wilful, obstinate, and *self-satisfied* stupidity. It is the *caricature of piety*. Accordingly, this image, like piety, is also missing from the Jews. There is no Jewish donkey.)[7]
>
> The goose, the dove, the hen, the parrot, the magpie, the crow, the duck – one finds them all represented, physiologically and characterologically, among human females. The males of these birds are henpecked husbands (with the exception of the rooster; parrot?)[8]

According to Peter Geach, Wittgenstein would classify his friends in Cambridge according to Weininger's specific classification of animal types; Barry Smith, who reports this story, also maintains that the chapter on animal psychology had a special importance for Wittgenstein.[9]

Lichtenberg: "Wherever We Look, We See Only Ourselves."

This paper looks at the role of the notion of "animal psychology" in Weininger and Wittgenstein, and the question of what we can learn from considering their attitudes to animals. I take as the point of departure for my discussion of Wittgenstein's interest in Weininger on "animal psychology" two passages from Lichtenberg's "waste books." There, he proposes that any observation or interpretation is ultimately a self-interpretation. These ideas play an important role in Weininger's metaphysics and "animal psychology"; following this Lichtenbergian leitmotif in Weininger and Wittgenstein will help us to see the connections between Wittgenstein's and Weininger's remarks about understanding animals. While both authors certainly read and appreciated Lichtenberg, I do not claim that he directly influenced them on this point.[10] Rather, the passages that follow are intended as striking illustrations of a particular train of thought that repeatedly arises in post-Kantian philosophy, a train of thought to which Weininger and Wittgenstein both respond.

> Certainly experiment and reflection enable us to introduce a significance into what is not legible, either to us or at all: thus we see faces or landscapes in the sand, though they are certainly not there. The introduction of symmetries belongs here too, silhouettes in inkblots, etc. Likewise the gradations we establish in the order of creatures: all this is *not in the things but in us.* In general we cannot remember too often that when we observe nature, and especially the ordering of nature, it is always ourselves alone we are observing.[11]
>
> In the preface to the second . . . edition of Kant's *Critique*. . . many singular things appear that I have often thought but never said. We discover no cause in things but notice only that which corresponds to something within ourselves. Wherever we look, we see only ourselves.[12]

The first remark from Lichtenberg sets out a central theme of Weininger's metaphysics: the structure of the world around us is ultimately a structure that we project onto it. Weininger's only reference to Lichtenberg is in connection with Lichtenberg's famous claim that to start from "I think" is to already presume more than we know from experience, and that we ought instead to say "it thinks."[13] However, the passage he quotes from Lichtenberg in his footnote begins with a sentence that raises a more general question, the very question under discussion here – namely, how, and whether, we can distinguish what we contribute to our experience from that which is independent of us: "We are conscious of certain ideas that do not depend on us; others, we believe at least, depend on us; where is the boundary?"[14]

Lichtenberg's second remark applies the idea that "wherever we look, we see only ourselves" to philosophical texts. The philosophers we read – not just our choice of philosophical heroes, but also the philosophies of the heroes we choose – are products of our own ordering activity. Such ideas teeter on the brink of an extreme relativism. If Lichtenberg avoids the relativism implicit in this Protagorean view, it is because he holds that the "ordering of nature" is not simply up to us: how we order nature – the kind of ordering that had been the traditional concern of metaphysics, and that informs Kant's theory of the categories – is determined by human psychology and the structure of the language we speak.

Wittgenstein's and Weininger's approaches to "animal psychology" can be seen as two related and connected developments of this Lichtenbergian topic.[15] Neither of them accepts Lichtenberg's psychologism, however; both are closer to Kant in their emphasis on the role of logic in structuring our thought, and their insistence that logic and ethics are independent from merely empirical psychology. However, both of them are acutely aware that what we take to be absolutely fixed, seemingly a matter of logical necessity, may later prove to be a product of our desire to find an objective order in the world. Weininger's idealist response to the Lichtenbergian question about the boundary between those ideas that depend on us and those that do not is to push that boundary out to its logical extreme, so that all ideas depend on us. Wittgenstein not only rejects this Weiningerian hyperbole, but also responds to Weininger by reflecting on the way our expectations inform how we look at, and talk about, other creatures.

In Chapter 4 of *On Last Things,* Weininger opens a discussion of symbolism, time, and motion by raising just this question about the nature and extent of our contribution to what we experience in connection with a discussion of the significance of symbols:

People have perceived many symbols of a higher reality in geometrical forms. We may leave undecided the question whether the reason for this phenomenon simply lies in the fact that what we are rediscovering in them is an a priori function of our own intuition, and no less, therefore, than something which has the properties and the value of the a priori, as Kant taught, or whether, on the contrary, we are only discovering in those laws those of our own imagination, and thus something that is rather more suitable for stripping them of all transcendental symbolism. Neither of the two answers really settles the question simply and in general.[16]

Thus, Weininger briefly mentions both the a priori Kantian approach and the a posteriori psychologistic response, only to put both of them to one side, claiming that neither of them can settle the question. Instead, he turns to a rambling, seemingly anecdotal, discussion of the significance of particular symbols, a discussion that leads up to far-reaching conclusions about the nature of time, morality, and the meaning of life. In the course of this discussion he begins to articulate a conception of symbolism that owes something to both Kant's conception of the a priori and a psychologistic reliance on empirical and introspective observation of particular mental processes. This question about the nature of symbols and our contribution to their significance is also a principal concern in the next chapter of his book, which contains the section on "animal psychology."

Weininger's "Animal Psychology"

Chapter 5 of Weininger's *Last Things* is entitled "Metaphysics," but he begins by warning the reader that what he sets forth "diverges from the usual notions": it is not about being and not-being, but "*symbolism,* universal symbolism."[17] Weininger's conception of "symbolism" diverges from the usual philosophical notions of a theory of symbols, too. What he claims to do is to specify the ultimate symbolic significance of each type of thing in the world. Drawing on an "introspective-psychological" method, he aims to uncover what "the sea, what iron, what ants, what the Chinese mean, the *idea* which they represent."[18] In the most general terms, what he aims to do is to state "*the meaning of everything particular in the totality.*"[19] The method is underwritten in part by the idea of the human being as a microcosm: because everything we know is interpreted through our psychological categories, to say what everything in the world symbolizes is ultimately to talk about human characteristics.

Although the chapter is less than twenty pages long, and trails off into a long list of examples of symbolist interpretations of particular types of plants and things, the author clearly conceived of it as the first chapter of a book draft:

> The fundamental thought and the presupposition of the book, the basis on which rests *all* that follows, is the theory of the human being as *microcosm.*[20] Because the human being stands in relation to all the things in the world, so all these things must surely exist in him. This thought about the microcosm is being taken seriously for the first time in this book: *according to it, the system of the world is identical with the system of humankind.* Every form of existence in nature corresponds to a characteristic in human beings, every possibility in humans corresponds to something in nature. Thus nature... is *interpreted* through the *psychological* categories *in* humans, and is regarded only as a symbol for them.[21]

However, while this makes Weininger's philosophy a form of idealism, he departs from the usual idealist view that both mental and physical phenomena are only appearances. Guided by what he calls "moral-theoretical considerations," he maintains that the mental has "more reality."[22]

Weininger's most well worked out example of a symbol's significance is his account of the dog, which he maintains is a symbol of a criminal.[23] Characteristically, his defense of this view depends on a detailed exposition of the "*essence of the criminal,*"[24] most of which will be familiar to the reader of *Sex and Character*: the criminal has no will, no judgment, no autonomy, continually commits sins, is only concerned with his pleasure, and lacks unity of consciousness. Unable to transcend the causal nexus, or the spatio-temporal present, he or she is bound to both things and people, either as master or as servant. Dimly aware of his potential for transcendence, the criminal is driven to negate everything that exists, to kill, to destroy, and to screw around ("From Don Juan to murderer is... only a step").[25]

Turning to "The Dog," Weininger finds all these traits writ large in the canine physiognomy. The evidence he offers is anecdotal, and is perhaps best understood as an invitation to interpret our experience of dogs in the light of the nexus of criminal traits just described. Characteristic canine behavior is construed as exemplifying Weiningerian criminality: "the dog's *barking* is decisive; it is the absolutely *negative* expressive movement. It proves that the dog is the symbol of the criminal."[26] "The dog's importunity, its jumping up on people, is the functionalism of the slave."[27] "*The dog's tail-wagging signifies that it recognizes every other thing as more valuable than itself.*"[28] "The dog's faithfulness [is] a symbol of baseness: the *slave mentality* (there is no merit in coming back after a beating)."[29] "The *sniffing* of the dog . . . indicates an inability for apperception . . . passively attracted by individual objects, without his knowing why . . . he simply has no freedom. The dog breeds with any bitch whatever, and this randomness also expresses that he has altogether given up choice."[30]

At first sight, Weininger's "animal psychology" provides us with an extremely personal philosophical pathology, a romantic metaphysics that objectifies his vision of good and evil as the structure of the world. If we are to take Weininger at his word, he asks us to believe that everything – not only animals, but ultimately also plants and even inorganic nature – is a symbol of a Manichæan conflict between mundane evil and the transcendent goodness that can only be achieved by the extraordinary genius.[31]

How are we to make sense of this extraordinary claim? Whenever a philosopher makes a claim that appears implausible, the usual interpretive strategies are either to defend the claim, perhaps by reinterpreting it or finding further support for it, or to concede that the claim is indefensible, and to provide an explanation as to why the philosopher was attracted to it. Defenders of Weininger's views on "animal psychology" have argued that they are best understood as a dramatic presentation of his conception of the nature of evil, and must be seen as complementary to his overall ethical views about the nature of human flourishing. Weininger's harshest critics have contended that his unrelentingly harsh treatment of animals is not just a natural extension of the misogyny, homophobia and anti-Semitism that pervades his work, but are a symptom of his extreme mental instability. Let us look briefly at each of these responses to Weininger's treatment of animality.

For Freud, Weininger was a perfect example of his psychoanalytic theories about the relation of circumcision to castration, Jewishness and femininity. Sander Gilman observes that "Weininger serves Freud as a touchstone for the definition of the diseased Jew . . . For Freud,

Weininger's disease is his self-hate, both as a Jew and a homosexual; the proof of his disease is his suicide."[32] Freud contends that because small boys unconsciously believe a mythical account of the nature of sexual difference, they fear that they could lose their penis and so become a woman, a fear of castration that can also manifest itself in the behavior of the adult neurotic. In a footnote to his seminal discussion of "Little Hans," Freud links anxiety about castration to anti-Semitism:

> The castration complex is the deepest unconscious root of anti-Semitism; for even in the nursery little boys hear that a Jew has something cut off his penis – a piece of his penis, they think – and this gives them a right to despise Jews. And there is no stronger unconscious root for the sense of superiority over women. Weininger (the young philosopher who, highly gifted but sexually deranged, committed suicide after producing his remarkable book, *Geschlecht und Charakter*), in a chapter that attracted much attention, treated Jews and women with equal hostility and overwhelmed them with the same insults. Being a neurotic, Weininger was completely under the sway of his infantile complexes; and from that standpoint what is common to Jews and women is their relation to the castration complex.[33]

One consequence of this view of the matter is that Weininger's beliefs are caused by his disease, and so the problem of whether one can give a rational explanation or justification for them falls away. Gilman, fittingly, spends most of the essay just cited showing how Freud's beliefs about Weininger have their origins in the ethnopsychological theories of the time, which held that there is a close causal relation between different ethnic body types and psychic constitution. From a Freudian standpoint, the more interesting question is the precise nature of the connection between Weininger's fears and his psychic condition.[34] There is a close connection between the fear of the Jewish, the feminine, and the animal in Weininger's psychic economy. While Jews and women amount to human incarnations of the irrational for Weininger, it is animals, and especially dogs, precisely because they are not human, yet take on a certain human character, that symbolize his greatest fear of all. This would hardly have surprised Freud; Little Hans's anxieties first presented themselves as a fear of horses. Artur Gerber, a close friend of Weininger's, related the story of a night in November 1902, when he talked Weininger out of killing himself. Ultimately, "in a voice as sinister, as icy cold, as desperate, and without hope as I have ever heard from a human being," he told Gerber the following:

I know that I am a born criminal. I am a born murderer. . . . I spent a night in a hotel room in Munich once. I could not sleep. Then I heard a barking dog. I have never heard a dog bark in such a terrifying way. It must have been a black dog. It was the evil spirit. I fought with it, I fought with it for my soul. In sheer terror I bit the sheets to shreds that night. Since that time I have known that I am a murderer. That is why I must kill myself!'[35]

It is unclear how reliable this memoir, published seventeen years after the event, actually is. Abrahamsen rehearses this issue at some length, pointing out that the account given by Gerber seems to telescope two separate events related by Weininger near the beginning of the discussion of "The Dog":[36]

The dog has a remarkably deep relation to *death.* Months before the dog became problematic for me, I was sitting at five o'clock one afternoon in a room of the hotel in Munich where I was staying, and reflecting on various things. Suddenly I heard a dog *barking* in a most peculiar and piercing way that was new to me, and simultaneously I had the irresistible feeling that exactly at that moment someone *was dying.*

Months later, on the most dreadful night of my life, although I was not ill I was literally wrestling with death – for there is no spiritual death without physical death for great men, because life and death are for them the possibilities which confront one another most powerfully and intensively. Just as I was thinking of succumbing, I heard a dog bark three times in the same way as that time in Munich. This dog barked the whole night, but these three times were different. I noticed that at this moment I bit into the bed sheet with my teeth, like a dying man.[37]

While the Freudian account can help us to see the tight nexus of associations linking these events in Weininger's life and thought, and the connections between his fear of death, dogs, Woman, and Jew, it does so at the price of treating his views as entirely explicable in terms of symptoms of mental illness. As Abrahamsen puts it, "his terror became clearer and clearer, and we may believe that out of necessity he gradually filled it with rationalistic content."[38]

We should not, however, dismiss Weininger's views as only symptoms of a struggle with insanity before we consider whether or not they can be rationally understood.[39] From such a perspective, his imaginative vision of how dogs symbolize evil is best understood as a further development of his reading of Ibsen's *Peer Gynt,* where the

Boyg and the Troll King epitomize the role of the subhuman and evil being. Allan Janik has recently provided an excellent exposition of Weininger's reading of *Peer Gynt,* and his conception of animality, along just these lines. Janik maintains that the point of Weininger's "proto-phenomenological description" of the Criminal is to give us a model of "*what it is to be immoral in itself,*" with the aim of pressing his reader "to reflect upon happiness and the good life by giving us the negative example of a life in which guilt and the idea of human limitation play *no role whatsoever*. . . . the polar opposite of Kant's autonomous human being."[40]

Consequently, Janik construes the "Metaphysics" chapter of *Last Things* as a commentary on the issues raised by Weininger's discussion of *Peer Gynt* in the first chapter of that book, a discussion that brings out the central place in that play of the relationship between the human and the animal, reason and instinct, and autonomy and heteronomy:

> Like Peer, the Criminal does not notice that he is actually the unhappiest of men despite his outwardly happy, hedonistic life and, like Peer seeking the center of the onion by peeling off its layers, he in fact destroys himself in rejecting both logic and ethics in his superficial search for self-fulfillment. However, Weininger recasts Ibsen's contrast between human and the sub-human trolls in *Peer Gynt* as a contrast between the Kantian autonomous rational agent and the fully heteronomous, self-willed, instinct-driven animal, which is only human in appearance. . . . Trolls lose themselves by being entirely self-serving, humans attain selfhood by overcoming selfishness.[41]

In short, Janik proposes that on a Weiningerian reading, *Peer Gynt* is "a drama of redemption, whose real hero is none other than humanity itself."[42] However, "humanity" turns out to mean those very few people who can live up to Weininger's inhuman ideals of denying everything in this world in order to strive for one's own salvation, a salvation that turns on dwelling on the dangers of damnation. Janik praises Weininger as rejecting modernist narcissism in favor of rigorous moral ideals, without sufficiently acknowledging that those ideals, which find their fullest expression in Weininger's reflections on animality, are curiously bifurcated. On the one hand, as Janik correctly stresses, Weininger's ethical outlook presents itself as nothing more than an unequivocal recovery of Kantian autonomy and traditional Christian duties. On the other hand, those very ideals are not presented as the deliverances of Reason or Revelation, but rather as arising out of the author's characteristically post-Kantian reflections on what is given to his consciousness, and his "theory of the human being as *microcosm*."[43] As a result, those ideals are an unstable product of what Sass, following Foucault, has called "transcendental narcissism."[44] For the very notions that underwrite Weininger's vision of moral redemption – the freedom of consciousness, its self-constituting character, and its status as the authoritative source of truth – can, with just a slight shift in perspective, be recognized as flawed and constrained. For consciousness has its limits and limitations: aspects of the macrocosm will always elude the grasp of the microcosm, and even within the microcosm, consciousness is not always transparent to itself. What is characteristic of Foucauldian "transcendental narcissism" is an oscillation between these two standpoints: the "solipsistic grandiosity" of the perspective of consciousness, and the "felt impotence and ignorance" that results from recognizing the limitations of transcendental reflection.[45] Janik's focus on Weininger's ethical doctrine helps us see how Weininger understood himself, but fails to do justice to the extent that his fears were intertwined with his hopes. The animal symbolizes not only our moral failings, but also the limitations of the transcendental perspective itself.

Wittgenstein's "Animal Psychology"

What did Wittgenstein see in the sketch of an extraordinarily speculative metaphysics that we find articulated in Weininger's canine characterology? To put the question a little more carefully, why did Wittgenstein so admire Weininger's vilification of those servile and craven, but also frightening and uncanny character traits that Weininger identifies as essentially canine? Was he attracted to Weininger's antimodernist moral vision, as Janik proposes? Or did he see it as a philosophical joke, an extreme example of the excesses that metaphysical speculation can yield? (Wittgenstein once said to Norman Malcolm that a philosophical book could be written that consisted entirely of jokes.) Perhaps the truth lies somewhere between these extremes; he may have been attracted to Weininger's Lichtenbergian insights into the ways we project ourselves onto our world, even as he was repulsed by the depth of Weininger's hatred for "man's best friend."

I suggest that the key to understanding the appeal for Wittgenstein of Weininger's shaggy dog story is to attend to Wittgenstein's discussion of the questions about both the differences and the similarities between humans and animals in the *Philosophical Investigations*.[46] Here, I will only be able to consider some of the leading concerns that connect the opening paragraphs of Parts I and II of that book, and the way they inform Wittgenstein's response to Weininger's view of animals.

The expression "animal psychology" occurs only once in the Wittgenstein *Nachlass*. The passage in question is part of of an extended critical discussion of the idea that one's knowledge of others' "states of consciousness" is a matter of an analogical inference. Its target is the idea that I infer what another thinks on the basis of observing the other's physiognomy, relying on what I know of my physiognomy when I am in certain mental states. Wittgenstein's narrator is driven to tell his interlocutor that he "must learn to think completely differently about the use of words." This is followed by a rather compressed example of the kind of change he is trying to bring about: "Animal psychology. Does a dog gnaw a bone involuntarily? Does he hunt game involuntarily? And what do we know of his kinaesthetic sensations?"[47]

If one thinks of what a dog does by analogy with our own lives, then one will be inclined to say, under certain circumstances, that a dog chooses to gnaw on a bone – perhaps when it lazily reaches over for one when it is tired and well-fed – and in other, equally imaginable circumstances, that it could not help itself. Similarly, sometimes a dog's owner may drag it away from the fire on a cold winter day to go hunting, and, on other occasions, it may eagerly go hunting. And one will think of the dog's sense of muscular effort that accompanies a voluntary motion on its part on the model of one's own first-person experience of such efforts.

In October 1916, in the context of an extended discussion of a number of Weiningerian themes, Wittgenstein had explored and criticized just this conception of psycho-physical parallelism as the basis for our knowledge of other minds. There he rejected it because he could find no suitable connection between one's psychic processes and a physiognomy, thus undermining the first step in the inference from knowledge of one's own mental states to knowledge of another's.[48]

In the *Philosophical Investigations,* Wittgenstein presents two leading objections to this anthropomorphic approach to animal psychology. First, it fails to do justice to the fundamental differences between ourselves and other animals, including dogs. Because they don't speak, it isn't appropriate to speak of them in ways that presuppose their mastery of a language, such as saying that they do something involuntarily. Although the passage just quoted provides no further support for the view that saying a creature does something involuntarily presupposes that the creature can speak a language, Wittgenstein does propose that attributing certain propositional attitudes to an animal presupposes that the creature can speak a language, and so it makes no sense to attribute such attitudes to creatures that cannot speak. The same goes for "voluntary" and "involuntary." Consequently, it is nonsense to say that the dog's behavior is "involuntary," for the term is only applicable to creatures that can use language.

On the Cartesian view of the nature of thought and the priority of inner mental processes over their linguistic expression, it is our capacity for thought that is the crucial distinction between us and other creatures. This naturally leads to a conception of mind in which each person knows what a mind is like from first-person experience, and then infers, on the evidence of others' actions, that they too are conscious. On this view, there need be no basic difference between one's grounds for attributing thoughts to other humans, and to dogs.

We can find an interlocutory statement of this anthropomorphic view of animal thought in a manuscript of Wittgenstein's from 1933, followed first by a challenge, then a brief exposition of the train of argument just discussed:

> "If a dog wags its tail, it means something by it." How could one justify that?
>
> If a crocodile approaches a person with open jaws, we would hardly ask if it meant something by it. And we would explain: the crocodile can't think and so there isn't any question of meaning here.[49]

Wittgenstein is not challenging the view that the dog's tail-wagging is significant, or meaningful – he considers it undeniable that the stereotypical signs of a happy dog are, under normal circumstances, signs that the dog is happy. What he does question is whether the dog means something, something propositional or linguistic, by the tail-wagging. Wittgenstein then reminds us that we would hardly ask the parallel question about a crocodile's approaching a person with jaws open, because we will all agree that a crocodile doesn't think, and so can't mean anything by its actions. (*Zettel*, ss. 521–2) A later version of this passage makes the point somewhat clearer by adding the following words to the first paragraph: "Does one also say: 'By drooping its leaves, the plant means that it needs water'?" The anthropomorphic dog-lover will, in all likelihood, reject the analogy, insisting that while plants, flies, and maybe even crocodiles can't think, dogs can. But here the tail is wagging the dog: what reasons do the defenders of animal thought have for this insistence?

Sex and Character and *Philosophical Investigations* both offer the same simple answer to this question: thought, propositional thought, presupposes talk, or at least the ability to talk. The narrator of the *Philosophical Investigations* tells us:

> It is sometimes said that animals do not talk because they lack the mental capacity. And this means: "they do not think, and that is why they do not talk." But – they simply do not talk. Or to put it better: they do not use language – if we except the most primitive forms of language.[50]

In other words, it is talk, not thought, that comes first. No language use, no thought. And the same goes for any other activity that depends on a grasp of language. "There is nothing astonishing about certain concepts only being applicable to a being that e.g. possesses a language."[51] Near the end of *Philosophical Investigations*, we are told that babies and animals cannot lie, or be sincere, for these are part of our linguistic form of life: "A child has much to learn before it can pretend. (A dog cannot be a hypocrite, but neither can it be honest.)"[52] Likewise, Weininger says in *Sex and Character* that animals "do not speak, and consequently do not lie."[53]

In a discussion of language, privacy, and our knowledge of others' experience in Part I of the *Philosophical Investigations*, Wittgenstein's interlocutor raises the question of whether our assumption that the smile of a small baby is not a pretense might be over-hasty. If a baby did have a private language, why couldn't it have the resources needed to deceive another? Just as in the case of the dog's wagging tail, Wittgenstein's narrator immediately asks how we know: " – And on what experience is our assumption based? (Lying is a language-game that needs to be learned like any other one.)"[54] In the next remark, the conversation turns to the case of a dog's faking being in pain, and gives a closely parallel answer.

250. Why can't a dog pretend he's in pain? Is he too honest? Could one teach a dog to pretend he's in pain? Perhaps it is possible to teach him to howl on particular occasions as if he were in pain, even when he is not. But the surroundings that are necessary for this behaviour to be real pretence are missing.[55]

If one does succeed in imagining that the dog has a mental life much like one's own, then one may be struck by the fact that dogs don't pretend, and look for an answer. Weininger thinks one can best understand oneself and one's world by seeing human nature writ large in the world around us; Wittgenstein offers the complementary approach of allowing us to accede to that temptation, only to remind us of the differences between animals and ourselves.[56] Weininger, as we have seen, expresses an extreme skepticism about dogs' friendly behavior, seeing it as evidence of dissimulation, concealing craven evil. Wittgenstein, on the other hand, maintains that this is nonsense. However, because animals do not have language, and so are not capable of those forms of deception that depend on a grasp of language, animal psychology is simpler than human psychology. Wittgenstein is often said to hold an "expressive" theory about mental states; perhaps the place where he comes closest to articulating such a view is in his discussion of the case of creatures that cannot speak.

Our pursuit of the connections between Weininger and Wittgenstein on animal psychology has led us to themes that figure prominently in the openings of both Part I and Part II of the *Philosophical Investigations.* Part I, section 1, of the *Philosophical Investigations* opens with a quotation from Augustine's *Confessions* in which he describes how he learned to speak. Augustine begins by telling us that he learned the names of objects by watching his elders make sounds and move towards particular objects. Wittgenstein's narrator takes the passage to give us a "particular picture of the essence of human language": words name objects, and sentences are combinations of such names. In this picture of language, he maintains, "we find the roots" of the idea that: "Every word has a meaning. This meaning is correlated with the word. It is the object for which the word stands."[57] In section 2, he asks us to imagine a language for which the description given by Augustine is correct, the "builders' language": Builder A has four words, "block," "slab," "beam," and "pillar," and his assistant B's job is to pass them to A in the order called out.

The story of the builders can seem quite simple until we consider the final sentence: "Conceive this as a complete primitive language." Can we really do this? We seem to face a dilemma. On the one hand, we have no trouble imagining what the scenario described in section 2 looks like; on the other hand, it is very hard, perhaps impossible, to fill it in fully, to imagine what life would be like for people whose language is so limited. The point of Wittgenstein's instruction, ("Conceive . . . "), like many of his questions, is not to lead us to an obvious answer, but to encourage us to stop and think about our grasp of language, by considering imaginary people who only share an extremely rudimentary language, a single language game. Part of the problem is that we are asked to imagine that these people think, and at first sight, that seems intelligible. Yet they are clearly unable to think as we do.[58] The builders' language, like the dog's beliefs, are what Wittgenstein calls "objects of comparison":[59] his aim in telling these stories is to get us to think about our grasp of language by reflecting on the similarities and differences between our lives and the lives of creatures without language, or with only the most rudimentary ability to respond to a few words.

Wittgenstein brings these concerns together in a striking passage from his later writings on the philosophy of psychology, where an interlocutory voice contends that we have more in common with dogs than beings like the builders: "A dog is more like a human being than a being endowed with a human form, but which behaved 'mechanically'."[60] This leads to a series of reflections on the variability, complexity and interwovenness of our lives, and the way in which any given behavior will be seen in terms of "its background within human life, and this background is not monochrome, but we might picture it as a very complicated filigree pattern, which, to be sure, we can't copy, but which we can recognize from the general impression it makes."[61] Subsequently, Wittgenstein explicitly extends the metaphor of the pattern of life to the case of a dog's deceiving us:

> Only in a quite specific context can something be an expression of pain; but only in a much more extensively determinate context can there be the pretence of pain.

> For pretence is a (determinate) pattern within the weave of life. It is repeated in never-ending variations.
>
> A dog can't pretend to be in pain, because his life is too simple for that. It doesn't have the joints necessary for such movements.[62]

Part II of the *Philosophical Investigations* begins by drawing our attention to just these questions about animals and language. The opening words revisit many of the themes just touched on, once again raising the question of the limits of animal psychology:

> One can imagine an animal angry, frightened, unhappy, happy, startled. But hopeful? And why not?
>
> A dog believes his master is at the door. But can he also believe his master will come the day after tomorrow? – And *what* can he not do here? – How do I do it? – How am I supposed to answer this?
>
> Can only those hope who can talk? Only those who have mastered the use of a language. That is to say, the phenomena of hope are modes of this complicated form of life. (If a concept refers to a character of human handwriting, it has no application to beings that do not write.)[63]

Here, Wittgenstein's narrator clearly does expect us to agree with him that a dog cannot hope, and gives us a reason: only "those who have mastered the use of a language" can hope. In other words: "the phenomena of hope are modes of this complicated form of life."[64] Likewise, Weininger draws a sharp distinction between those capacities that are part of animal forms of life, and those, such as hope and memory, that are characteristically human, although his exposition is in terms of differences in mental complexity, rather than linguistic ability:

> If we now, in conclusion, ask the question whether organisms other than man possess a similar capacity for remembering earlier moments of their lives, *reviving them again in their entirety*, then the most probable answer must be in the negative. Animals could not remain, as they do, for hours at a time, motionless and peaceful on one spot, if they were capable of thinking back about their past or of looking ahead to the future. Animals have a sense of familiarity and feelings of expectation (that of the dog greeting his returning master after twenty years away; the pigs at the slaughterhouse door, led to the appointment by a mare); but they possess no memory and no hope. *They are capable of recognition* (thanks to familiarity), *but they have no memory.*[65]

Wittgenstein's first objection to the idea of animal thought, then, is that it underestimates the differences between us and creatures that cannot speak a language. His second objection to the anthropomorphic approach to animal psychology is that it fails to do justice to the similarities between ourselves and dogs. For what we say, both about animal psychology and human psychology, is not ordinarily based on an inference from observed behavior to unobserved mental states, but rather is based on what we see.

Wittgenstein is not simply replacing the classical humanist idea that the mind of another is an unseen, inner realm by the bald naturalist conception of the mind as analyzable into behavior, and dispositions to behavior.[66] Nor should he be read as replacing this hoary false dilemma, often described as the choice between a "Cartesian" or a "behaviorist" view of the mind, with the "Wittgensteinian" criterial view that there is an internal relation between behavior and mental states that underwrites a refutation of skepticism about other minds. The core of the alternative approach that Wittgenstein elaborates is his idea that my grasp of an animal's, or a person's, psychology is a matter of my seeing what they do in a certain way, a form of response that we already take for granted in our everyday lives, but fail to properly appreciate.[67] Characteristically, we attend to the face, or the gestures of a person, or an animal, and see how they feel.[68] In a remark composed in December 1933 that occurs with minor variations in several places in the *Nachlass,* including source typescripts for the *Philosophical Investigations,* Wittgenstein writes:

> If I say this face has the expression of kindness, goodness, or cowardice, then I don't just seem to mean that we associate such and such feelings with the look of the face, rather, I'm tempted to say that the face is itself an aspect of cowardice, goodness, etc. (Compare, e.g. Weininger.)[69]

This is not only a rejection of Weiningerian psycho-physical parallelism, but also an expression of Wittgenstein's attraction to the diametrically opposed view, that the friendliness or goodness is present in the face itself, although Wittgenstein expresses unease about the best way of putting this point. A passage written shortly afterward, that makes strikingly un-Weiningerian use of Weininger's technical term, "symbol," makes the opposition to Weininger's views even more explicit:

> One can say: the dog's friendly eye, friendly mouth, wagging tail, for instance, are primary – and independent – symbols of friendliness. I mean by that: they are parts of the phenomenon one calls friendliness. If one wants to conceive of

other appearances as expressions of friendliness then one sees those symbols in them.[70]

The friendliness is not inferred, a further object lying behind the appearance, but is actually seen in the dog's comportment. The relationship between the rejection of a conception of thought as a hidden inner process and the soul as the receptacle within which those processes occur is particularly clear in an exchange in the *Philosophical Investigations,* where Wittgenstein's narrator asserts that "We don't say that *possibly* a dog talks to itself."[71] His interlocutor, assuming that such assurance could only be justified if we had direct access to the dog's inner states, replies "Is that because we're so minutely acquainted with its soul?"[72] Wittgenstein's narrator responds by offering us a different way of looking at things: "Well, one might say this: If one sees the behaviour of a living being, one sees its soul."[73]

This way of responding to Weiningerian animal psychology is a significant step away from the Kantian, and Lichtenbergian, way of putting the problem of delimiting the boundary between those aspects of the world that depend on us, and those that do not. For it involves rejecting the false dilemma that either the friendliness is something objective, the result of an inference from what is seen to another's mental state, or it is something subjective, the result of the observer's spreading his or her inner states onto the observed object. On the approach Wittgenstein begins to articulate here, the friendliness is objective, in that it is present in the face of the friendly creature, yet it also has a subjective aspect, in that it takes a suitably equipped observer to attend to that aspect of what is seen. What I see in the other's face is not something I can choose at will, but that I see it is partly due to my abilities. Nor is there anything about this way of conceiving of the other creature that requires him or her to be human; we can also see happiness in a dog's face.

Conclusion: Looking, and Seeing Differences

The broad outline of Wittgenstein's approach to the principal similarities and differences between dogs and ourselves has much to recommend it. It provides a basis for a principled critique of Weiningerian anthropocentrism and the false dilemma on which the only available positions appear to be a baldly naturalist conception of human behavior as nothing but behavior, and the classical humanist conviction that the mind is something behind the behavior. It also begins to do justice to the character of our awareness of others' psychology, both animal and human. However, it is surely too schematic and simple, if taken by itself, to do justice to the full extent of those similarities and differences.

The further similarities between ourselves and dogs have to do with the complexity of the ways in which dogs' lives and our own can be interwoven. For while dogs can only respond to certain quite limited aspects of human language, they do share people's lives in ways that create a richly significant fabric, a background against which a dog's behavior can express a subtle grasp of its circumstances. Here is an example of the kind of "being with dogs" that I have in mind:

> There is (what I definitely want to call) a game I used to play with my mother's dog Sophie, in which we would run around a small pond. My aim was to catch her; hers to avoid being caught. Sometimes we would find ourselves facing each other, almost motionless, on either side of the pond, each of us watching the other for movements indicating a direction of pursuit or flight. I would try faking a movement; starting to the left but running to my right. Sophie would sometimes be foxed, but would always correct her run when she saw me coming the other way.
>
> Sophie has a lot of Collie in her and I never caught her. But one day while we [*we*] were playing this game I slipped as I tried to change direction too quickly on damp grass. Almost immediately Sophie ran straight up to me. I was unhurt, but she licked my face anyway.
>
> I do not see why this cannot be counted as a case of "mutual intelligibility." The dog could see my distress, and I could see her sympathy.[74]

Part of the appeal of this story is that it is such a good example of the extent of the mutual sympathy that can arise between human and animal, the interwoven pattern of activity within which the other creature enters our lives, yet it does not ventriloquize a voice for Sophie, or place a thought bubble over her head.

The other side of the story is that it also hints at the ways animals escape our grasp: Sophie always avoided being caught. The further differences between animals and ourselves have to do with the extent to which their lives are quite different from our own, an aspect of our relationship to animals that the discussion so far has barely touched on.

Guido Frongia reads some of Wittgenstein's later remarks on animals as suggesting the following line of thought concerning the radical otherness of animals' lives. If as we take the mastery of language not only as a necessary condition for full personhood, but also as the yardstick by which we measure the significance of other creatures, then animals will only take on significance in relation to ourselves, as a means of one kind or another. But Wittgenstein also emphasizes the difficulties involved in applying our concepts to what animals do, especially if the animals in question have their own system of communication, such as birds do, or are sufficiently alien to us – such as a crocodile or a fly. The danger here is of taking our own concepts as the only possible yardstick by which to judge animal behavior. Wittgenstein is often taken to be arguing that we have no alternative, but in fact, in stressing the need for the philosopher to "regard man here as an animal,"[75] he does develop just such an alternative. For we not only reason about whether animals have certain feelings, weighing the analogies and disanalogies with our own case; we also experience instinctive and unreflective responses to animals' feelings. These include not only the familiar case in which we see the dog's happiness, but also the more unsettling case where we feel an instinctive uncertainty about an animal's psychology, precisely because it is so different from us.

> Think of the uncertainty about whether animals, particularly lower animals, such as flies, feel pain.
>
> The uncertainty whether a fly feels pain is philosophical; but couldn't it also be instinctive? And how would that show itself?
>
> Indeed, aren't we really uncertain in our behavior towards animals? One doesn't know: Is he being cruel or not.[76]

Indeed, it is this kind of uncertainty about the significance of the suffering of pain in species very different from our own, and the differences between people as to their "spontaneous sympathy"[77] for animals that is partly responsible for the deep disagreements between vegetarians and meat eaters. Frongia proposes that in asking us to see the use of language as only one form of interaction between humans and other animals, Wittgenstein's later writings open up the possibility of "considering every living being (to whatever species it may belong) *not only* as a means, *but also* as an end in itself. They tend to give us back the sense of a radical diversity of the various species of animals which surround us, a diversity which the use of (human) language does tend to make uniform."[78]

We have come a long way from our starting point, the Weiningerian proposal that we understand animals entirely in terms of the extent to which they express characteristically human concerns. Weininger's basic idea is that their real significance is an ethical one, because they are a means of human self-improvement: they provide a vivid typology of human ethical failings. Wittgenstein, on the other hand, provides a perspective from which the ethical significance of our relationship to animals is that they help us to see the dangers in taking man to be the measure of all things.

Notes

A first draft of this essay was presented at the Wittgenstein/Weininger symposium at the May 2001 meetings of the Canadian Philosophical Association in Quebec City. I am grateful to Steven Burns, Cheryl Herr, Allan Janik, Joachim Schulte, Daniel Steuer and Béla Szabados for their extremely helpful suggestions and criticism.

1. McGuinness 1996, 30.
2. McGuinness 1996, 82. In *Young Ludwig* (1988) McGuinness asserts that *Sex and Character* was of more importance to Wittgenstein than *On Last Things*, but changed his mind after editing this correspondence (2002 40, n. 33.) It was *Sex and Character* that Wittgenstein recommended to English-speaking friends, but that may well have been because it was the only translation available. In a letter Wittgenstein wrote to Moore in 1931, he called the translation "beastly" (Wittgenstein 1995, 250). Both books were popular among German language readers at the time. Indeed, some Germanists maintain that *On Last Things* had a greater impact on German readers than *Sex and Character* (see Weininger 2001, x–xi.) As we shall see, there are close connections between Wittgenstein's treatment of "animal psychology" and passages in both of Weininger's books.
3. Weininger 1997, 70; 2001, 53.
4. Wittgenstein, *Culture and Value*, 1980, 19; 1998, 16. That list of influences is part of a passage that addresses prototypically Weiningerian themes: the relationship between originality and reproductiveness, genius and talent, and the character of the "Jewish thinker" and "Jewish spirit." For further discussion of this passage, see the Introduction to this volume. On the dating of Weininger's influence on the *Tractatus*, see Haller 1988, Janik 1985, 65, n. 8, and 2002, n. 31.
5. See Janik 1985, 65 and 2002, n. 23. The "animal psychology" section is the third of the five sections of Chapter 5 of *On Last Things*, which is on "Metaphysics."

6. Weininger 1997, 136; 2001, 108.
7. Weininger 1997, 136–7; 2001, 108. For discussion of Wittgenstein and Weininger on "the Jews" and "Jewishness," see McGuinness 2001 and Stern 2000 or 2001.
8. Weininger 1997, 137; 2001, 109.
9. Smith 1985, 228, n. 6.
10. On Wittgenstein's relationship to Lichtenberg, see von Wright 1942, Stern 1959, and McGuinness 1988.
11. Lichtenberg 1908, J375, 71; 1990, 129; 2000, 141.
12. Lichtenberg 1908, J550, 100; 1990, 136; 2000, 104–5.
13. Weininger 1980, 198. On Wittgenstein's interest in using a Lichtenbergian subjectless language for immediate experience, see Stern 1995, 72–87.
14. Lichtenberg, quoted in Weininger 1980, 526, note to 198. My translation.
15. I had hoped to include some discussion of Lichtenberg's *On Physiognomy: Against the Physiognomists* (1778), which was brought to my attention by Daniel Steuer, but that has proved impossible within the scope of this essay. The essay contains Lichtenberg's critique of Lavater, who founded the "science" of physiognomy, which aimed to deduce character and personality traits from a person's face. Weininger's animal psychology is part of that physiognomic tradition, and Wittgenstein's objections to Weininger echo aspects of Lichtenberg's critique. While we do not know if Wittgenstein read Lichtenberg's *On Physiognomy,* there would have been remarks on physiognomy in the material Wittgenstein did read, and he was certainly acquainted with Schopenhauer's summary of those arguments in *The World as Will and Representation* I s.12 (1958). For a brief discussion of Lichtenberg's antiphysiognomy, see Stern 1959, 88–92.
16. Weininger 1997, 104; 2001, 82.
17. Weininger 1997, 122; 2001, 96. The subtitle is rather more informative: "Containing the idea of a universal symbolism, animal psychology (with a fairly complete psychology of the criminal) etc."
18. Weininger 1997, 122; 2001, 96.
19. Weininger 1997, 122; 2001, 96.
20. See Wittgenstein, *Notebooks 1914–1916,* 84; *Tractatus,* 5.63.
21. Weininger 1997, 122–23; 2001, 96.
22. Weininger 1997, 123; 2001, 97.
23. Weininger 1997, 124; 2001, 98.
24. Weininger 1997, 124; 2001, 98. The discussion of the criminal character, the first part of the section entitled "Animal Psychology," occupies 7 pages of *Über die letzten Dinge* (124–31), and 5 pages of *On Last Things* (98–103). The remainder of this section consists of subsections on "The Dog," "The Horse," and "General remarks." The final two sections are "Plants," and "Inorganic Nature" (1997, 131–40; 2001, 103–11.)
25. Weininger 1997, 130; 2001, 103.
26. Weininger 1997, 132; 2001, 104.

27. Weininger 1997, 132; 2001, 105.
28. Weininger 1997, 133; 2001, 105.
29. Weininger 1997, 133; 2001, 105.
30. Weininger 1997, 133–4; 2001, 106.
31. Weininger 1997, 138–40; 2001, 109–11.
32. Gilman 1995, 105.
33. Freud 1980, 198 fn.
34. For further discussion of Weininger and Freud on Jews and gender, see Gilman 1995 and Le Rider 1993, ch. 9.
35. Weininger 1919, 19–20. This translation is from Abrahamsen 1946, 92–3. The text omitted between the second and third sentences consists of Gerber's description of the circumstances, and does not contain anything said by Weininger.
36. Abrahamsen 1946, 96–7; see also 94–6.
37. Weininger 1997, 130; 2001, 103–4.
38. Abrahamsen 1946, 97.
39. One should also note that Abrahamsen's remarkably confident psychohistorical diagnoses are based on scanty evidence.
40. Janik 2002, main text, between notes 32 and 33 (the document is a web page and so has no standard pagination).
41. Janik 2001 64; the relationship between Weininger and Ibsen is the topic of his ch. 3. See also Janik in Weininger 2001, xxvii–xxxiii.
42. Janik 2001.
43. Weininger 1997, 122; 2001, 96. This passage is quoted in full at the beginning of my section entitled Weininger's "Animal Psychology."
44. Sass 1994, ch. 11, and especially 327–31; see also Foucault 1972, 203, and 1973 318–35.
45. Sass 1994, 331.
46. For a related but rather different treatment of this topic, see Janik 2002.
47. Wittgenstein, *Wittgenstein's Nachlass,* MS 134, 115–16; 7 April 1947. *Du mußt fundamental umlernen über den Gebrauch der Wörter. Tierpsychologie. Nagt der Hund unwillkürlich am Knochen? Hetzt er das Wild unwillkürlich? Und was wissen wir von seinen kinästhetischen Empfindungen?*
48. Wittgenstein, *Notebooks 1914–1916,* 84–5.
49. Wittgenstein, *Wittgenstein's Nachlass,* MS 115, 39; 14 Dec. 1933. "*Der Hund meint etwas damit, wenn er mit dem Schwanz wedelt.*" *Wie könnte man das begründen?*

    Wir würden kaum fragen, ob das Krokodil etwas damit meint, wenn es mit offenem Rachen auf einen Menschen zukommt. Und wir würden erklären: das Krokodil könne nicht denken und darum sei eigentlich hier von einem Meinen keine Rede.
50. Wittgenstein, *Philosophical Investigations,* s.25. Wittgenstein translations are based on published translations, when available, but I have made a number of changes.
51. Wittgenstein, *Zettel,* s.520.
52. Wittgenstein, *Philosophical Investigations,* II, 229.

53. Weininger 1980, 384; not in 1906 translation. The context, however, is quintessentially Weiningerian; it comes from his discussion of the essence of Woman, where it qualifies his statement of the thesis that an animal "has just as little metaphysical reality as the true woman." ("*Das Tier hat zwar ebensowenig metaphysische Realität wie die echte Frau; aber es spricht nicht, und fölglich lügt es nicht.*")
54. Wittgenstein, *Philosophical Investigations*, s.249. The parenthetical remark forms a self-contained paragraph, and so has the tone of a comment on the previous exchange, and a reminder of something everyday, rather than a continuation of either of the previous voices.
55. Wittgenstein, *Philosophical Investigations*, s.250. See also *Zettel*, s.389 and s.518.
56. It is relevant here that he once considered King Lear's "I'll teach you differences" as a motto for the *Philosophical Investigations.*
57. For further discussion of *Philosophical Investigations* s.1 and the sections that follow, see Stern 2004, ch. 4.
58. See Wittgenstein, *Zettel*, s.99 and s.390; *Remarks on the Philosophy of Psychology, II*, s.623. See also Stern 2004, ch. 4, and Schulte (forthcoming).
59. *Philosophical Investigations*, s.130.
60. *Remarks on the Philosophy of Psychology, II*, s.623.
61. *Remarks on the Philosophy of Psychology, II*, s.624.
62. *Last Writings on the Philosophy of Psychology*, ss.861–2.
63. *Philosophical Investigations*, II, 174. The second paragraph echoes s.650, where a similar question is raised, but not answered: "We say a dog is afraid his master will beat him; but not, he is afraid his master will beat him to-morrow. Why not?"
64. For some further discussion of the issues raised by this cryptic but suggestive final sentence, see Hacker 1993a, ch. 4, and 1993b, 36–46, s.3; Garver 1994, ch. 15, s.3, and Stern 1995, ch. 6, s.4.
65. Weininger 1980, 186; my translation. Weininger 1906, 145. This leads Weininger to maintain that memory is essentially human, and closely related to both logic and ethics.
66. "Bald naturalism" is taken from McDowell 1994, and "classical humanism" from Glendinning 1998.
67. Mulligan (1981) provides a complementary perspective on Wittgenstein's break with the subject/object distinction, and its relationship to Weininger's treatment of animals.
68. Allan Janik has drawn my attention to Spengler's discussion of dogs, language, and the primacy of nonverbal communication as a source of this train of thought: "He who would penetrate into the essence of language should begin by putting aside all the philologist's apparatus and observe how a hunter speaks to his dog." Spengler 1939, vol. 2, ch. 5, part iv, 131.
69. Wittgenstein, *Wittgenstein's Nachlass*, MS 115 23–4, Wittgenstein, *Philosophical Grammar*, p. 176. For later versions of this passage, see *Wittgenstein's Nachlass*, MS 146, 82; MS 228 117, and MS 230, p. 18 s.65. The topic is discussed at length in the *Brown Book*, pp. 162–180 and in *Philosophical*

Investigations II xi. See also Szabados's essay in this volume. Compare this to Wittgenstein's question in *Notebooks 1914–1916*, 84: "Is, e.g., an angry face angry in itself or merely because it is empirically connected with bad temper?"

70. Wittgenstein, *Wittgenstein's Nachlass*, MS 115, 25–6. See also *Philosophical Grammar*, 178 and *Zettel*, s.506.
71. *Philosophical Investigations*, s.357.
72. *Philosophical Investigations*, s.357. See also *Philosophical Investigations*, II iv–v.
73. *Philosophical Investigations*, s.357.
74. Glendinning 1998, 142.
75. *On Certainty*, s.475.
76. *Remarks on the Philosophy of Psychology*, II, s.659.
77. *Remarks on the Philosophy of Psychology*, II, s.699.
78. Frongia 1995, 352.

References

Abrahamsen, David (1946). *The Mind and Death of a Genius.* New York: Columbia University Press.

Foucault, Michel (1972). *The Archaeology of Knowledge and the Discourse on Language.* Translated by A. M. Sheridan Smith. New York: Pantheon Books.

——— (1973). *The Order of Things: An Archaeology of the Human Sciences.* New York: Vintage Books.

Freud, Sigmund (1977). *Case Histories I: "Dora" and "Little Hans."* Translated by Alix Strachey and James Strachey. Harmondsworth, Middlesex: Penguin.

Frongia, Guido (1995). "Wittgenstein and the Diversity of Animals." *The Monist* 78 (4): 534–52.

Garver, Newton (1994). *This Complicated Form of Life: Essays on Wittgenstein.* Chicago: Open Court.

Gilman, Sander (1995). "Otto Weininger and Sigmund Freud: Race and Gender in the Shaping of Psychoanalysis." In Nancy A. Harrowitz and Barbara Hyams, eds., *Jews and Gender: Responses to Otto Weininger.* Philadelphia: Temple University Press, 103–20.

Glendinning, Simon (1998). *On Being With Others: Heidegger – Derrida – Wittgenstein.* London: Routledge.

Hacker, P. M. S. (1993a). *Wittgenstein: Meaning and Mind. Part I – Essays.* Oxford: Blackwell.

——— (1993b). *Wittgenstein: Meaning and Mind. Part II – Exegesis.* Oxford: Blackwell.

Haller, Rudolf (1988). "What Do Wittgenstein and Weininger Have in Common?" In Haller, *Questions on Wittgenstein.* Lincoln: University of Nebraska Press, 90–9.

Harrowitz, Nancy A., and Barbara Hyams, eds. (1995). *Jews and Gender: Responses to Otto Weininger.* Philadelphia: Temple University Press.

Hyams, Barbara, and Nancy A. Harrowitz (1995). "A Critical Introduction to the History of Weininger Reception." In Harrowitz and Hyams (1995), 3–20.

Janik, Allan (1981). "Therapeutic Nihilism: How not to write about Otto Weininger." In Barry Smith, ed. *Structure and Gestalt: Philosophy and Literature in Austria-Hungary and her Successor States.* Amsterdam: John Benjamins B. V., 263–92.

——— (1985). *Essays on Wittgenstein and Weininger.* Amsterdam: Rodopi.

——— (1995). "How Did Weininger Influence Wittgenstein?" In Harrowitz and Hyams (1995) 61–72.

——— (2001). *Wittgenstein's Vienna Revisited.* New Brunswick and London: Transaction Publishers.

——— (2002). "From Logic to Animality or How Wittgenstein Used Otto Weininger." *Nomadas* 4. *http://www.ucm.es/info/eurotheo/nomadas/n4-ajanik1.htm.*

Janik, Allan and Stephen Toulmin (1973). *Wittgenstein's Vienna.* New York: Simon & Schuster. 1996, revised second edition, Chicago: Ivan Dee.

Le Rider, Jacques (1993). *Modernity and Crises of Identity: Culture and Society in Fin-de-Siècle Vienna.* Translated by Rosemary Morris. First published in French in 1990. New York: Continuum.

Lichtenberg, Georg Christoph (1778). *Über Physiognomik; wider die Physiognomen* [On Physiognomy: Against the Physiognomists]. Second edition. Göttingen: Dieterich. Reprinted in volume IV of the 1844 edition of Lichtenberg's *Collected Works.*

——— (1908). *Aphorismen,* vol. 4. Edited by Albert Leitzmann. Berlin: Deutsche Literaturdenkmale des 18. Und 19. Jahrhunderts, #140. Reprinted by Kraus Reprint, Nendeln, Lichtenstein, 1968.

——— (1990). *Aphorisms.* Translated by R. J. Hollingdale. London: Penguin.

——— (2000). *The Waste Books.* Translated by R. J. Hollingdale. New York: New York Review Books. Reprint, in a new edition, of Lichtenberg 1990.

McDowell, John (1994). *Mind and World.* Cambridge, MA: Harvard University Press.

McGuinness, Brian (1988). *Wittgenstein: A Life. Young Ludwig* (1889–1921). London: Duckworth.

——— (2001). "Wittgenstein and the Idea of Jewishness." In James Klagge, ed., *Wittgenstein: Biography and Philosophy.* Cambridge: Cambridge University Press, 221–36. Reprinted as "The Idea of Jewishness," in McGuinness 2002.

——— (2002). *Approaches to Wittgenstein: Collected Papers.* London: Routledge.

McGuinness, Brian, Maria Concetta Ascher, and Otto Pfersmann, eds. (1996). *Wittgenstein Familienbriefe* [Wittgenstein Family Letters]. Vienna: Hölder-Pichler-Tempsky.

Mulligan, Kevin (1981). "Philosophy, Animality and Justice: Kleist, Kafka, Weininger and Wittgenstein." In Barry Smith, ed., *Structure and Gestalt: Philosophy and Literature in Austria-Hungary and her Successor States.* Amsterdam: John Benjamins B. V., 293–311.

Sass, Louis (1994). *Madness and Modernism: Insanity in the Light of Modern Art, Literature and Thought.* Cambridge, MA: Harvard University Press. First published by Basic Books, 1992.

Schopenhauer, Arthur (1966). *The World as Will and Representation.* New York: Dover. Translation of *Die Welt als Wille und Vorstellung,* by E. F. J. Payne.

Schulte, Joachim (2004). "Primitive Language-Games." In Erich Ammereller and Engen Fischer, eds., *Wittgenstein at Work: Method in the Philosophical Investigations.* London: Routledge.

Smith, Barry, ed. (1981). *Structure and Gestalt: Philosophy and Literature in Austria-Hungary and her successor states.* Amsterdam: John Benjamins B. V.

——— (1985). "Weininger und Wittgenstein." *Theoria* 5: 227–37.

Spengler, Otto (1939). *The Decline of the West.* Translated by C. F. Atkinson. New York: Knopf.

Stern, J. P. (1959). *Lichtenberg: A Doctrine of Scattered Occasions.* Bloomington, IN: Indiana University Press.

Stern, David G. (1995). *Wittgenstein on Mind and Language.* Oxford: Oxford University Press.

——— (2000). "The Significance of Jewishness for Wittgenstein's Philosophy." *Inquiry* 43: 383–402. Reprinted in Stanford M. Lyman, ed., *Essential Readings on Jewish Identities, Lifestyles and Beliefs: Analyses of the Personal and Social Diversity of Jews by Modern Scholars.* New York: Gordian Knot Press, 2003.

——— (2001). "Was Wittgenstein a Jew?" In James Klagge, ed., *Wittgenstein: Biography and Philosophy.* Cambridge: Cambridge University Press, 237–72.

——— (2004). *Wittgenstein's* Philosophical Investigations: *An Introduction.* Cambridge: Cambridge University Press.

von Wright, Georg Henrik (1942). "Georg Christoph Lichtenberg als Philosoph." *Theoria* 8: 201–17. A revised and abridged version of this article, in English, can be found under "Lichtenberg" in *The Encyclopedia of Philosophy,* ed. Paul Edwards.

Weininger, Otto (1906). *Sex and Character.* An anonymous abridged translation that omits footnotes and appendixes. New York: Heinemann. Reprinted in 2003 by Howard Fertig, New York.

——— (1919). *Taschenbuch und Briefe an einen Freund.* Leipzig: E. P. Tal.

——— (1980). *Geschlecht und Charakter: Eine prinzipielle Untersuchung.* Munich: Matthes & Seitz. First published in 1903.

——— (1997). *Über die letzten Dinge.* Munich: Matthes & Seitz. First published in 1904.

——— (2001). *A Translation of Weininger's Über die letzten Dinge (1904/1907)/ On Last Things.* Translated by Steven Burns. Lewiston, NY: Edwin Mellen Press.

Wittgenstein, Ludwig (1922). *Tractatus Logico-Philosophicus.* Translation on facing pages by C. K. Ogden. London: Routledge & Kegan Paul. Second edition, 1933.

——— (1953). *Philosophical Investigations.* Edited by G. E. M. Anscombe and R. Rhees. Translation on facing pages by G. E. M. Anscombe. Oxford: Blackwell.

______ (1958/1964). *The Blue and Brown Books.* Edited by Rush Rhees. Oxford: Basil Blackwell.

______ (1961) *Notebooks, 1914–1916.* Edited by G. H. von Wright and G. E. M. Anscombe. Translation on facing pages by G. E. M. Anscombe. Second edition, 1979.

______ (1967). *Zettel.* Edited by G. E. M. Anscombe and G. H. von Wright. Translation on facing pages by G. E. M. Anscombe. Oxford: Blackwell. Second edition, 1981.

______ (1969). *On Certainty.* Edited by G. E. M. Anscombe and G. H. von Wright. Translated by G. E. M. Anscombe and D. Paul, Oxford: Blackwell.

______ (1969). *Philosophical Grammar.* First published as *Philosophische Grammatik,* German text only, edited by Rush Rhees, Oxford: Blackwell. English translation by A. Kenny, 1974, Oxford: Blackwell.

______ (1980). *Remarks on the Philosophy of Psychology, Volume I.* Edited by G. E. M. Anscombe and G. H. von Wright. Translated by C. G. Luckhardt and M. A. E. Aue. Chicago: University of Chicago Press.

______ (1980). *Remarks on the Philosophy of Psychology, Volume II.* Edited by G. H. von Wright and H. Nyman. Translated by C. G. Luckhardt and M. A. E. Aue. Chicago: University of Chicago Press.

______ (1980/1998). *Culture and Value.* First published in 1977 as *Vermischte Bemerkungen,* German text only, edited by G. H. von Wright and Heikki Nyman, Frankfurt: Suhrkamp. Amended second edition, with translation by P. Winch, 1980, Oxford: Blackwell. Revised second edition with new translation by P. Winch, 1998, Oxford: Blackwell. Translations are taken from the 1998 edition.

______ (1982). *Last Writings on the Philosophy of Psychology, Volume I: Preliminary studies for part II of the "Philosophical investigations."* Edited by G. H. von Wright and H. Nyman. Translation by C. G. Luckhardt and M. A. E. Aue. Chicago: University of Chicago Press.

______ (2000). *Wittgenstein's Nachlass: The Bergen Electronic Edition.* Oxford: Oxford University Press. References are to the von Wright (1982, *Wittgenstein,* Oxford: Basil Blackwell) numbering system.

unity
peace
clarity
unsayability
(vs tragic)

CV 60 ↓ bel: c Co

clarity 42 *

✓ thot re: relig due:
corrected way of see
- diff μεθ